WALKING A GOLDEN MILE

WALKING
A
GOLDEN
MILE

WILLIAM REGAL
with NEIL CHANDLER

World
Wrestling
Entertainment®
BOOKS

POCKET
BOOKS

NEW YORK
LONDON
TORONTO
SYDNEY

POCKET BOOKS, a division of Simon & Schuster, Inc.
1230 Avenue of the Americas, New York, NY 10020

Photo credits
Pages 5, 7, 13, 21, 29, 31, 42, 46, 48, 55, 60, 65, 77 (top and bottom), 82, 87,
96, 98, 118, 130, 153, 158, 244 (top), 272, 286–287 Courtesy of William Regal.
Pages 72, 73 Courtesy of Express Newspapers.
Pages viii, 9, 93, 104, 111, 114, 117, 120, 124, 128, 132, 139, 142, 150, 155,
161, 162, 164, 183, 225, 230, 233 Courtesy *Pro Wrestling Illustrated*
Photographs.
All other photographs Copyright © 2005 World Wrestling Entertainment, Inc.
All Rights Reserved.

ISBN-13: 978-0-7434-7634-8
ISBN-10:   0-7434-7634-4

First Pocket Books trade paperback edition August 2005

10 9 8 7 6 5 4 3 2 1

Cover designed by Dave Barry
Book designed by M Roles, London

Visit us on the World Wide Web
http://www.simonsays.co.uk
http://www.wwe.com

Manufactured in the United States of America

For information regarding special discounts for bulk purchases,
please contact Simon & Schuster Special Sales at 1-800-456-6798
or business@simonandschuster.com

This book is dedicated

to the memories of

my grandfather William Matthews,

and to Bobby Baron.

ACKNOWLEDGEMENTS

I would like to thank my wife Chris, my sons Daniel, Dane, Bailey, my dad, and the rest of my family.

To the people whose teaching and advice helped shape my wrestling career; Robby Brookside, Marty Jones, Steve Peacock, John Pallo, Dave Taylor, Dave "Fit" Finlay, Skull Murphy, Johnny Saint, Johnny South, Frank "Chic" Cullen, Dennis "Rocky" Moran, Rene Lassartesse, Terry Rudge, Ray Steel, Tony Francis, Mark "Roller Ball" Rocco, Jimmy Breaks, Pete Roberts, Mal Saunders, Tony St. Clair, Mick McMichael, and "Cyanide" Sid Cooper.

To the McMahon family for everything; Jim Ross, for believing in me; Gerald Brisco and Bruce Prichard, for being there when I was at my lowest point; Pat Patterson, Jack Lanza, Sgt. Slaughter, the Hebner's, Timmy White, and even Tony Garea.

Johnny, Arn, Ricky, Dean, Steve and everyone who works at the WWE for being the best at what they do.

Jim Weigel and the staff at TRC.

Neil Chandler, Dave Rodgers in Blackpool, Dr. Ken West, Dr. Bruce Grundy, Kelly Carr, Matt Fury, Mickey Brett, Lynne Pearce, Barrie Knight, Graham Quinn, Davey Coates, Dominic Hayes, Chin, and Anthony Cali.

To Paul (H), a true friend.

Jason Singh, Doc Dean, Dave Taylor, Marty Jones, Mal Saunders, Steve Gray, Bobby Eaton, Chris Benoit, Eddie Guerrero, Bryan Danielson, Eugene, Tajiri, Steve Austin, Peter Thompson, Glen Walsh, Stuart, Alan, Dennis (Joe), Steve Breani, Howard Finkel, Peter and Teresa Lyons, Jayne Porter, Bill and Kevin at N.E.R.D., and Robyn at ProExotics for their friendship.

CONTENTS

PROLOGUE

Sitting in the Gutter, Looking Like a Star

I'd always wanted to be a professional wrestler. Don't ask me why. I can remember when I was about four or five, sitting down in front of the television at 4 p.m. every Saturday afternoon and watching the wrestling on ITV's *World of Sport*. I just knew that was what I wanted to be.

And in my chosen profession I'd gone far further than I ever expected. I'd appeared before the British public on those same Saturday afternoon shows, alongside icons like Big Daddy and Giant Haystacks. I'd wrestled all over the world. I'd been one of the very few to cross the Atlantic and make it big in the glitzy world of American pro wrestling.

It was December 1998. Just a few months beforehand, I'd signed a lucrative contract with World Wrestling Federation – the biggest and most successful wrestling company the world has ever seen. I'd already been a star of their deadly rival, World Championship Wrestling. But my new deal was going to put me right back on the map.

I was back home in England for Christmas with my wife and kids, ready to have a good time. It was a chance to catch up with the family, meet friends and celebrate my good fortune. The holiday started well enough when I managed to meet up with an old friend who sorted me out with my three favourite drugs. He gave me 500 Valium; some Hypnoval, which knocks you out completely; and a load of Nubain. That's an opiate.

Over the next two weeks I took Valium every day – enough to put a dozen donkeys to sleep. By day I injected Nubain. By night I shot Hypnoval into myself, passing out for a couple of hours and shooting more whenever I woke up throughout the night until I'd had enough. I couldn't even consider getting out of bed in the morning until I'd swallowed ten Valium.

Everyone was acting a little strangely that Christmas. My wife wouldn't talk to me. None of her family – with whom we were staying – would speak to me either. My Blackpool mates seemed a bit off, too. I told my friend Glen not to worry because I was going into rehab once I got back to the States. I didn't know until much later just how worried he was.

And it was exhausting, staggering around Blackpool trying to catch up with my old friends. Buying wraps of speed – amphetamine sulphate – seemed to be the only way to keep going.

It was Christmas Eve. I was a World Wrestling Federation Superstar and I was going to celebrate the fact. There was an off licence – a liquor store, Americans would call it – at the end of the road. I went in and bought as many bottles of alcopops as I could carry. They all had daft names – Hooch, Two Dogs – I didn't care. I just wanted them to wash down the Valium. I dropped ten pills and sat down in the gutter to drink my way through every bottle I had. Dogs looked at me as they moped by.

Earlier in the day I'd had to ring my dad and confess that I had a drug problem. I never wanted to tell him. He'd brought me up single-handedly after Mum left, and he meant more to me than anyone else in the world. But I had to tell him. It was the only way to explain to him why Chris and the kids wouldn't be coming with me to see him on Boxing Day. My wife couldn't even stand to be in the same room with me by then.

I spent several days at my dad's. My godparents' son Adrian came to try to talk some sense into me. He was older than me but we'd always been close. I told him what I told everyone else: that none of it was my fault. Everyone was against me. No one understood the pain I was in. I had to work with injuries. No one knew how tough my job was. I made excuses left, right and centre. And every single one of them was bullshit.

My cousin Graham had no better luck than Adrian. We'd grown up together and we were like brothers, but I wouldn't listen to him either.

New Year's Eve, back in Blackpool. On the door of the Heaven and Hell club was my friend Stuart, with another lad called Murray whom I'd met the year before. I asked them where Glen was and they wouldn't tell me. Even in my drug-fuelled state I could see they were uncomfortable with my being there. They were friends of mine but they just didn't want me around.

On January 2 we flew back to America. I fished around in my pocket for some Valium to get me through the flight and I only had three-and-a-half pills left. There was no way that was going to be enough. I snuck to the back of the plane where the stewardesses kept the drinks trolley and got hold of as many miniature bottles of gin I could. I never normally drank gin; but on that flight I downed bottles and bottles of it.

It was two days before I was due to check into the rehabilitation clinic. I had just fourteen weeks to save my life.

How had I let my life become such a mess? It's a long story . . .

A Wrestler, a Comic or a Clown

1

I'm not as old as you might think. It's just that I've been wrestling a long time. There's very few on the current World Wrestling Entertainment talent roster with more experience on the job than I have. The fact is I was born Darren Matthews on May 10, 1968 in a little village in the middle of England – Codsall Wood in Staffordshire. Not a lot goes on in Codsall Wood. My dad Don Matthews is a builder and he built the house I was born in, just fifty yards from my grandfather's house, where my dad himself was born.

Wrestling is one of my earliest memories. Whenever I could, I'd watch it on TV. I also loved that old show *The Comedians*, all those old gag-a-minute northern stand-up comics, and I loved Slade too, the glam rock band. Wrestling, comedy and showbusiness – they were always going to play a big part in my life.

I was seven when my mum Paula left us. Mum and Dad had a massive row and my dad took me out in the car to see some of the houses he was building. He said to me: "What would you think if you got home and your mum wasn't there?" I don't remember being too bothered. I'd always looked up to my dad and he was the one I wanted to be around. But it must have affected me, because I took my frustrations out on other kids. They'd tease me in the playground, shouting, "Where's your mum?" For the only time in my life, I turned into a bully. There's nothing I hate worse now than a bully. That or a liberty-taker. I've no time for bullies – and I met plenty of them when I became a wrestler. I try to live my life without having regrets, but the fact that I bullied other kids all those years ago is something that troubled me for a long time.

I used to be a right naughty lad. But then when I was about fifteen I woke up one day and the thought struck me: "This is not the way to be." I couldn't carry on the way I had been. That was it. Simple as that. I've prided myself on my politeness from that day.

I hated every single minute of school. It's a terrible thing to admit when I know so many kids watch me on TV every week, but it's true. I detested it. My first school was a Catholic school, St Joseph's Convent, even though I'm not a Catholic. Mum leaving when I was so young didn't help matters, but I would never have been able to handle being preached at by those nuns in any case. I never liked being told that I'd go to hell if I didn't do what some nun told me to.

Just about the only highlight I remember from school was being taken on a trip to Chester Zoo when I was eight. My best friend was a lad called Andrew who had this curly thick white hair. He began pulling faces at a gorilla who retaliated by throwing a big pile of shite at him, hitting him square in the face. All you could see of Andrew were his eyes, peering through this steaming mask. The nuns were running around, shouting and screaming. It was like a *Tom and Jerry* cartoon. If that was the only thing I can remember from school, you can imagine how mind-numbing I found the place.

Then when I was nine I went to the middle school – and was soon faced with another confusing situation. My mum had run off with this bloke and my dad ended up marrying his wife. It got pretty complicated. I've a half-brother who's my mum and step-dad's kid, and a step-sister.

My dad had custody of me and I'd go to stay with my mum in the school holidays, but I didn't like going. She lived in Bristol, a hundred miles away. When I was there I never saw much of my brother, who was always out with his friends. I didn't really know him, though we do keep in touch today. He's nice enough. But most of the time I didn't want to be there because I wanted to stay at home with my dad, granddad and the close family who lived nearby: my uncles, aunties and cousins – especially my cousin Graham. He's older than me, but we spent so much time together growing up that he's more like a brother to me than anything else.

But my dad was always the one I looked up to. To this day he's the nicest man I've ever met – and I'm not just saying that because he is my dad. He is the kindest person. I've never heard him swear or even say a bad word about anybody. He's a real hard worker, too. You never saw my dad without a pair of overalls on. He would come home covered in cement and has always worked hard for his living.

He doesn't need to work these days but he still does. He still gets up early every morning and never stops all day. If he didn't work he wouldn't know what to do with himself. Lately he has had problems both with his leg and with his arm but nothing stops him. I've seen him shovelling stuff with one hand. If he gave it up now he'd have no financial worries but that is who he is – a grafter. But what it meant for me when I was growing up was that dad was often out at work. That meant I spent a lot of time with his father, my granddad.

Granddad's name was William Matthews, known as Bill, and he was probably the biggest influence in my life. In his younger days he was a bit of a rogue, well known for fighting and drinking. He'd do a bit of wrestling, a bit of boxing, a bit of running – anything to make a few quid. He'd tell me stories about how he used to wrestle at a place called the Pear Tree pub. Back in the 1920s and 1930s

My dad is still my greatest inspirat
Here we are backstage at Birmingham in 2
with my stepmur and my old frienc Jason Singh.

they had a ring up in the beer garden where he used to do his stuff. He packed it in back in 1933, aged just thirty-two, because he came down with pleurisy and pneumonia. He also worked in Blackpool for a while. He was a navvy and there had been a lot of work going there when he was younger, on the sea walls and the like.

He used to tell me all these stories about him fighting when he was younger. He was a big, powerful fellow, over six feet tall, and he was a great character. He used to joke around and would teach me all these dirty stories and poems. He'd tell me all these things and whenever I repeated any of them to my mum, I'd get a thick ear for it. I've still got a picture of him in a suit and the older I get, the more I look like him.

He died in 1990, when he was eighty-nine. He loved it when I started wrestling and travelling around the world. Even when I'd moved to Blackpool, I'd come back to see him more than I would most people. Whenever I was passing through the Midlands on the wrestling trips that would take me all over the country, I'd stop over with him.

My granddad William
Matthews in his suit.
Note the family
resemblance . . .

He drank all his life and smoked a pipe. He'd had every disease you care to name but in the end, the only reason he died was because he had got fed up with living. My gran had died a few years before and he used to tell me there was nothing on TV he wanted to watch any more, nothing he wanted to do. The last time I saw him, he told me: "I'm going to die, son."

He used to tell me all these stories about him fighting when he was younger. He was a big, powerful fellow, over six feet tall, and he was a great character. He used to joke around and would teach me all these dirty stories and poems. He'd tell me all these things and whenever I repeated any of them to my mum, I'd get a thick ear for it. I've still got a picture of him in a suit and the older I get, the more I look like him.

"Don't be so soft," I said. I told him I was due to go to South Africa two weeks later to wrestle.

"Don't stay," he said. "Get yourself gone."

He died soon after. I did what he'd told me and went to South Africa. That was the way it was between him and me.

When I got to Codsall High School I had the same trouble as before. It bored the life out of me. Things that I liked, I did okay at, such as woodwork. But something I didn't like – French for example – was another matter. I got thrown out of French for being a disruptive little git.

If there is anything I want to learn about I'll do it on my own. I read constantly these days, and have always tried to educate myself. But when they tried to teach me a load of old cobblers it drove me up the wall. I was one of the lads sitting at the back of the class, being sarcastic and messing around all the time. Because I never thought I'd need any of it. I'd always known what I was going to do. I was going to be a wrestler.

I remember one of my last days at Codsall High, when I was sent to see the careers officer. "What are you going to do?" he asked me. "Are you going to get a trade?"

"No," I said. "I'm going to be a wrestler."

He threw me out of the office and told me to come back when I wanted to talk some sense. I expect he's still there today.

Relaxing with my mum.

Now mine is not a rags to riches tale. I didn't become a wrestler because I wanted to be rich and famous. We weren't badly off. My dad owned his own business and we lived in a lovely village, in a beautiful home, because my dad had built it. I was fortunate. We'd go on good holidays – Jersey, Guernsey, Spain, Tunisia. We never went without.

But when I became a wrestler, I made myself poor. Some of my friends and family were almost as surprised as the careers officer had been. Everyone expected me to take over the family business from my dad, but I knew I could never work a regular job. Even when I helped my dad out at weekends, I knew I couldn't hack that life. I'm not decrying anyone who can – good luck to them. My dad's a grafter, and my mum too – she's a nurse. But it wasn't for me.

One reason was the way I saw people treat my dad. He'd do jobs for them and then they wouldn't want to pay him. It used to drive me wild. I was going to be a wrestler and that's all there was to it. A wrestler or a clown or a comedian. I've ended up becoming a mixture of all three.

My dad used to take his young, wrestling-mad son to Wolverhampton Civic Hall every two weeks to see Dale Martin's shows. It was great. I watched all the stars of the day, people who affected me and whose inspiration I still use in my own act now. There was Giant Haystacks, Big Daddy, Kendo Nagasaki, The Royal Brothers, Mick McManus and Cyanide Sid Cooper – I was always a huge fan of his and use a lot of his material today.

On my eighth birthday I was taken to see Mick McManus at Wolverhampton Civic Hall and it must be the greatest birthday present anyone has ever given me. Around 1975 I saw Dynamite Kid there when he was just sixteen and he was awesome. He was only a little kid and he wasn't flying around like he did later in his career, but you could already tell how good he was going to be. He was full of energy, moved like a sparkplug.

One night he wrestled another guy I liked a lot, Tally Ho Kaye, in a street fight. Tally Ho did a foxhunting gimmick and the idea was for the two of them to fight in their street clothes. Tally Ho had a really posh outfit on, all polished boots and brass buttons, and Dynamite turned up in a sports jacket, tie, jeans and a pair of Doc Martens. Tally Ho used Dynamite's tie to strangle him – it was brilliant stuff. I was intrigued by all this drama and theatre. I didn't care about all those people who said it was bent. I was hooked.

I used to run round collecting autographs from all the wrestlers. That's why I always give autographs now, as long as I have the time – I can remember when I was the excited kid with the pen and the notebook. I can't always oblige. If I'm rushing for a plane it can be difficult, but I'll always apologize if I can't. I always used to sign for everyone who asked but these days it is less likely to be a handful and more likely to be hundreds or thousands. Sometimes, if I see 250 kids and I know I'll only be able to do two or three, I'd rather not do any at all

> I used to run round collecting autographs from all the wrestlers. That's why I always give autographs now, as long as I have the time – I can remember when I was the excited kid with the pen and the notebook. I can't always oblige. If I'm rushing for a plane it can be difficult, but I'll always apologize if I can't.

and let them think I'm a bit of a dick. I would feel badly for all the people I couldn't do.

My being such a starstruck wrestling fan wasn't so unusual back then. All of Britain was hooked on it. They say that in the 1960s, a couple of matches between Mick McManus and Jackie Pallo, which were put on before the FA Cup final, the biggest sporting event of the British year, drew more viewers than the football – eleven or twelve million. That's more than one fifth of the population. Even the Queen and Prince Philip were fans. Everyone went to the wrestling at their local town hall or swimming baths; it was a British tradition. And I loved it more than anybody.

When I turned fifteen I started taking the bus into Wolverhampton on my own to go to the wrestling. By this time I had new heroes: Dave "Fit" Finlay and Mark "Rollerball" Rocco. But what I liked most were the villains. It was the way they could control people. It was only natural that I'd end up playing a villain myself. In life as well as wrestling, I've always admired the rogues.

Soon my wrestling education expanded as I travelled further afield to watch my heroes. I'd go to Rhyl town hall in North Wales, where the promoter Oric Williams used to put on shows. Here were all these other guys, ones you never used to see on TV. The independent scene, I

Fit Finlay was one of my earliest heroes.

suppose you'd call it now – shows put on by Oric and Brian Dixon.

Oric used to have all these monsters. One guy was called the Wild Man of Borneo. He was a Sikh who used to come out with all his long hair down and hair all over his body. You'd see people like Crusher Mason and Adrian Street, very different from the guys you saw on TV. Giants like Klondyke Bill and Klondyke Jake. And after I'd seen a few of these shows I was even more enthralled. I loved all the over-the-top stuff. The crazy gimmicks and the face-pulling.

It wasn't long before I realized there was a great deal more to this wrestling caper than what you saw on Saturday afternoons on *World of Sport*. Some were just entertainers. Others were very skilled wrestlers. But the ones who were both, who had the whole package, were the ones to emulate. I began to watch the wrestlers who made me believe that what they were doing in the ring was real. As far as that goes, England has the best wrestlers in the world – or did in those days, at any rate. I was determined to learn that really serious style. I wanted to be a wrestler whose matches were completely believable.

Looking back, I was lucky to be trying to break in when I did. In the late 1970s and early 1980s there were so many amazing guys in Britain to watch and learn from. There was Rocco, Finlay and Marty Jones – someone who became a big influence in my career later on. There was Satoru Sayama who wrestled as Sammy Lee and later became the original Tiger Mask in Japan, and sometimes the Dynamite Kid.

These people revolutionized the wrestling business in England. They had a style that no one else could do. They wrestled really well. They did flying moves but it was all part of a believable, hard-hitting style – my favourite. I recently watched a video of Marty Jones wrestling Rocco in 1977 and it still stands up today. It was the first time they ever wrestled each other on TV and you wouldn't know it wasn't a modern match – in fact, it was better than a lot of what you see today. Incredible wrestling.

But wrestling isn't the easiest thing in the world to get into. You can't just look in the Situations Vacant column and answer the ad that says "Wrestlers wanted". There weren't any textbooks telling you how to get into the business. You had to work it out for yourself.

My uncle Eddie provided my way in. He used to drink in a pub in Wolverhampton with a guy who did a lot of wrestling. He did local shows, carnivals, that kind of thing. So I met this fellow and started putting up the ring with him – the traditional first job for anyone starting out in the business.

On Tuesday afternoons I would go to Wolverhampton Civic Hall and hang around. I'd watch while they put up the ring and after a while I began to meet a few people involved in the shows. I hung around with them and whenever there was an opportunity, I'd get in the ring and I'd try out different things. I'd done a little bit of judo when I was younger, just enough to know how to fall properly. I didn't know anything else, so I started to figure things out for myself.

There weren't any wrestling clubs in Wolverhampton, so I went to a boxing club to get fit. As a schoolboy I was a fat kid – when I was ten I weighed ten-and-a-half stone (147 pounds). But I started getting into shape at the boxing club, and all because I wanted to make it as a wrestler. I was determined to find a way in somehow.

Watching these guys in Wolverhampton, I'd figured out all these falls. So I started practising them at home in my dad's back garden. I made a frame of two-by-two wood, put two eight-by-four sheets of plywood on top and a blanket on top of that to make my own improvised ring and I used to throw myself around on that all the time, trying to teach myself how to fall. I'd backdrop myself off walls onto the grass and fly all over the place.

All of this was with just one goal in mind. My dad would encourage me, but I'm sure he thought it was just a passing phase, not something to which I'd stay committed.

Soon I started to get quite tall. Most people today don't realize I'm 6 feet 4 inches. As a villain, I crouch down to look smaller than I am. I want the fans to think they can beat me themselves because they'll hate me all the more when I get away with some in-ring villainy. It's one of the tricks I've picked up along the way.

So I was tall enough to be a wrestler, but there was a problem: I had no athletic ability whatsoever. I'd never done any sports, watched any or cared about them, for that matter. At school I'd get out of them any way I could. So pretty early on I recognized I couldn't be a high-flying wrestler, even if it was my favourite style to watch. I just didn't have the ability for it. When I tried to fly I looked like a very sad sack indeed. I'd never be a performer like Rocco in the past or Eddie Guerrero and Chris Benoit today.

That's why I decided I had to concentrate on mat wrestling and entertaining. Making my matches look more believable and fluid became my obsession.

Before we go any further I think I should explain a few things. I have a tremendous respect for the wrestling business. It has given me every material possession that I own, allowed me to feed my family and taken me around the world. But I owe it to you to tell the truth and that means telling you things about my chosen occupation that I wouldn't have told you ten years ago.

When I started in the wrestling business it was part of our job to defend the legitimacy of our sport. Nowadays it's very different. In the 1990s, World Wrestling Federation acknowledged that wrestling was entertainment. Nothing that most people didn't already know or at least suspect. Today, people watch wrestling and enjoy it for what it is. They don't feel as though they are having their intelligence insulted. But I personally do not like to overexpose the business – more on that later.

Throughout this book I will write honestly about my life and the business I am in. I will be explaining certain aspects of what goes on behind the scenes. So I will start by telling you this – yes, a professional wrestling match is "fixed". But it is not fake. It's fixed because the participants know what the outcome of the match is going to be when they start. It is not fake because the action you see is genuine – it really does hurt. We are skilful but we are not magicians. No matter what you do, when a man weighing 300 pounds lands on you from a great height, it is going to hurt.

People say we know how to fall, meaning we can fall in a controlled way. Yes we can – but in a wrestling match, with so many things going on at the same time and so many switches of momentum, too many things are outside your control. You can't help but fall in an uncontrolled way. That's why there will be so many injuries discussed in this book.

As a seventeen-year-old rookie I practised my moves at every opportunity.

Not only was I dead set on becoming a wrestler, I was dead set on being a wrestler in Blackpool. It wasn't that far away from Staffordshire and when I was a little kid we used to go there for days out. Even then I used to say I would live there one day, because it was like wonderland to me.

Blackpool is the biggest holiday resort in Europe and, I believe, the second most-visited destination after the Vatican. There's nothing cultural about the place. It promises cheap and cheerful entertainment for the masses. It boasts a giant amusement park, known as the Pleasure Beach – one of the biggest in the world.

It's got three big piers, an enormous sandy beach and non-stop entertainment. There's a huge stretch called the Golden Mile – actually seven miles long – which is lit up in the winter by the famous Blackpool Illuminations. There's so much to do there – everything a kid would want. Circuses, amusement parks, arcades full of games and machines. It was a magical place for me when I first set eyes on it and it still is. A lot of people say it's past its heyday now but I don't see that. When I go back there, I still see it as a fairytale place.

> People say we know how to fall, meaning we can fall in a controlled way. Yes we can – but in a wrestling match, with so many things going on at the same time and so many switches of momentum, too many things are outside your control. You can't help but fall in an uncontrolled way. That's why there will be so many injuries discussed in this book.

Unsurprisingly, one of my first memories of Blackpool revolves around wrestling. We went to the Pleasure Beach one day when I was nine or ten. We walked round the corner of the beautiful old White Tower building there to be confronted by this row of wrestlers. They looked like monsters to a little lad like me. There was a Red Indian, a Viking, a few masked men and some women. They were throwing out challenges to the crowd, daring them to step in the ring.

Years later I'd get to know the truth behind some of these people. Radnor the Viking, for example, was a fellow called Dave from Ellesmere Port in Cheshire. I wrestled him later on. But as a youngster, this was the most impressive sight I'd ever experienced. Scary too. When they were challenging the crowd to a fight, I was convinced they were challenging my dad. As far as I was concerned, my dad was the biggest, strongest fellow in the world; but Radnor the Viking was enormous and had a big axe!

The moment we went in to watch their show, I was hooked. I looked at those men in that ring, with the crowd in the palms of their hands and thought: "I'm going to work here one day. I'm going to be a wrestler at Blackpool Pleasure Beach."

And a few years later, I was.

I remembered that first view of Radnor the Viking when I was fifteen and went back to the Pleasure Beach to see the wrestlers again. Again, the same experience – I walked round the corner, saw the wrestlers and knew more than ever this was what I wanted to do. So I started out like many people do in the wrestling business – from then on, while I was still at school, I went to the Pleasure Beach every weekend and hung around. The promoter, Bobby Baron, was a lovely man who really looked after me. After a few weeks of hanging around, I plucked up the courage to tell Bobby what was on my mind.

> **I went up to him and blurted it out: "I want to be a wrestler."**
>
> **Bobby took out the pipe that was permanently clenched in his teeth and said: "Eee," which was how he started all of his sentences. "Eee, I bet you do, kid."**
>
> **"No, I really do," I insisted.**

And that led to my first ever match. My opponent was a man called Shaun who later became Colonel Brody. At the time though, he wrestled as a gay character called Magnificent Maurice. He was 6 feet 6 inches, with an impressive handlebar moustache and a big, bald head. Already, in the short time I'd been hanging around the wrestlers, I'd seen him knock several people out. And there was me, a little fifteen-year-old.

Still, I got in the ring with him. "I know what this wrestling's all about," I thought. All that training in the back garden would stand me in good stead now. I started by throwing some weak, fake punches at him. He just glared at me. Then, BAM! He whacked me on the back of my head and I went down. He picked me up and proceeded to throw me all over the ring. Soon after – though the match felt plenty long enough to me at the time – he got me in a single-leg Boston crab and I tapped out. Either he'd thought I was just another wannabe from the crowd or Bobby had told him to slap me around a bit to get rid of me. But throughout the beating, there was skill there too. He could have hurt me badly, but he didn't. He humiliated me instead.

I wasn't going to give up after just one match. I went back the next weekend and I kept going back. Within a few weeks, they took pity on me and took me in. They had a lot of guys who never became real wrestlers but just worked as plants in the crowd, and they thought I could be one of them. When I got the chance to, I'd jump in the ring and roll about, teaching myself some moves.

> Steve would get on the mic and use the same spiel he always used. "What we're looking for are fighting men. Anybody who can have a fight. We want boxers, wrestlers, judo men, karate men, poofs, queers, perverts, Len Faircloughs, anybody who can fight."

The way it worked was this. The wrestlers lined up outside – just as they had when I'd seen them as a nine-year-old – while Steve Foster from Wigan, the man on the microphone, would get everyone going. Punters were challenged to get in the ring with the wrestlers. The matches were of three three-minute rounds. Challengers would get £10 for every round they lasted, and £100 if they lasted all three or knocked the wrestler out.

Steve would get on the mic and use the same spiel he always used. "What we're looking for are fighting men. Anybody who can have a fight. We want boxers, wrestlers, judo men, karate men, poofs, queers, perverts, Len Faircloughs, anybody who can fight."

Now Blackpool's a tough place. There'd be gangs of lads who would have been roaming around, drinking all day, and they'd be up for it. First a smaller guy, one of our plants, would step up to accept the challenge. That would get the crowd going. Then Steve would ask: "Is there anybody else?" and a bigger guy would step in. Now the crowd would be on the hook. They'd *ooh* and *aah*, thinking the big guy was bound to have a great chance. Then everyone would file in and pay their money to see the matches.

Sometimes the wrestlers would have to go out and do this routine two or three times to fill the place up before the show started. It was a great place to learn about crowd psychology. When the big fellow got in to have a go, you could tell everyone was thinking: "Now here's someone who can win."

The wrestlers who took the challenges usually wore masks. There were a couple of reasons for that. Firstly, it made you look more like a monster when you were standing outside and Steve was getting people in. Secondly, if trouble really kicked off in the shows – which it did – or if you had to give someone a really good hiding, you could bugger off when the police came because no one knew what you looked like. The crowds used to be so programmed by TV that they'd shout at the challengers to tear the wrestler's masks off. No good advice, like "Punch his head in!" or "Kick him in the balls!" Just, "Tear his mask off!" That always used to make me laugh.

At the end of that summer season, I had to go back to Codsall to finish my last year in school. Now I had had a taste of this intoxicating new world, school managed the impossible and became even drearier than it had been before. I still went to Wolverhampton when I could to hang around and talk to some of the wrestlers. But I was fixated on getting to the Pleasure Beach. And I wasn't going to stay in school one second longer than I had to.

When I finally took my exams, I just did them and left. Never even looked at the results. My dad has probably got the certificates somewhere but I've never looked at them. It was May 18, 1984. I was a few days past my sixteenth birthday and about to become a professional wrestler.

The wrestlers who took the challenges usually wore masks. There were a couple of reasons for that. Firstly, it made you look more like a monster when you were standing outside and Steve was getting people in. Secondly, if trouble really kicked off in the shows – which it did – or if you had to give someone a really good hiding, you could bugger off when the police came because no one knew what you looked like. The crowds used to be so programmed by TV that they'd shout at the challengers to tear the wrestler's masks off. No good advice, like "Punch his head in!" or "Kick him in the balls!" Just, "Tear his mask off!" That always used to make me laugh.

2

Wrestling in Wonderland

Before I left home to go to Blackpool I worked for six weeks to get some money together. I did jobs for my dad but most of the time I worked for my uncle Bill, Dad's oldest brother and one of the funniest people I have ever been around. Life's always much better when you are around funny people and more often than not I've been lucky enough to have that. I did six weeks of labouring for Bill and he made me laugh every single day.

Before I left for Blackpool I went to see my granddad, who was very proud I was going to become a wrestler. My dad let me go but I don't think he believed I would last for very long by myself in the big outside world. I wanted to prove to him – and myself, I think – that I could succeed on my own. As I said, everyone had expected me to take over his business, which as far as I was concerned meant taking from him for the rest of my life. I could have done that quite easily, but it was the last thing I wanted.

He was a self-made successful man, and I wanted to be too – in my own chosen field. I didn't want to take anything from him and I never have. It wasn't rags to riches, more like riches to rags. I went from living in a very nice house to just scraping by in Blackpool.

And yet, when I was sixteen and working at Blackpool Pleasure Beach, that was all I ever wanted out of life. I never wanted to go any further and would have been happy if I'd stayed there until my dying day. I earned £5 a job. I stayed in Belmont Avenue in a house owned by Steve Peacock, one of the wrestlers, where he lived with his wife and kids. My room was a small bedroom at the back of the house.

Soon I was working hard but not making any money. Bobby Baron ran the wrestling at the Pleasure Beach and also did a few shows around the area with his little Blackpool crew. Bobby had a deal with Pontin's holiday camps for whom we'd do shows as part of the entertainment. Also the Carla Gran caravan park in Fleetwood, the Ponderosa holiday park in Grange-over-Sands, and whatever other odd jobs came up. Shows at the holiday camps meant two singles matches followed by the four men who'd already wrestled in those in a tag match to make up an hour's show. Sometimes there would be a break after the singles matches while everyone got down to bingo before the tag match started.

The crew was Steve Peacock, my friend Peter Thompson, who wrestled as Steve Fury and with whom I'm still in touch today, and

> Shows at the holiday camps meant two singles matches followed by the four men who'd already wrestled in those in a tag match to make up an hour's show. Sometimes there would be a break after the singles matches while everyone got down to bingo before the tag match started.

another guy called Dave Duran. I'd been taken on as an apprentice so as the new boy I had to do whatever little jobs needed doing. I'd put up the ring with Michael Jessop, an infamous name in the wrestling business. He has been putting up rings for forty years and still hasn't got a clue how to do it. But we all liked Mike and took care of him.

We would go into these places carrying our little ring and put it up. I would carry the bags, make the tea and do whatever needed doing. Sometimes I would wrestle. Other times I would referee. Afterwards I would drop the ring, get it into the van and off we would go to the next job. Often we would do two or three shows a day. It might be the Carla Gran in the afternoon and then Pontin's in Morecambe at night. Sometimes we would do something at the Pleasure Beach and then go and do something else in the evening. There was a lot of work around so we were on the go non-stop.

Peter was a big help to me in those early days. He was about ten years older than me so he took me under his wing and smartened

Peter Thompson really looked out for me in those early days. Here we are with Pedro the Gypsy.

me up a lot. He told me what to do – and warned me what I should avoid. He always dressed really well; he looked the part. He used to say that there was no disgrace in being skint – just in acting skint. And he was the world's best wind-up merchant. He always took the greatest of pleasure in playing tricks on me whenever he could.

When we wrestled, there would be a piece of paper with the wrestlers' names on for the ring announcer to introduce us before each match. The other boys always took great delight in dreaming up the daftest names they could for me when I was wrestling. Bertie Bassett from Littlehampton was one favourite. Phil Hiscock from Cockermouth – you name it, I've been it. Peter always thought that was hilarious.

When I think of some of the stunts he pulled, I really have no idea why I'm still his friend today.

When we wrestled, there would be a piece of paper with the wrestlers' names on for the ring announcer to introduce us before each match. The other boys always took great delight in dreaming up the daftest names they could for me when I was wrestling. Bertie Bassett from Littlehampton was one favourite. Phil Hiscock from Cockermouth – you name it, I've been it. Peter always thought that was hilarious.

There was only one problem in my happy new life – I was an absolutely rotten wrestler. I learned this awful fact in my first week on the job. We went to Pontin's in Morecambe, where I was due to referee. Even wrestling fans might not understand this, but refereeing is a very hard job. Good refs are a vital part of our business. A good referee can make a bad match look good, and a bad ref can make a good match look bad. He's got to be in the right place, doing the right things at the right time.

But this night I wasn't even going to start to learn to referee. Because a friend of mine George Burgess said: "No, I'll referee, you wrestle." That put me in a right panic. I'd only ever done stuff in the ring at the Pleasure Beach and this was going to be in front of a thousand people in the ballroom at Morecambe. They always packed out the hall because it was part of the entertainment they'd paid for when they booked their week at the camp. On my first official day in the job, this was pretty daunting. There were 500 or 600 screaming kids in the audience and my bottle was going. But I was thrown out there and told to get on with it.

I was up against a Manchester wrestler called Paul Tompkins who was going by the name of Tiger Tompkins. Now, I didn't have much of a clue but there were a few things I did know how to do. My opponent could

> I got knocked about every single day. Soon everything hurt. I had a really bad back. I got used to going into the toilets and coughing up blood. He was determined to do me in – and he did a good job of it.

throw me off the ropes and I could do a cartwheel or take a bump. So when Paul threw me off the ropes, I went to do my cartwheel. As I went up on one arm, the other one buckled and I landed flat on my face. The crowd went: "Oooh!" and burst out laughing. I felt like I'd died a thousand deaths. It didn't really help that this came after being introduced as Bertie Bassett from Littlehampton. We struggled through the match somehow, but I'll always remember the embarrassment.

There was obviously plenty to learn inside the ring. Soon I realized I had a great deal to learn outside it, too. There were very few positions in this company, we were a small crew. This meant that their places were jealously guarded by some of the guys who were already there. Most of them were all right but they made sure I had a hard time – they wanted me to earn my place and that was fair enough.

Steve Peacock was always okay with me. But Dave Duran spent the next two years beating me half to death. He physically hurt me as much as possible. He had a knack of getting me to give him money and never giving it back. I didn't know any better and, to tell the truth, I was a bit scared of him. He was a big heavy man in his mid to late twenties and he used to enjoy giving me beatings. I got knocked about every single day. Soon everything hurt. I had a really bad back. I got used to going into the toilets and coughing up blood. He was determined to do me in – and he did a good job of it.

You expect to get it hard when you start out, but this guy was going over the top to hurt me. I'm not complaining about it because it gave me a lot of respect for what we do. I do think that when you are learning the ropes you should be leant on a bit, and every hold should be applied at full force so you have a respect for it and to toughen you up. The constant hidings did teach me something else, too – not to be worried about getting into a fight with anyone. The worst anyone can do is beat you up, and I'd had plenty of that. I don't consider myself a hard man, and getting proper hidings doesn't happen much nowadays.

But it certainly happened then. Dave was doing his best to scare me off, and make sure I didn't come back. I felt differently: I was determined that he wouldn't succeed. For the whole of that summer season, my first, it went on day after day. But I just kept going. Dave Duran wasn't going to get the better of me.

Bullying wasn't the only out-of-the-ring activity I learned about. Every book has got to have at least one sex story. Good for sales, they say. So here's mine.

Back then I was a little lad who'd never had a girlfriend at school, doing the job I wanted to do but getting knocked around a lot for the privilege. One night at the beginning of September we were at the Carla Gran in Fleetwood. We'd done a couple of matches and were waiting around to do the second half of our show while they were having a knobbly knees contest, or something equally glamorous.

The next thing I knew, this girl came up and stood next to me. We started chatting. We established that she was from Liverpool and I was sixteen. Then, bold as brass, she said: "Are you going to take me outside then?" My jaw dropped, but I managed to stammer: "All right." So I took her outside and we climbed into the back of the ring van. She pulled her skirt up, I dropped my strides and I started doing my best to give her the most enjoyable five seconds of her life.

I'd no idea what I was doing. But just as we were coupled, I noticed that sitting in the front of the van were Steve Peacock, Peter Thompson and everybody else working on the show, all watching us and laughing. The girl started laughing as well. I was lying there, dying from embarrassment and wishing everyone would leave me alone. I didn't know where to put myself. Then the ring music started up – and I realized I was supposed to be refereeing the tag match. And because I was referee, that meant I had to be in the ring first.

I valiantly left this girl lying in the back of the van, pulled my trousers up and sprinted to the ring. I ran through the mud, straight in the back door, across the stage, through the curtains, into the ring and stood there in the corner, sweating and thinking: "This can't be happening to me." One by one, the wrestlers came to the ring. I was just about to bring them to the middle when Steve Peacock turned to the crowd and said: "Ladies and gentlemen, we can't wrestle with a referee who's got a hard-on."

> **Steve Peacock turned to the crowd and said: "Ladies and gentlemen, we can't wrestle with a referee who's got a hard-on."**

It was true, too. I didn't know where to put myself. So I lost my virginity in the back of a ring truck. It's fair to say my whole life has been entangled in wrestling in one way or another.

I was happy wrestling but I wasn't making any money. The £5 a job was the normal rate but it was well nigh impossible to live on that, even then. Steve Peacock knew the people who ran an Indian restaurant called the Star of India on Central Drive and he got me a washing-up job there. I'd finish wherever I was wrestling and get there for 10 p.m. to wash up, wait on tables or whatever they wanted me to do. They used to shut at 2 so it would be 3.30 a.m. by the time we got out. For this I got the princely sum of one pound an hour.

One night I brought out a curry and it turned out it was for the comedian Lenny Henry, who'd popped in for a meal. I'd only ever seen him on TV and he was enormous in real life. Lenny was in

Blackpool doing a summer show, one I got to see a few times that summer. And that was another reason why Blackpool was so great.

I've always admired stand-up comedians because I think they have one of the hardest jobs in the world. I used to love watching stars like Bernard Manning, Frank Carson, Mick Miller and the Grumbleweeds. I'm also a big fan of Tommy Cooper, Morecambe and Wise, Les Dawson and many of the classic British sitcoms like Only Fools and Horses and Steptoe and Son. Newer shows like Alan Partridge, The Royle Family and Peter Kaye's Phoenix Nights are great too. But I must say that Billy Connolly is the funniest guy I've seen.

For a big comedy fan like me, it was heaven. All the biggest names in British comedy would play Blackpool.

I've always admired stand-up comedians because I think they have one of the hardest jobs in the world. I used to love watching stars like Bernard Manning, Frank Carson, Mick Miller and the Grumbleweeds. I'm also a big fan of Tommy Cooper, Morecambe and Wise, Les Dawson and many of the classic British sitcoms like *Only Fools and Horses* and *Steptoe and Son*. Newer shows like *Alan Partridge*, *The Royle Family* and *Peter Kaye's Phoenix Nights* are great too. But I must say that Billy Connolly is the funniest guy I've seen.

Being a comedy fan is a big help if you're a wrestler. I've borrowed off all of them and am always throwing lines of theirs into the show. Les Dawson was a great face-puller, and it's no coincidence that my facial expressions are one of the things I'm best known for today. When I later became Lord Steven Regal in WCW (World Class Wrestling), a lot of my act was inspired by Terry-Thomas, the gap-toothed comic actor from the 1950s and 1960s.

Because of the character I play, I can do all this stuff and people don't laugh – they hate me for it instead. The only strange thing is that being such a serious student of comedy, I still don't understand what makes Americans laugh. I can watch a show like *Friends*, one of America's most-watched sitcoms, and think it is a nice enough show, but it doesn't make me laugh.

Working at the Star of India wasn't all about seeing the stars, however. To make sure I'd have something to eat the next day, I used to take some chicken, wrap it up in a parcels and put it on the top of the back wall. Then I'd go round the back after work to pick it up. This little dodge meant I had something to eat. One night I went round into the alley to find a dog and a cat fighting over my chicken, which had fallen off the wall. I went hungry the next day.

Blackpool is a seasonal place and once the summer season is over and all the holidaymakers have gone home, it can be a grim one too. There was no wrestling at the Pleasure Beach, for a start. The restaurant job finished too. Taken altogether, it meant a very lonely winter in Blackpool trying to make ends meet. I did what wrestling work I could and ended up moving into a house with my friend Peter.

That was great for me, although it did give Peter plenty of opportunities to wind me up on a daily basis. But living with him did me a lot of good. He was like a wiser older brother. I'd go round town with him and meet a lot of people. Peter was well known in Blackpool because he had lived there since the age of sixteen. Everybody knew him. And he was always trying to teach me things. One day he took me into a bookmaker's and put a great big bet on a horse. It lost and he said: "That's the reason you should never gamble." I took it to heart and never have. He smartened me up to a lot of things like that.

Things were tough that winter. Having no money meant I had to go and sign on to get unemployment benefit – not an experience I wanted. When it came round to Easter time, there was some wrestling work. But after that was another dead period until June when the summer season kicked in. In that period, for the one and only time in my life, I bit the bullet and got a proper job.

There was an engineering factory in Blackpool advertising for workers. "Earn £40 a week", the advert said. I thought it might suit me for a couple of weeks until the summer season started. I went along to the place and they put me on a machine. There were these little ten-inch-long metal bars and I had to put them in the machine and cut them in half. By lunchtime, I couldn't take any more. I thought: "These people are mental for doing this, how can they do it?"

I walked out. I do not understand how you can do that for a living. I know people work in factories; some do it all their lives and are perfectly happy. Good luck to them. But it's beyond me. The only normal job I ever had and it lasted four hours.

Working in a nightclub was different. When I turned seventeen I heard that they needed glass collectors at a local place called the Tangerine Club. I started working there at weekends and sometimes also nights in the week when they needed me to go in for a few hours.

Soon it was summer again – which meant another whole season of Dave Duran. At the start of the season he took me aside.

> **"We can have this summer easy or we can have it hard," he told me. "Either you give me some of your wages and I won't beat you up so much – or you don't and I beat you up."**

> **"Bollocks!" was my reply. "You're going to have to beat me up then."**

And that is exactly what he set out to do. I thought the year before had been tough, but it was nothing compared to what was happening now. He really hammered me, to the point where I thought I couldn't take it any more. He was smacking me about something terrible. I was still getting bigger and thought to myself: "I'll stick it out." But it meant some terrible beatings in the ring. He was a naturally strong man, eighteen stone (252 pounds), and I was twelve stone tops (168 pounds).

It got to the stage where this daily punishment was really getting me down. My body was starting to protest. I had pain shooting down both legs. I was coughing up blood. My neck was so stiff I could hardly move my head. I was in a bad way, and thought I couldn't take much more. I'd had enough. Then just when I was at my lowest, something wonderful happened. Dave went away to work for someone else for a week and they brought in a replacement. It was Ian Wilson, still a good friend of mine, who wrestled as Mad Dog Wilson.

Throughout his wrestling career Ian has held down a day job as a postman. He's a terrific fellow who is good at his job and he made a superb villain, as he was great at riling up fans. So I got to wrestle him. I'd met Ian a few times before and he had stood out every time. When you are young you get used to the older wrestlers being standoffish towards you – they want you to respect them. But whenever I was throwing myself around the ring trying to learn how to do things, Ian would always come up with a quiet word of advice.

My match with him was a revelation. He threw himself all over the ring for me. "This is how it is meant to be," I thought. I

One of my earliest matches, against Ripper Raven. I'd have been sixteen or seventeen. Bobby Baron is the referee.

dropkicked him a few times. He threw himself over the top rope, and let me do all the moves I wanted. Duran had never let me do anything. I never learned much by wrestling him. It hardened me up all right, and taught me to take a lot of punishment without moaning, but that was about it.

The only times I'd ever learned anything up until then had been in the ring with Steve Peacock, who was a great wrestling comedian. He did a gay gimmick as Gaylord Steve Peacock and would put on a comedy match. He'd wrestled all the top comedy wrestlers who used to be around – Catweazle, Kevin Connelly and Pedro the Gypsy. These were all funny guys, especially in the ring. They did routines made famous by Les Kellett, a man before my time. I learned a lot of comedy off Peacock which I do in my act now.

So having the sort of match I had with Ian was stunning. I thought: "Right, this is it. I'm going to keep on at this." Of course Dave Duran came back a week later and started hammering me again. But now it didn't matter. I'd seen just how good wrestling could be and knew it was what I wanted to do.

Come September, I moved back in with Steve Peacock. By this time I had graduated to the bigger, front room. A girl who lived close by used to come round often. She lived in the next street and I knew her brother and sister. They were little kids who used to play with Steve's youngsters. She was a hairdresser who used to do the hair of Steve's wife Julie. She also used to babysit for Steve so I'd see her all the time. She was a bit older than me so I was a bit shy around her at first. But soon I had the perfect opportunity to speak to her.

Bobby Baron had decided he wanted me to wrestle as a cowboy. I went out and bought a cowboy hat and got my hair dyed blond. I hated it. The hat was ten sizes too big for me and I looked properly crap in it. I knew how to look good in the ring – or thought I did. I had black wrestling boots so I sprayed one of them gold and one of them silver. I wanted to get two silver streaks bleached into either side of my blond hair and that would be it – I'd look fantastic.

So I asked this girl to do it. Her name was Chris and she refused

I knew Chris was the one for me. With us is my brother, Lee.

to take any payment from me. I said I'd thank her by taking her out to the Tangerine Club. I was seventeen and she was eighteen. We went out that night and we are still together today. Chris became my wife.

The Tangerine Club was looking for doormen and since I was collecting glasses there anyway, I got the job. I'd already had to lie about my age to become a glass collector and being just seventeen, I shouldn't have been working as a bouncer. Back then

I thought I was filling out but when I look at old pictures now, I realize I was really skinny.

Working the door at the club was a lot of fun. People from the football club used to go there and it was a great scene. The doormen were good too. There was a rugby player called Dave Secca and Dave Beatty, one of the football crowd, and between them they taught me how to be a proper doorman.

I've never believed in banging on about how hard you are, but we were good at our job. The secret of being a doorman is to be polite. We didn't growl at people when they went in. We'd ask how everyone was doing. If you stand there trying to intimidate people, they get the hump straight away. Then they'll be drinking in a club with the hump on – and that usually means trouble. Learning that stood me in good stead later on.

> There have been times when there hasn't been much wrestling work around and I have always been able to get hired as a doorman because people knew I could do the job.

There have been times when there hasn't been much wrestling work around and I have always been able to get hired as a doorman because people knew I could do the job. The Tangerine was the sort of place where there would be a fair bit of trouble. It wasn't exactly a glamorous establishment. It was the kind of place where even the piano had a bandage on its leg. When the Blackpool Illuminations were on and the town was at its busiest it would get mental in there.

When you arrived at 6 p.m. it would already be heaving. Because of the football club connection and their links with other football and rugby clubs, lots of parties would take a day trip to Blackpool and then book into the Tangerine for the night. The coaches would drop them off at six and they would be drinking there until it shut. There was never anything major but things did kick off quite regularly and as a doorman, you'd have to do your job.

I discovered another passion of mine at the Tangerine – soul music. Particularly Motown and what's called Northern Soul, which is rare soul music. When I worked there it was just after the heyday of Northern Soul in England but people would come up to the DJ and ask him to play "casino music", which was what they called it. The DJ only had three Northern Soul tracks. "Needle In a Haystack" by the Velvelettes, "There's a Ghost In My House" by R Dean Taylor, and "The Snake" by Al Wilson. They kicked me off on Northern Soul and they are still three of my favourites today.

There was a lot of fun to be had in the Tangerine Club. They had a band and a DJ called Guy Francis who would do an hour-long stint. Every night for his last set he would dress up as something, which usually made for a lot of laughs because he'd pull a girl and take her home wearing his outfit and get changed at home. I hadn't

I discovered another passion of mine at the Tangerine – soul music. Particularly Motown and what's called Northern Soul, which is rare soul music. When I worked there it was just after the heyday of Northern Soul in England but people would come up to the DJ and ask him to play "casino music", which was what they called it. The DJ only had three Northern Soul tracks. "Needle In a Haystack" by the Velvelettes, "There's a Ghost In My House" by R Dean Taylor, and "The Snake" by Al Wilson. They kicked me off on Northern Soul and they are still three of my favourites today.

seen his set one night so my first sight of Guy was when he came walking out of the club blacked up like a Zulu with a grass skirt on and a big comedy bone through his nose. He was hand in hand with a girl – they walked out, calm as you like, got in his car and drove off.

When I wasn't wrestling, working at the Tangerine Club kept me going. That and helping out a wrestler friend of mine, Tony Francis, who ran a second-hand cooker shop on Central Drive. He'd always give me work, shifting cookers and the like around. I grew up a bit doing jobs like that. The following year, 1986, I moved into a flat with Chris. She and I got engaged and were married on November 8, fourteen months after we first went out together.

Before that, though, I met one of the most important men in British wrestling – Max Crabtree. Tony Francis took me to a Dale Martin show, which was Max's company. That was the night I also met Marty Jones.

Max wanted me to work for him, and laid it out. "It's no use doing all that fairground stuff if you want to come and work for us. Marty's got a gym in Shaw near Rochdale and you've got to go there on Sunday mornings."

Marty was a good guy to meet. He's one of the best wrestlers you'll ever see – what we call a great worker. He has wrestled in some of the best matches I've ever seen. That 1977 match he had with Rocco was awesome. Another match he had in 1985 when he wrestled Owen Hart was electrifying. The best match I ever saw him work was in Durban, South Africa. It was an open air stadium and when it got to 5 p.m. that afternoon it poured down. The stadium held five or six thousand fans but when we arrived there must have been only a thousand or so die-hards, sitting out in the rain under their umbrellas. I went on early and did what I could before Marty wrestled a guy called Gama Singh from Calgary in Canada. They did a full hour in that torrential downpour – 12 five-minute rounds with no falls. It was an incredible showcase of wrestling skills. It was just like the end of that film *Paradise Alley*, if you've ever seen it. I sat out in the rain and watched every moment, enthralled.

So now I'd wrestle all week and work at the nightclub at weekends, get home at 3 a.m. Sunday morning and get up early to go to Shaw, to Marty's gym. I couldn't drive in those days so we'd borrow Chris's stepdad's car and she'd drive me, or I'd take the bus, which used to take forever. But it was all worth it to go and work out with Marty. He helped me tremendously. When I started with him, I was able to do a couple of bumps and a bit of comedy. But Marty taught me to wrestle.

One Sunday I got there and Max turned up to watch us. He had a

Marty was a good guy to meet. He's one of the best wrestlers you'll ever see – what we call a great worker. He has wrestled in some of the best matches I've ever seen. That 1977 match he had with Rocco was awesome. Another match he had in 1985 when he wrestled Owen Hart was electrifying. The best match I ever saw him work was in Durban, South Africa. It was an open air stadium and when it got to 5 p.m. that afternoon it poured down. The stadium held five or six thousand fans but when we arrived there must have been only a thousand or so die-hards, sitting out in the rain under their umbrellas. I went on early and did what I could before Marty wrestled a guy called Gama Singh from Calgary in Canada. They did a full hour in that torrential downpour – 12 five-minute rounds with no falls. It was an incredible showcase of wrestling skills. It was just like the end of that film Paradise Alley, if you've ever seen it. I sat out in the rain and watched every moment, enthralled.

notepad out and was pretending to write things down, though in reality I reckon he was just doodling to look good. He said he'd give me a few jobs but I had to stop working for Bobby Baron. That was something I wasn't prepared to do. I never stopped working for Bobby – he'd given me my first break and been very good to me. Right up until the time I came to America, I worked for Bobby whenever I could. Even when I was travelling the world, if I came back and had only one day spare and Bobby had a show on, I'd be there.

How did I clear it with Max? I didn't. Blackpool was its own little place and no one was going to report me to Max if I did the odd show here and there. If I did shows for Bobby on the quiet, no one was going to pick up on it. Bobby was very good about it because he liked me, so he would arrange things around any commitments I had with Max.

But as far as Max was concerned, he was the only one in the business who had any idea and I needed to work for no one but him.

I took the job from Max – what else was I going to do? It wouldn't be long before I was on television myself, and Bertie Bassett from Littlehampton would be a memory. I was about to become Steve Regal.

3
Steve Regal and Big Daddy

My first job for Max was in Skegness against a Blackpool pal of mine, Barry Sherman – a councillor by day who used to wrestle as Rex Strong. But I was still the man with no name. I was still using whatever was made up for me on the day. Some were memorable, like Mick Malone the Scrapman's Kid. Others were rotten.

One day I was sitting in the cooker shop, talking with Tony Francis. We were reading a wrestling magazine and there was an article in it about an American wrestler called Steve Regal. "That's a good name for you," said Tony. I liked it – it just sounded right. I never dreamed I'd ever wrestle in America, so bumping into the first Steve Regal didn't seem a problem. Luckily I never have – he finished before I got over here. Steve Regal was my ring name from then on.

I was dead set on the name but Max was dead set against it. Probably because he didn't think of it first. "We've got too many Steves," he told me. "Let's think of something else. I know, let's call you Roy Regal." Roy Regal! I hated it. It needled me to death. It made me sound like a gay cowboy.

For the next few months I was Steve when I worked for Bobby and Roy when I worked for Max. I don't know why the name Roy bothered me so much – I should have shrugged my shoulders and got on with it. But it really drove me mad.

Working different shows for these two promoters I started meeting some very talented wrestlers. I was on shows with Marty Jones and Fit Finlay. There was a guy called Ray Steele who was really good. Another one was Terry Rudge. They all did extremely believable-looking wrestling, just the style I liked. Whenever they went at it in the ring it was as real as wrestling ever got because they'd knock the hell out of each other. They used to work so hard and when they came out of the ring, drenched in sweat, it looked like they'd had a real battle. They used great psychology too.

> I never dreamed I'd ever wrestle in America, so bumping into the first Steve Regal didn't seem a problem. Luckily I never have – he finished before I got over here. Steve Regal was my ring name from then on.

The only trouble was Max hated this kind of stuff – he thought it didn't draw money. He was more interested in his brother Shirley – or Big Daddy, as he was better known. But there was one very good thing about working for Max – TV.

After doing a few jobs for Max I got my first televised match in Southport in 1986. It was a very big deal to me. It came just after another big deal, which was getting to wrestle at Blackpool Tower Circus. It was a beautiful circus which had stood there for more than 100 years and had an incredible atmosphere when you wrestled there. The circus would be on six days a week and on a Sunday night they'd have a Dale Martin wrestling show. I used to go to watch even before I was working for them. It was my favourite venue then and remains so to this day.

So things were looking up when the TV offer came along. It was in Southport, and getting there was a story in itself. I hadn't got a ride; I couldn't afford a car and wouldn't ask anyone for money to get one. I'd have to ask Terry – better known as Spit. Terry used to hang around at Blackpool Tower and he dreamed of being a ring announcer. Brian Crabtree, Max's other brother, did that job and always looked very smart. So Terry used to dress up like Brian and hand him the microphone at the beginning of the show. Everyone called him Spit but I'd never spoken to him and didn't know why. I asked someone one day, and they said: "Go and talk to him, you'll soon find out."

So I did. This poor fellow, whose one ambition in life was to be a ring announcer, used to work on the trams in Blackpool. One day he was working on top of one and got caught up in the electric cables and was electrocuted, or so I was told; although now I think about it, he may have had Tourette's Syndrome.

Anyone who spoke to him would soon discover how it had affected him. He'd start off normally: "Hello Darren, how are you?" And then, in the middle of a sentence, he'd break off and start spitting and barking. "WHOO PTT PTT PTT!", he'd go. So he got the nickname Spit the Dog.

But Spit was my only ride to Southport. Because it was such a big deal for me, I was taking Chris with me. She'd never met Spit before, but she found out all about him soon enough.

Chris was in the back and I was in the front passenger seat. As soon as we had got outside

of Blackpool, Spit started barking: "WHOO WHOO WHOO WHOOF!" and the car went all over the road. Chris didn't know what was going on.

It was like this all the way to Southport. "WHOO! – lovely weather isn't it, it's going to be a – WHOO GNAA GNAA GNAA, GNAA GNAA GNAA PTT! – great show tonight."

By the time we arrived Chris was a nervous wreck, and I wasn't much better.

I was wrestling Marty Jones, who had a vicious dropkick which he used to knock me out. That Saturday night, after the match had been on telly in the afternoon, I happened to be working at the Tangerine Club. As I walked through the door, everyone there shouted: "Nine, ten, out!"

So working Dale Martin's shows for Max had got me on telly, but I wasn't happy working for him. Instead of wrestling all the good workers who were around, I got thrown straight into the Big Daddy tag matches. For those who don't know, throughout the 1970s and 1980s Big Daddy was a legitimate superstar in England. Everyone in the country knew who he was, and they still do. Even Margaret Thatcher was a fan.

His was the ultimate big man act. He was in his fifties and weighed about 35 stone (490 pounds) without a single pound hanging the right way. He was a rotten wrestler, absolutely awful. But he had a charisma about him, and his brother Max Crabtree had made him into a superstar.

Like a lot of guys, I was given the role of his tag partner. Every Big Daddy match was the same. His partner would be beaten half to death by the two villains and then Big Daddy would get in and squash them in seconds. I didn't like getting dragged into this role. I really wanted to learn how to wrestle properly, and doing nothing else but that, I wasn't learning anything.

I was working quite regularly for Max at that time so I did about four TV matches for him. He kept putting me in these tag matches, one of which was quite possibly the worst match in television history. It was me, Big Daddy, my friend Richie Brooks, Giant Haystacks, Cyanide Sid Cooper, and a manager called Charlie the Gent, who wasn't even a wrestler. It was so awful, that finished it for me. I thought: "This is useless, I'm not learning anything."

I could see plenty of talented wrestlers around who weren't having to get themselves beaten up to make Big Daddy look good. Great wrestlers like Tony St Clair, Ray Steele, Terry Rudge and Dave Taylor; heavyweights who would travel all over the world. Whenever you saw them they'd be wearing Japanese wrestling T-shirts, or T-shirts from Germany, which I thought was very exotic. I started to find out more about the work they were doing in all these countries and I thought: "Now that's for me."

I knew I hadn't the ability of a Dynamite Kid, but I was getting bigger all the time and I wanted to be one of those solid heavyweights who wrestled really hard. That was my ambition, but I still wasn't very good at it. I had never had the real opportunity to learn how to wrestle that way.

The money was another problem. I'd started out getting a fiver a job from Bobby. Soon I graduated to £10 and then £15 when I turned eighteen. When I went to work for Max Crabtree he cut me back down to a tenner. When you were wrestling on television everyone watching would assume you were making big money, but it was only £60 a job. It was the same for everyone. Max made a lot of money but no one else did. So working for Max meant a pay cut. It was one reason I was still working for Bobby and doing whatever else I could to earn a few quid – I needed to get a house.

At that time the wrestling TV situation in Britain was strange. Dale Martin and Max had half of the television shows and an independent promoter called Brian Dixon had the other half. They'd alternate week by week. Brian had people like Mark "Rollerball" Rocco and Dave Taylor on his shows and they were the real deal.

Originally you could only work for one side or the other. Then suddenly it changed and both sides started using everybody. One day I bumped into Frank Cullen – Chic Cullen as he was known – who was a Scottish wrestler. I really admired his style in the ring.

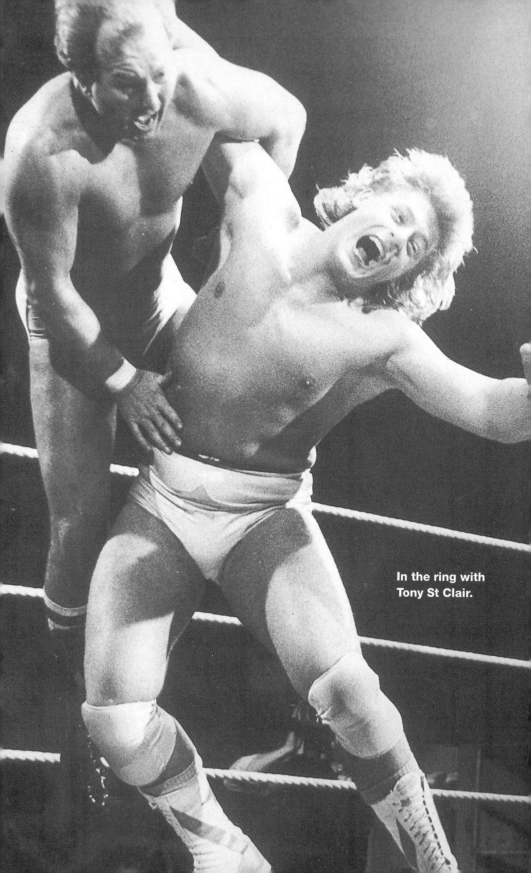

In the ring with
Tony St Clair.

I knew I hadn't the ability of a Dynamite Kid, but I was getting bigger all the time and I wanted to be one of those solid heavyweights who wrestled really hard. That was my ambition, but I still wasn't very good at it. I had never had the real opportunity to learn how to wrestle that way. The money was another problem. I'd started out getting a fiver a job from Bobby. Soon I graduated to £10 and then £15 when I turned eighteen. When I went to work for Max Crabtree he cut me back down to a tenner. When you were wrestling on television everyone watching would assume you were making big money, but it was only £60 a job. It was the same for everyone. Max made a lot of money but no one else did. So working for Max meant a pay cut. It was one reason I was still working for Bobby and doing whatever else I could to earn a few quid – I needed to get a house.

He had worked with the famous Hart family in Calgary and had a very believable style. He did things differently from everybody else I knew. I was chatting to Frank and a friend of his, Rocky Moran from Northern Ireland, about the problems I was having working for Max. They suggested I give Brian Dixon a call.

I did and Brian said straight away: "I've got fifteen jobs for you next month." I told him how I wanted to be a great wrestler like all the guys I admired. "Then those are the guys I'll put you on with," he said. I rang Max and told him I was quitting. Everyone thought I was mad – Max in particular. "You can't quit," he told me. "This is Dale Martin's. This is the biggest promotion in Britain."

One of my last matches for Max was my most enjoyable. Shortly before I was due to get married, I wrestled Pete Roberts – someone I really looked up to. Most people won't know him, but any British wrestler worth his salt would put him in his top three. An absolute class act in the ring and a gentleman outside it too. He was a wrestler's wrestler, who used to work in Japan all the time. His stuff was so far above anybody else's. I was just a green eighteen-year-old wrestling one of my heroes.

> I rang Max and told him I was quitting. Everyone thought I was mad – Max in particular. "You can't quit," he told me. "This is Dale Martin's. This is the biggest promotion in Britain."

He gave me a piece of advice I've never forgotten. He said: "Make everything you do in there mean something, otherwise don't bother doing it." I know it sounds simple – but it's the key to being a good wrestler. It's about everything you do in the ring – how you get hit, how you react; every single thing you must make mean something, or otherwise don't do it. That's how I work and how I teach people too. People think I use lots of tricks in the ring but I don't – it's all about the little things. The way I move and the way I react to things.

Guys who figure out how to make every little motion mean something know this. It means you have no problem in making people believe what you are doing for the whole time they are watching it. Or even if they don't believe it, they want to watch it because they can see how hard you are working.

Wrestling Pete Roberts that night was an honour because he was the absolute best.

Two days later was one of the best days of my life – I got married to Chris. All the family came over from the Midlands and it was a wonderful occasion, one that I'll never forget. But there's no time for a lengthy honeymoon when you're a wrestler. You probably can't afford one anyway. Within a week I was having my first matches for Brian Dixon. I still didn't have a car but Johnny Saint, who lived in Blackpool, used to drive me to matches. Johnny is the best lightweight wrestler I've ever seen – watching him inside the ring, you saw a master at work. My first match was against Rocky Moran, who did a hard, aggressive style like Finlay and Rocco, so I loved wrestling him.

Working for Brian I palled up with another of his wrestlers, Robbie Brookside, whom I'd first met a few months earlier when he worked for Bobby Baron for a while. Robbie had studied under some very good teachers, and after I hooked up with him he would pass on some of his knowledge to me every day, either with a chat or by showing me a particular move or technique in the ring. He and I became a tag team called the Golden Boys, since we both had bleached blond hair and gold trunks with gold stars on – we looked like a couple of overworked drag queens. A proper pair of tarts, basically.

There were plenty of other great guys to learn from too. I wrestled against Dave Taylor, Pete Roberts, Terry Rudge, Johnny South, Ray Steele – all of them very hard, physical matches.

Through the winter time we did the regular towns where Brian Dixon always put on shows. Then in June, July, August and September we did the seaside towns. But we also had the Butlins circuit. While Bobby had the Pontin's contract, Brian had Butlins. Butlins

The day Chris and I got married was one of the happiest of my life.

and Pontin's are both British institutions, pretty much like wrestling. They offer cheap, cheerful holidays with laid-on entertainment for working folk and are sewn into the fabric of British life. And back then, part of that entertainment was us wrestlers. Doing the Butlins circuit was good fun but it meant an insane schedule. The loop we used to do went something like this:

On a Saturday I would wrestle for Bobby Baron at Blackpool Pleasure Beach. On Sunday I'd get picked up at the Tickled Trout in

Preston and we would start on our travels. In the car would be Brian Dixon, who would referee, plus four wrestlers and all our bags.

Our first destination would be Ayr in Scotland. We would wrestle there on the Sunday afternoon, which also meant having to put the ring up and take it down afterwards. Once we'd finished in Scotland we would drive to Skegness in Lincolnshire and stay there on Sunday night. We'd do a show there on the Monday afternoon as the first half of a double, with the second show somewhere like Bognor Regis at night – another long drive. We'd do the show in the holiday camp that evening in Bognor and stay the night there in staff chalets which were about as charming as a concentration camp. We'd do another show there on the Tuesday afternoon and double up again with a drive to Croydon or Eastbourne. On Tuesday night we'd drive to Minehead in Somerset, a hell of a drive which would get us there at three, four or five in the morning.

Butlins and Pontin's are both British institutions, pretty much like wrestling. They offer cheap, cheerful holidays with laid-on entertainment for working folk and are sewn into the fabric of British life. And back then, part of that entertainment was us wrestlers.

Next morning we'd get the ring up at eleven, wrestle at 1 p.m., drop the ring, drive back to do another show on the south coast before we'd drive to Selsey to get ready for a show on a caravan park on the Thursday afternoon. There might be another show there on Thursday night or if not we would drive to Pwlhelli in north Wales. We'd stay there on the Thursday night and wrestle there on a Friday afternoon and as long as there was no Friday night show we'd drive back to Blackpool where I would begin again for Bobby on a Saturday.

We did that for twenty weeks straight. That was ten to twelve shows a week, and probably several thousand miles by the time we'd criss-crossed Britain from top to bottom several times. On top of that was the Pleasure Beach, which would start at eleven and finish at five and could be as many as five shows in the day. Those twenty weeks in the summer of 1987 were a great deal of hard slog, a lot of laughs and the best wrestling education you could get.

A right pair of tarts ... Robbie Brookside and me as The Golden Boys.

I worked for Brian that winter but the next summer I decided I wanted to spend more time in Blackpool than the year before. I worked at the Pleasure Beach when I could and I would do Pontin's shows for Bobby, too. His little Pontin's empire was expanding into Southport, Morecambe and other places along the north-west coast so I could stay busy enough and spend more time at home.

It was a real good team of fellows, too. A lad called Jimmy Munroe, a Wigan rugby player named Steve Brenie, Duggie McDonagh from Blackpool; I wouldn't want to forget them. By this time my training was paying off and I was getting big and strong. I'd even earned the respect of Dave Duran because I had endured all the batterings he gave me. He was actually a funny bloke as it turned out when you got to know him, and from then on I got on with him okay.

By this time Chris and I had bought a house, a little terraced number in Blackpool, for £18,500. We had that house from the beginning of 1987 until I came to America. All the while I had been wrestling, Chris had been doing three jobs to save up enough money to buy the house. The hairdressing place she'd worked at had shut down but she worked at a fish and chip shop in the evenings, in the bar at her auntie's restaurant and in another shop in the daytime.

So we were doing all right. One day my dad came to see the wrestling and by then I was on top, taking the challenges myself. Not on this day though – I was having one of the wrestling matches

> *By this time Chris and I had bought a house, a little terraced number in Blackpool, for £18,500. We had that house from the beginning of 1987 until I came to America. All the while I had been wrestling, Chris had been doing three jobs to save up enough money to buy the house. The hairdressing place she'd worked at had shut down but she worked at a fish and chip shop in the evenings, in the bar at her auntie's restaurant and in another shop in the daytime. So we were doing all right.*

we sometimes put on to keep people entertained while we were pitching outside for challengers to fill the place up for the challenges themselves. There were a few odd fellows who used to hang around all the time. One was called David Davis, a very strange-looking creature. He wore an old raincoat down to his ankles and the worst wig you have ever seen. It was terrible. It had bits sticking out where he had combed it.

David used to fancy himself as a magician and sometimes Bobby would put him on between matches. He used to be like my comic hero Tommy Cooper in that he'd do tricks badly – except that unlike Tommy Cooper, whose unsuccessful magic was part of his act, David was attempting to do them properly. Halfway through a trick he'd realize it wasn't working, say "Oh well" and abandon it for the next one. Holidaymakers had been having a grand day out at the Pleasure Beach and then they would find themselves in a dark room watching a guy with a terrible wig, a gown and a raincoat, doing these lousy tricks.

Bob never used to pay him anything but David hung around anyway because he was a wrestling fan. There were always a few people hanging around at the Pleasure Beach who weren't the full shilling. My friend Peter had a great knack for collecting them – he would bring them in and get them to do odd jobs for him. Peter thought all this was very funny, but these people used to drive me nuts.

There were always a few people hanging around at the Pleasure Beach who weren't the full shilling. My friend Peter had a great knack for collecting them – he would bring them in and get them to do odd jobs for him. Peter thought all this was very funny, but these people used to drive me nuts.

So this particular day my dad was there to see just what sort of a world his son had given up everything for. I'd done my bit and I was watching David Davis up on the stage, facing the ring and the crowd. Behind him there was a flashy curtain. Dave Duran climbed in to the ring with a mask on because he was due to wrestle one of the challengers from outside. Something went on between the two Daves and before you knew it, Duran had hit Davis.

Davis fell backwards so all you could see through the curtain were his feet sticking out. Duran reached behind the curtain, grabbed Davis's wig and threw it out into the crowd. There was a water bucket and a bottle by the side of the ring and the wig landed on the bottle, just balancing on it. Then Duran came back through the curtain, grabbed the wig again and hurled it out into the crowd. They all started tossing it about. Davis came out from behind the curtain. I hadn't known this beforehand, but he had alopecia. He had no eyebrows and not a single hair on his head – he looked like Uncle Fester from *The Addams Family*. And he wasn't happy.

"Who's got me syrup?" he shouted, meaning his wig, and jumped into the crowd to try to get it back. This only spurred the crowd on, who were throwing the wig around with more abandon than ever. Steve Foster, who was on the microphone, laughed so hard he fell off the stage onto the floor. My dad was stood next to me, watching all this chaos going on. I hadn't been there long and he still wasn't sure about wrestling, knowing there was his business at home for me to take over. He looked at me and his face was a picture. That look said it all. "What on earth are you doing here, son?"

My dad was stood next to me, watching all this chaos going on. I hadn't been there long and he still wasn't sure about wrestling, knowing there was his business at home for me to take over. He looked at me and his face was a picture. That look said it all. "What on earth are you doing here, son?"

Another day we were standing outside in the rain with our masks on; me, Dave Duran and Benny Railings from Liverpool, when another guy walked past wearing a rotten-looking wig. It was one of those red wigs with silver hair underneath. He was obviously fascinated by us. "Get those masks off!" he shouted. Dave shouted back: "Okay – if you take your wig off!"

"All right," he said, and a crowd started to gather. "You first," we told him. He grabbed both sides of his wig in two hands and lifted it straight off the top of his head. "Your turn now," he said triumphantly. "Get your masks off."

"Fuck off!" we shouted at him. He tried his best to keep a shred of dignity, replaced his wig and walked away. We nearly wet ourselves laughing.

There was no shortage of colourful characters at the Pleasure Beach. There was a midget who worked with us called Pat. He had been one of Bob's crew from years before and hadn't wrestled in twenty years, but he just turned up one day, completely drunk. There was a reason for that – he was never sober. I used to stand him on a stool next to me and you would have to keep hold of him so he wouldn't sway off. It made the pair of us look like a ventriloquist act. All the kids would think this was cute, but Pat hated kids. They'd come up and say: "Hello, Mr Midget," and he'd snarl at them to fuck off.

Wrestling in England meant long matches. Most of them were six five-minute rounds and so you learned how to wrestle for long periods of time. To keep people interested, you had to learn a lot of moves. You had to learn the psychology of it too. Wrestling at its best is high drama and, just like drama, psychology is so important. A lot of people don't understand that – they just think it's two blokes screaming and shouting. But if you are a real aficionado, the matches we did back then were superb. They were longer and emphasized storytelling, an important part of a good wrestling match.

Pat had a rival midget at the Pleasure Beach. There was a circus next door where there was this fat little midget, who was round like a little ball. Pat hated him. This fellow used to advertise the circus so he would walk around with his face painted like a clown's, leading a camel or a llama to advertise their show. But the paint didn't help because he always looked thoroughly miserable. Whenever the poor bloke came around, trying to drum up trade, Pat would say: "Look at this wanker. Fucking Laughing Boy."

Pat always wanted to fight everybody. Sometimes we used to let him get in the ring and have a match. He'd wrestle one of the women or Duggie McDonagh. I couldn't work out why Pat drank so much, so one day I decided to tackle him about it. It was eleven in the morning but he was already completely gone.

I said: "Pat, you're a bloody nuisance. Why are you always drunk?"

He looked at me sternly and said: "You do realise dwarves don't live much past fifty?" I didn't – and I told him so.

"Well," said Pat, "I'm forty-nine."

And I said, "Oh. Do you want a drink then?"

Sure enough, the booze ended up doing for Pat. He was drunk one day as usual and accidentally killed himself when he jumped out of a taxi.

The Pleasure Beach was always entertaining. But, as I've said before, you had to find other ways to pay the bills in the winter. Through the winter of 1987 I was back working for Brian Dixon – and learning more and more about the job. Brian had been as good as his word and I got in the ring with several great wrestlers who also became good friends. Mal Sanders and Steve Grey in particular were two guys I grew to think the world of. We travelled all over the country and for the first time I felt I was getting a grip on the job and learning to do it well.

Wrestling in England meant long matches. Most of them were six five-minute rounds and so you learned how to wrestle for long periods of time. To keep people interested, you had to learn a lot of moves. You had to learn the psychology of it too. Wrestling at its best is high drama and, just like drama, psychology is so important. A lot of people don't understand that – they just think it's two blokes screaming and shouting. But if you are a real aficionado, the matches we did back then were superb. They were longer and emphasized storytelling, an important part of a good wrestling match.

I learned how to tell the story of a fight, how to build it and build it until everyone would be going crazy at the finish. It made for great matches. I used to sit and watch everyone else's matches as well, something I've always done. If you sit and watch the rest of the show, it means you are constantly learning. If you can't be bothered, it means you aren't taking the time to learn everything you possibly can. And that means you are never going to be as good as you can possibly be.

We'd go anywhere to do a show – even the Shetland Isles. But the Butlins run was the bread-and-butter. I've explained how tough the schedule was but not how it was the best wrestling education you could get. Not only were you working a lot of shows, you were also working in front of fairly large crowds because they had paid for entertainment and were going to watch every part of it.

Butlins taught me the importance of entertaining people. Years before I had learned how to do comedy matches with the likes of Steve Peacock but now I really learned how you had to entertain everyone, whether they were wrestling fans or not. There would be a lot of children in the audience which meant you had to do a plenty of comedy or pantomime – whatever was needed to keep them into your match.

Brian Dixon always used to tell me: "You've got to show out more." What he meant was you had to work the crowd more. And that's what I learned to do. Butlins camps were the greatest places in the world to teach you that. Top British comedians and entertainers have learned their craft in Butlins and Pontin's. They

Brian Dixon always used to tell me: "You've got to show out more." What he meant was you had to work the crowd more. And that's what I learned to do. Butlins camps were the greatest places in the world to teach you that. Top British comedians and entertainers have learned their craft in Butlins and Pontin's. They learned the art of capturing and entertaining their audience. It's the best schooling entertainers could have and wrestlers are no different. It was a great opportunity to learn how to be not just a wrestler but a sports entertainer, which is what I've become today. Nowadays it is all about entertainment and that's why I'm good at what I do – because I had all those years soaking up that invaluable experience.

learned the art of capturing and entertaining their audience. It's the best schooling entertainers could have and wrestlers are no different. It was a great opportunity to learn how to be not just a wrestler but a sports entertainer, which is what I've become today. Nowadays it is all about entertainment and that's why I'm good at what I do – because I had all those years soaking up that invaluable experience.

Butlins was good fun, too. During 1987 and 1988, the two years we did Butlins, the crew consisted of Brian, me, Robbie Brookside and a lad called Ian "Doc" Dean. I don't know where he got the Doc nickname from but he started working for Brian when he was fourteen and he'd have been no more than fifteen or sixteen when we did those trips.

There would be the three of us wrestlers plus a fourth, who would change from week to week. One was Sandy Scott, a

Robbie Brookside had his trademark long hair by the time my third son Bailey was born. Holding Bailey is Ian "Doc" Dean.

Scotsman who lives in Norwich these days, who was known then as The Dragon. He was quite possibly the funniest person you could ever wish to meet. When we met up at Preston on a Sunday morning and Sandy was in the car, you knew you'd be in for a good time. He would make you ill from laughing so hard. To say he used to like a drink and a smoke would be an understatement – he liked them as much as any person ever has.

At one time he had worked the Butlins circuit full time so he was well known everywhere we went. By this time he'd got a regular job with an engineering firm, but he still loved to wrestle and would save up his holidays and use them on a week of Butlins jobs with us. Everyone who had worked the camps for a long time knew him; he was a real Butlins celebrity.

One night we arrived at the camp in Bognor Regis and we were approached by a new guy who was the bar manager, or something like that. He came up and said to Sandy: "I believe you're The Dragon."

"Yes I am," said Sandy. The other guy said: "I believe you like a drink." "I've been known to have a few," Sandy replied. And this guy said: "Well, I bet you can't keep up with me."

A big mistake. This was at seven o'clock. I didn't really drink then so I was able to watch everything that went on. By nine o'clock the bar manager was stood on a table in one of the Butlins' bars with his trousers round his ankles dipping his own dick in his own pint of beer. He was absolutely paralytic.

This was the kind of thing The Dragon did with people. Hungover and bleary-eyed, he would walk into the restaurant where all the holidaymakers were having their breakfast and walk right up to a table, make a drum-roll sound and grab hold of the tablecloth as if he was going to drag it off and leave everything standing behind it on the table, like the magicians do. And the perfectly quiet family would scatter for cover.

They were juvenile jokes really, but with all the miles we did and the little money we earned, having Sandy around helped to lighten things up and make a tough life seem better. I've always found that if people can make you laugh, it doesn't matter what else is going on – everything's always a thousand times more bearable.

I didn't really drink then so I was able to watch everything that went on. By nine o'clock the bar manager was standing on a table in one of the Butlins' bars with his trousers round his ankles dipping his own dick in his own pint of beer. He was absolutely paralytic. This was the kind of thing The Dragon did with people. Hungover and bleary-eyed, he would walk into the restaurant where all the holidaymakers were having their breakfast and walk right up to a table, make a drum-roll sound and grab hold of the tablecloth as if he was going to drag it off and leave everything standing behind it on the table, like the magicians do. And the perfectly quiet family would scatter for cover. They were juvenile jokes really, but with all the miles we did and the little money we earned, having Sandy around helped to lighten things up and make a tough life seem better. I've always found that if people can make you laugh, it doesn't matter what else is going on – everything's always a thousand times more bearable.

Another funny guy, although in a completely different way, was Dave Taylor. I got to know him on my first foreign wrestling tour when I went to Tel Aviv in Israel in the summer of 1987. Dave was on that trip along with Klondyke Kate, Kendo Nagasaki and his manager Gorgeous George Gillette, Shane Stephens, Brian Dixon, who refereed, and his wife Mitzi Mueller, who was also a wrestler.

On that jaunt Dave and I struck up a friendship which holds fast to this day. Nowadays we live near each other and I see him all the time when I'm at home. He's the funniest guy I have ever met in my life who doesn't have a sense of humour. He's like Victor Meldrew with a suntan. Dave hates everything and everybody in the world. He'll always tell you his difficulties, how he's struggled to get through a day without screaming and shouting and wanting to kill people. It's a great tonic to listen to. I've been with Dave all over the world since that first trip, and he always makes me laugh.

My career was on the up. I'd got bigger and taller. I had grown to 6 feet 4 inches, which is tall for England. In America I might look average, but at that height and seventeen stone (248 pounds) I was definitely a British heavyweight. I was bigger thanks to my training regime in Blackpool. I made some good friends in my Blackpool gym. People like Glen, who used to pick me up and run me to shows when I didn't have transport so that I could earn a few quid. He'd do a lot of things for me most people wouldn't. He ran security for different events in Blackpool and would always offer me work if I wasn't wrestling at the time. A great guy, the absolute best.

Or Alan, the hardest-training man I've ever seen. The gym used to be freezing, especially in the depths of a Blackpool winter, but he wouldn't bother with a T-shirt and would train wearing just a pair of shorts. The sweat would pour off him. And a New Zealand rugby player called Joe. Those guys and my friend Peter are still the people I go to see when I am home in Blackpool.

It was lucky that things were getting better for me personally, because they were about to get a whole lot worse for the British wrestling scene. Butlins finished at the end of 1987 and we carried on working for Brian Dixon. I still tagged with Robbie Brookside and wrestled as a single occasionally. I did a few TV shows for Brian, but then, in 1988, the axe fell. No more wrestling on British television. Most British wrestlers had been on TV hundreds of times. I'd done six televised shows.

A new man called Greg Dyke had been brought in to take charge of the ITV network and he simply didn't want wrestling on his channel. It didn't have the right image. He was embarrassed by it and thought he knew what was best for the British public. He must have had a God complex to think that he knew better than his viewers. He didn't though. Dyke went on to greater things, becoming Director General of the BBC until he resigned in January 2004. But taking wrestling off British television was a big mistake.

I believe he had a long-term plan to get rid of it. First he moved the show from its regular 4 p.m. Saturday slot to 12 noon. Most wrestling fans were working-class people who would work half days on Saturday mornings or else would go out shopping. So in the new time slot, viewing figures immediately fell by half. Within a short period of time, Dyke had the excuse he wanted to take it off television.

It was a great shame because millions people in Britain used to watch it. And it really hit many wrestlers badly because without television, wrestling wasn't as popular. Attendance at the shows dropped and it was a tough time for a lot of the guys who had to go out and get regular jobs. Luckily I never had to. I was bigger and more skilled than I had ever been.

I was starting to get a reputation as someone who could have long, serious matches. It meant that although the British scene was entering a real slump, I could still find plenty of work. But I would have to go abroad.

At twenty, I'm about to embark on one of my first world tours.

4

Learn a Trade, See the World

Business was going down for British wrestling, but not for me. You could tell things were bad. Max Crabtree would never use anyone who wrestled for someone else, but now even he had to scrap his golden rule. So while I was still working for Brian Dixon I started doing shows for Max at Dale Martin's again. My growing reputation meant I was never without work. I'd made my name wrestling against people like Terry Rudge, Dave Taylor and Johnny South. I was envious of them, because along with Tony St Clair, they'd only ever do a month at a time in Britain. The rest of the time they were travelling the world, wrestling in Germany, Japan or Africa. I wanted some of that.

In that summer of 1988 I still did the odd week for Brian Dixon at Butlins and shows for Bobby Baron in Blackpool or his new extended Pontin's run. But the most exciting thing was an opportunity to wrestle in France. My friend Richie Brooks had already been going over there for a few weeks when he would go for five days or a week at a time and then fly back to England. It sounded perfect so I started going with him. Over the next couple of weeks we went eight times.

On my first day I flew into Paris to be picked up by a guy with one arm driving a Porsche. I was a bit worried he wouldn't be able to drive us to the arena safely. When we got there we saw it was an outside show in a small arena with stadium seating.

When I looked at the ring I was dumbfounded. I looked at Richie, and at the ring again, and at Richie again. I could see the ring moving.

"Is this a wind-up?" I asked Richie. "What's going on here?" He said: "Oh, you don't know about that do you?"

"Don't know about what?"

"In a lot of the places here they don't have too many decent venues for wrestling," Richie explained. "So they either run it in circus tents or on swimming pools."

When we walked towards the ring I could see what he meant. It was in the middle of a large swimming pool, supported by four 4-foot-square floats, one at each corner. Getting to the ring for a match was a performance in itself. There was a rope running from one end of the pool to one of the ring corners. I had to get in a little rubber dinghy and they would pull me along the rope to the ring where you would get out. At the time I was working as a babyface – a good guy – which meant having to stand up in the boat on your way to the ring, desperately trying to keep my balance as I smiled and waved at the crowd. I looked like a complete prat. Then, when I got into the ring, it was moving. Every time I took a step it would sway in the water. It was unreal.

The wrestling in France was horrendous. In my first match I was up against a great big giant of a guy, a huge monster. I was really into the strong style of wrestling then so I knocked hell out of him, but he wasn't used to that at all. He was okay about it but, to the French, wrestling was like ballet. They didn't consider themselves athletes or wrestlers. They used to call themselves artistes, which didn't sit well with me.

Every night I would watch Richie in these tag matches. He was really into the strong style as well but these other guys would bounce around like fairies. It was dreadful. But at the time work in England paid £20 a job and here I was getting £80 a day, plus my food and hotel and the cost of flying me in and out all the time. On top of that we got to travel all over France, which was a bonus.

They had no idea how to set up a tour properly so in a five-day stint you would do an incredible amount of travelling. One of the women wrestlers used to drive Richie and me in one of those big Citroëns. One day we'd be right in the north of France and the next day you would be deep in the south. Sometimes we would drive for fifteen hours from Paris to a show in the south, then the next day we would be up in Normandy, then back in the south, then back to Paris, and then a show near the Belgian border. It was insane. And for the first time in my life I wished I hadn't got kicked out of French lessons for mucking about. None of the French people seemed to like us very much and without any of the language, it was hard work. The French wrestlers wouldn't help us in any way, shape or form.

> At the time I was working as a babyface – a good guy – which meant having to stand up in the boat on your way to the ring, desperately trying to keep my balance as I smiled and waved at the crowd. I looked like a complete prat.

A lot of these shows were in small towns or villages. We would arrive and there'd be a big circus tent put in a field with the ring in. We would turn up at 5 p.m. and the show wouldn't start until midnight. The other wrestlers used to drop us off and disappear, leaving Richie and me without anything to eat. We used to have to wait until they'd set up the stands selling hot dogs and French fries for the show so we could get something to keep the hunger at bay.

It was a very strange way to do business. They wouldn't put the show on until enough people turned up. Sometimes it would get to ten o'clock at night and no one would be around. Then suddenly people would arrive from all over the place. They'd be drinking wine and eating at these cheese stalls and having a good time when suddenly someone would say, "Right, we'll start the show." There was no set time. The people would pile into the tent and we would go on.

Perhaps the strangest place I ever wrestled was out at sea. It was in the bay at St Tropez. The ring was floating there in the middle of the bay, with all these yachts around with people watching. We went to the ring by speedboat. We must have looked like ants to anyone trying to watch the wrestling. An interesting experience, to say the least.

Other opportunities to work abroad were starting to open up. The year before the French trips, I had been wrestling Dave Taylor a lot and he asked me if I wanted to go to Germany. I said yes, but it didn't come off. However, the next year the chance came up again because Dave used to work in Hamburg every year for a promoter called Rene Lassartesse for a six or seven-week run. This year, Dave had got to work with another promoter called Otto Wanz, who ran Austria and Germany for a whole six months. So Dave put a word in for me and I got his spot in Hamburg for that September.

Before I went I was still working all over the place – France, Pontin's, Butlins and the Pleasure Beach – it was a great summer. As always, the Pleasure Beach was top entertainment. There was myself, Peter, an ex-pro rugby player called Steve Breaney, Jimmy Monroe from Liverpool, John Raven, Drew Macdonald. Everyone on that team was big and handy so if it kicked off – which it used to do

Dave Taylor was great company on tour. This is in Germany, 1992.

frequently – you could count on all of them. Another guy working there then was Johnny Howard from southern Ireland who used to wrestle as Rasputin. He had long hair and a great big beard and used to wear a monk's robe. He was a real character.

There was only one cloud on the horizon. Chris was pregnant with our first son, Daniel. So it was time for a big decision. It was shaping up to be my first trip to Germany, which I hoped would become my bread and butter. It was a good career move because once I had established myself there I would be able to work for months at a time, and the money was good. But it also meant I wouldn't be present at Daniel's birth.

I put my career first. It was a hard thing to do and Chris wasn't happy with my decision. But we needed the money and my career needed the boost. When it came to the day to leave, it was hard. Chris was devastated – but I went anyway. I got into Johnny

Howard's Mercedes and we drove to Dover, got the ferry to France and then drove on to Germany.

The wrestling in Germany and Austria was different from that in England. It was run in tournaments. That year, Hamburg was a seven-week tournament. It was in a big tent on the Heiligingeistfeld, which is at the top of the Reeperbahn, and was run in a league form. You'd have the same wrestlers there every night of the week and over the tournament everyone would wrestle everyone else. There was a points system and a big scoreboard kept track of the points totals of the fifteen or sixteen wrestlers. It worked its way down to the last week and the last night, when the two guys with the most points would wrestle each other for the trophy.

There would be speciality matches like chain matches, or extended time matches which meant you would go to a finish if it was a draw at the end of normal time. If it was a draw after the regulation five four-minute rounds we would wrestle a sixth round of ten minutes. Sometimes if that was a draw we would wrestle again.

The variety made it interesting for the fans and a fair-sized crowd would come. On Friday and Saturday nights we would fill the tent with 500 or 600 people. Tuesday night was *damentag* – ladies' night when women would get in free with a man, so that was always sold out. Some nights in the week you might only wrestle in front of fifty people but it worked out overall.

On that first trip I was getting 185 marks a night, which was about £60 or £70. Seven nights a week for six or seven weeks added up to a lot of money for me, considering I was just twenty and had a baby on the way. On my first night there I was with Terry Rudge, one of my favourite people of all time. He was a great London guy who'd make me laugh constantly – and he was a top wrestler too.

We were sat next to each other in the little locker room they had in the back of the tent. On my other side was Franz Van Boyton – a Belgian I hadn't met before, who looked a bit like Errol Flynn. Getting changed in this tiny room, it soon became apparent that his face wasn't the only similarity to the great actor. He dropped his strides to reveal the biggest dick and pair of bollocks I had ever seen. You couldn't help but look. This thing like Popeye's forearm with coconuts for knackers flopped out next to me. I was aghast.

Terry Rudge took one look at me and said: "Well, I'd rather he fucked me than hit me on the head with it."

It was the best one-liner I'd ever heard, and Terry didn't hesitate in following it up. "You know whose wife is his, don't you?" he asked me.

"Who?" I responded.

"The one with the cauliflower arsehole!" Figure that one out. My first experience of Germany, and even aged twenty I already realized that life in Hamburg was going to be a bit different.

It was a dream place for a wrestler. Working in front of the same crowd every night meant you had to keep varying your matches, putting new moves in all the time which was a valuable learning experience. And being in the same place for that length of time was unheard of for us. We stayed in caravans in a small campsite just outside the town – much better than the poxy hotel rooms which were all we could have afforded.

You could cook in the caravans too. I rented one and enjoyed an idyllic seven weeks. I rode to the tent every day with

> Everyone knows how the Beatles learned their trade there and here I was doing the same thing – there's not much these showbiz types have done on their way up that I haven't.

Johnny Howard. We got to sample the sights of Hamburg while we were there, and it became one of my favourite cities in the world. Working there reminded you that you weren't very different from other entertainers. Everyone knows how the Beatles learned their trade there and here I was doing the same thing. Clubs and Butlins in England, Hamburg – there's not much these showbiz types have done on their way up that I haven't.

Saturday, October 6, 1988 was one of the biggest nights of my life – our son Daniel was born. It was a bittersweet moment for me. Of course I was delighted. But at the same time I was sad that I wasn't able to be at home for his birth. I had chosen to do what I thought was right at the time; for the money and for my career.

Whether it was a selfish choice or not, I don't know. I think I did the right thing – working in Germany stood me in good stead for the rest of my career. As soon as the tournament was finished I hurried back to Blackpool and my first opportunity to hold my son in my arms. It's an indescribable feeling, to hold this little tiny baby and know he's yours.

I might have missed out on Daniel's birth, but circumstances would soon mean I got to be there for plenty of his earliest moments. Going to Germany had been worthwhile at the time – and would be so in the long run – but it had taken me away from the wrestling circuit in England. When I got back, until the end of that year I couldn't get much regular work, only odd days here and there. Chris was working in a carpet factory in Blackpool so I was wrestling what nights I could and the rest of the time I was looking after Daniel.

The nights I was wrestling, Daniel would go to a childminder. If I was away all week, I reckon the childminder was getting paid more than Chris was; but that's what we did to keep our heads above water. It was one of those times when work was short, but I have never been tempted to give up on wrestling. All my life there have always been plenty of people who've tried to tell me to pack it in and get a proper job. I won't name them – they know who they are. But I never lost faith that I could get on in this business, so I stuck it out.

It worked out for me and that's what I tell people today – always live your dreams and don't let other people put you off. They're usually the ones who have failed themselves or never achieved their ambitions. They don't want you to get on because they've never done so. I never listened to any of them and I'm glad I didn't.

At one show in 1989 I met an Indian fellow from South Africa who asked me if I'd like to go and wrestle there. One of my friends, Dalibar Singh from Leeds, was always a very big draw in South Africa. The Indian community there adored him. Dalibar was working for this promoter, and he asked me to go in place of the Iron Sheik, the Iranian who'd been a World Wrestling Federation star in the 1980s. He had caused all kinds of problems out there, so I came in at the last minute to replace him.

We left in March. Another wrestler on the same trip was Kashmir Singh from Wolverhampton. I'd known Kashmir – Jason was his real name – since our Butlins days. He was a gentleman and we'd always been good friends. On our first night there we wrestled a tag match at Pietermaritzburg with myself and a great big Afrikaaner called Verdie the Hammer against Dalibar and Kashmir Singh. It wasn't a massive building but we certainly caused a reaction – the crowd nearly rioted. People were pulling out knives at ringside. Not quite like working Butlins.

Kashmir had to leave after the first week – he was booked on another trip to the Middle East – but I stayed there for three weeks and absolutely loved it. We stayed in Durban, which was wonderful. It was a holiday town like Blackpool, except with sun. We wrestled two or three times a week and I spent the rest of the time lying on the beach, watching the surfers. The only thing I didn't do was go in the water. I wasn't reassured by all the shark nets that ringed the bay in spite of the fact that the locals insisted that swimming was perfectly safe – those nets were there for a reason.

All my life there have always been plenty of people who've tried to tell me to pack it in and get a proper job. I won't name them – they know who they are. But I never lost faith that I could get on in this business, so I stuck it out. It worked out for me and that's what I tell people today – always live your dreams and don't let other people put you off. They're usually the ones who have failed themselves or never achieved their ambitions. They don't want you to get on because they've never done so. I never listened to any of them and I'm glad I didn't.

We only had one problem on this trip – the promoter disappeared with all the money. You hear a lot of horror stories from other wrestlers about not getting paid, or when promoters have stiffed them, but this was the only time in my life that it happened to me. The promoter disappeared with my plane tickets, which meant that I couldn't get home. Dalibar sorted it out. On the last night, he went to the ticket office and got the cash out of there. I ended up £50 short in my wages, but it could have been a lot worse. Dalibar sorted my tickets too. It didn't spoil the experience – I still have a great fondness for South Africa.

Time at home still meant time with Daniel, in between jobs for Bobby and Brian. I was lucky to get to spend time with him when he was young. When our second son Dane came along in 1991 I didn't have the same luxury. I was there when he was born – just as I was for our third son Bailey too – but after that it got difficult. I was travelling too much and then came to America. I try to make up for it now by spending all my spare time at home with my children, but you can't really make up for something like that.

That year I was also working for Oric Williams, who was based in Rhyl in Wales. For Oric you would do two- and three-week tours to Scotland, which was new for me. We used to stay in all the little towns and villages – it was beautiful. One day we got to drive all the way around Loch Ness – something not many people get to do in the course of their usual employment. We didn't see the Loch Ness monster, though.

> I was travelling too much and then came to America. I try to make up for it now by spending all my spare time at home with my children, but you can't really make up for something like that.

Oric also did tours in Ireland. We'd travel round both the north and the south, from top to bottom, working in villages and towns. We didn't just do Dublin and Belfast, we went all over the island. The only hard thing was the little bed and breakfast places you had to stay in, where you'd have to contend with lumpy porridge and cold so intense it would stick the bedsheets together.

Working for both Oric and Brian, I got to wrestle Giant Haystacks many times. Most days we would travel in his car. We'd leave later than most people which meant more time at home, then we'd meet up in Manchester. He'd drive us in his big car and he would always leave immediately after the show, which meant getting home at a decent time. So I spent a lot of time with Haystacks and enjoyed his company most of the time. He was a very witty guy who knew something about everything. On a road trip he would always have a bucketload of stories about his adventures in life, and whether they were true or not didn't really matter.

I was with Haystacks when I went back to Germany. I did the Hamburg tournament again for six weeks, and loved the fact you could get in a little routine every day. Gym in the morning, eat, sleep, do the show and then out afterwards until all hours. It didn't get boring because Hamburg is such a great city. There was always something to do.

As soon as I got back I got a call from Oric asking me if I wanted to go to Brehmen for November and December. This was good news. The big tour in Germany was for a company called CWA, the Catch Wrestling Association, run by Otto Wanz. He and his partner Peter Williams ran a tour from June to Christmas. It started with three weeks in Graz in Austria, a beautiful place, seven weeks in Vienna, another tremendous city, ten days of one-off spot shows as we moved into Germany, then nine weeks in Hanover followed by a week off before five weeks in Brehmen.

> I spent a lot of time with Haystacks. He was a very witty guy who knew something about everything. On a road trip he would always have a bucketload of stories about his adventures in life, and whether they were true or not didn't really matter.

The Brehmen tour was the big prize because it wasn't in a tent or anything so basic but inside in the Stadthalle. It insulated you against Christmas, always a tough time for wrestlers because many of the places which did wrestling shows for the rest of the year put on Christmas shows in December instead. So everyone wanted to get on that tour because it was good money. And everyone who was already on it wanted their pals to get on it.

Because places on that tour were so coveted, it was a tight knit circle, so to get the chance with Otto Wanz was a great opportunity. But from day one, for whatever reason, Otto hated the sight of me. We did not get on. I don't really care now looking back on it, but Otto had a real knack for making you feel absolutely worthless. He certainly

Giant Haystacks was one of British wrestling's biggest characters – in every sense. I was lucky enough to wrestle him many times.

made me feel that way; but all the same I still enjoyed the tour. It was the first time I met Scott Hall, who was working there. There were a lot of great guys: Dave Taylor, Tony St Clair, Dave "Fit" Finlay and Colonel Brody – the man who'd given me my first match back in 1983.

I went with Haystacks and got my little caravan set up behind the building. Haystacks' real name was Martin but he introduced himself to me as Luke so that's what I called him. A lot of wrestlers have several names – people call me Darren, Steve, Lord, Commish (for commissioner), William, all sorts. I used to go shopping with Haystacks and my sole entertainment every day was to wind him up. The devil got into me because I was spending all my time with the same person.

He didn't like going into the supermarket because he was 6 feet 11 inches and 45 stone (630 pounds), with long hair and a beard; and he hated people staring at him. So he would ask me to go in for him. The first day we were there he picked me up at 9 a.m. and drove to the supermarket, where he presented me with a little list

aystacks could
ertainly put on a
t of pressure.

of things he wanted. He made a point of saying: "Please get me some nice French ham." Luke Haystacks was a huge man with huge hands, but he had the most delicate mannerisms – he used to pick things up and move them round very precisely. So he described this French ham very particularly and you could tell it meant the world to him. I couldn't read German so when I got to the delicatessen, I picked up the first thing that looked like ham, asked them to wrap it and took it out to him.

On our way back in his Mercedes, he put the shopping bag on my knee and began lifting items out one by one and looking at them. When he got to the ham he pulled it out, opened it, peered at it, nibbled it, smelled it, wound the window down and threw it out of the car. He looked at me and said: "You must be the stupidest bastard on God's green earth." That wasn't French ham, he scolded me, it was such-and-such.

That set me off laughing. Luke got mad as hell and started calling me all kinds of names. So from that day on it didn't matter what he asked me to get him, I always got the wrong thing just to wind him up. A little thing, I suppose, but it used to make me laugh and it passed the time.

My favourite Haystacks story is the time when, at the end of the first week, he came and asked if I wanted to go to the laundrette. My clothes needed doing, so I agreed. Dave Finlay and his first wife Paula, who used to manage him as Princess Paula, went with us. I was dreading it. I thought Luke would do his usual thing and ask me to do everything for him again, and the last thing I wanted to do was handle his underwear and socks. But when we got there and walked in, this huge laundrette was empty so Haystacks was happy to do his own stuff. He didn't ask me to do anything for him and was happily laughing and joking.

The four of us went back the following week, but this time it was packed with people, several of them students. Everyone stopped and stared at Haystacks, who looked mortally embarrassed. He froze and didn't know what to do. Attracting all this attention when we were out and about was always his greatest fear. One lad in there was drawing on a sketchpad to pass the time. He stopped what he was drawing, turned around and started sketching Stacks. Poor

Stacks didn't know where to put himself. Then the woman who ran the place came out from the back holding a pair of his underpants which he'd left the week before. You can imagine the size they were and she was holding them out at arm's length, like they were an enormous flag.

She said in German: "Are these yours?" Everyone in the place burst out laughing. Stacks just looked at me and said: "There's no fucking need for that, is there?" I started laughing myself and I couldn't stop, even though I felt sorry that he was so mortified. The poor bastard.

I have a lot of fond memories of Haystacks and a lot of sad ones, too. In 1995 he came to WCW where they wanted to try him out as a big monster. He wrestled for a few months under the name Loch Ness but his health was beginning to fail. His knees were troubling him badly and his back was bothering him too. He was trying his best but he was really struggling. I felt very sorry for him. He really loved his wife and she had had a lot of problems battling cancer. She got ill again and he went back to England and that was the last I ever saw of him. Cancer got him, too, in the end. When I heard he had died, I was very sad, because deep down he was a really good guy.

In the early nineties I did more foreign trips. In 1991 Dave Rees, a Dale Martin's referee, lined up a week in Tenerife. Our second son Dane was only four months old. I had managed to be there with Chris at the birth this time and it was such an overwhelming experience that it was still all a bit much for me. So I told Dave Rees that I'd do Tenerife only if I could take my wife with me. I had plenty of other work going on and could afford to turn it down if I had to.

We left Daniel with Chris's mum and stepdad, took Dane with us and had a wonderful week. It was a nice little break – I only had to wrestle three times so it was like a paid holiday. I was also working for a German promoter called Gerdt Vollink. He was a really nice guy who'd fly you in, pay you very good money and ask you to bring a couple of other British lads with you for two or three shows. It was good. You would go home after three days with a chunk of money.

By this time I was one of the better-paid guys in England, earning £30 a night. I know it sounds pitiful now; but I'd never been so busy at home, working six and seven nights a week and some doubles as well. Then Gerdt offered me a trip to Spain. Everything would be paid for, plus we would earn something like £3,000 for two months' work. It sounded like a nice easy summer and I planned to bring Chris and the kids out later on. But I should have known it sounded too good to be true.

I drove down with Steve Casey, the man who'd originally got me in working for Gerdt. He took his caravan, which he was going to stay in while we were there. The first night saw us in the bullring in Benidorm, which holds 15,000 people. Twenty-eight turned up. The following night they gave out 300 free tickets to try to drum up some interest. That night twenty-five came. It just wasn't working.

> There was a great big crew of us there, wondering what on earth we were supposed to do. Looking back, I don't even know why they'd planned the tour at all. There hadn't been wrestling in Spain for years; there was no television to promote it and the few who turned up certainly didn't know who the stars were.

There was a great big crew of us there, wondering what on earth we were supposed to do. Looking back, I don't even know why they'd planned the tour at all. There hadn't been wrestling in Spain for years; there was no television to promote it and the few who turned up certainly didn't know who the stars were.

For the next week and a half we had crisis meetings trying to figure out what to do. Gerdt and his wife would take us out to a succession of local restaurants while we pondered our predicament. After I'd bathed in the sun for two weeks and eaten all I possibly could, the promoter decided it wasn't worth running anything. He said he'd pay us the month's money, fly us home and call it quits. "Thanks very much," I thought. We had no contracts, just a verbal agreement, and he wasn't obliged to pay us anything at all, if he wasn't a gentleman. He was a real good fellow.

This meant I had six weeks without a booking in sight, since I'd expected to be in Spain. So it was back working for Bobby Baron and Max Crabtree again. I'd do the fairground for Bobby and also

From the family album: Chris's mum and stepdad, Patricia and Terry.

My dad and stepmum with Daniel, Dane and my nephews
Andrew and Steven.

Pontin's in Morecambe, Prestatyn and Southport. On Saturdays I'd do the fairground and then the Blackpool Sandcastle at night for Max. On Sundays it would be the fairground followed by Morecambe. Mondays I'd do Bridlington over in Yorkshire for Anne Relwyskow, a promoter based in Leeds. There weren't too many women promoters around, but Anne's dad George had been in wrestling for many years, and she took over from him. A woman in a man's world, she was a wonderful lady who knew the business and took no nonsense from anyone, even if they were twice her size.

At the Sandcastle we would wrestle in the theatre part at the back. The front part upstairs was a nightclub called Bedlams. Some of my friends worked the door there and the manager asked me to help them out on a Saturday night. So Saturdays now became very busy – at the Pleasure Beach in the day, wrestling at night in the Sandcastle and then as soon as I'd finished I would go on the door from 10 p.m. to 2 a.m., and I did the door there on a Friday too. It all added up to a great summer. Very easy work, lots of money coming in and home every night to see Daniel, Dane and Chris.

In September I went to Hamburg to do the tournament for my third and last time. Robbie Brookside was there on his first visit, which was a bonus. Also with us were Terry Rudge, who was later to play a key role in introducing me to the company, and Indio Gujaro from Colombia. Indio did this cool witch-doctor gimmick and was one of the best wrestlers I'd ever been in with at that time. With his talent and that gimmick, he could have made a fortune in World Wrestling Federation in the 1980s. People hated him instantly. He just had that natural heat off people. As well as being a tremendous wrestler, he certainly looked the part – he had a huge Afro and carried a collection of shrunken heads around with him.

I also did a week in Belgium which turned out to be pretty bizarre. Franz Van Boydon, the trouser beast, ran this show in his home village there. I travelled with Andrew Blackwell from Flint in north Wales, who was known as Blackie; Johnny South and Drew Macdonald. There wasn't a single hotel in the village so Franz put us wrestlers up in his friends' places, two and three at a time. I was with Johnny and Blackie in a little farmhouse – it was brilliant.

Everyone treated us like kings and we had a really top time.

We were wrestling in the local town hall, which was only a small building. Franz gave us a pep talk before the first match: "Look, these people have never seen wrestling. They don't know what it is. All they know is that I'm a wrestler. So I want you to go out there and wrestle without doing much, because if you do anything complicated, it'll be too much for them to follow and they won't understand it. So for five rounds go in there and just stick a headlock on, or an armlock or a leglock."

That's what he wanted out of the matches and it worked. The people were going absolutely insane. You would put a hold on, keep it on for most of the round, and if towards the end your opponent managed to get out of it the crowd would cheer the house down. Very strange – but a memorable trip.

Of all the travelling I've done in my career, the most enjoyable was a 1991 tour of South Africa. It was my second visit there and I went with Terry Rudge, who has always been one of my favourite people to be around. In South Africa, it's the Indian population who are the biggest wrestling fans. Traditionally they ran the fruit businesses over there, and they looked after us very well. We were there for two weeks, working for a first class promoter called Ish Maharaj.

Ish put us up in an apartment just off the seafront in Durban and all the time we were there, he made sure that we didn't want for anything. In the second week my mentor Marty Jones arrived and with him along, the trip got even better. It was on this tour that Marty wrestled Gama Singh in the pouring rain, while I wrestled Gama's brother Akkam. He was a talented guy and we had some excellent matches.

My days of going to Hamburg were over, however. I had a falling out with the promoter Rene Lassartesse – or more to the point, with his money man. A lot of the act I do today, like walking to the ring with my nose in the air, is taken from Rene. When I knew him he was getting on in years but still wrestling in his own tournament – and I thought he was a tremendous wrestler. He had that extra ingredient, that little something special, that made the crowd hate him passionately.

I'd been asked to do a show for Rene's rival Gerdt Vollink, fifteen minutes outside Hamburg and long before Rene's own tournament started; and Rene's money man told me that if I did it, I couldn't work for them. I wouldn't stand for that. The other show wasn't in the same town; besides, I had to make money for my family and Gerdt was paying me well. I told them what they could do with their ultimatum, which meant that September would now be Hamburg-free.

So I was doing my usual thing around Blackpool when I had my first contact with World Wrestling Federation.

One fine day in September 1991, a FedEx truck rolled up outside my house. I don't think a FedEx truck had ever seen the streets of Blackpool. It delivered a letter from the company, asking me if I could come to their Pay-Per-View at the Albert Hall in October for a try-out.

It was completely out of the blue. I was totally shocked – I'd no idea that something like this might have been on the horizon. I contacted them immediately, telling them I'd be there. I found out later I had my good pal Terry Rudge to thank. Lord Alfred Hayes had an office job for the company at the time and Terry had known him twenty years before. Terry hadn't spoken to him in donkey's years but he called him up specifically to tell him about me.

On the big day, I got into my smartest light grey suit and drove down to London. I was nervous and had a hell of a job finding the Albert Hall – to this day, my sense of direction isn't the best. The sweat was pouring off me. So when I got there and got to the door with my bags, the security guard asked: "Have you leaned against something?" The whole back of my trousers and jacket was one big sweat stain. I looked like a right pillock. But there was nothing for it. If I took my jacket off, you could still see the stain on the trousers. So I had to half-walk, half-shuffle along the wall so no one could see.

Eventually I found Jack Lanza, the agent I was supposed to meet. He's still there now, and a bloody good agent too. He told me to go and get something to eat, but food was the last thing I wanted to think about; my nerve was totally going by this point. This was my big chance. I dreamed of going to America; and I wanted more than anything to work for them. I used to watch a lot of American wrestling on tape: World Wrestling Federation and National Wrestling Alliance, which later became WCW. I really wanted it.

Just as I was wondering who I would be wrestling, I bumped into an old buddy Wayne Bridges, who was with another wrestler, Brian Maxine. He used to wrestle as Brian "Goldbelt" Maxine, and the two of us were on first. It was my first time in the Albert Hall, which was an incredible building: a massive circular structure with an ornate exterior, and one of London's biggest venues. The night was a complete sell-out and I was very nervous, but Brian made me look like a million dollars, and I've always thanked him for that. Jack said: "That was great. Come with us to Wembley tomorrow so we can talk to you."

So the next night I duly travelled out to the Wembley Arena to talk to some of the agents. They told me they didn't have anything for me just then, but they'd let me know when they had. In those days the company was very gimmick based. There are very few true gimmicks left these days – you are more likely to play a character or an extension of your own personality, not a true gimmick character. But that wasn't the case back then, and they said they wouldn't bring me in until they could think of something for me to do.

I left there that night feeling on top of the world. But it was a long time before I would work for Vince.

Even when I came to America I was still getting letters from the company at my house in Blackpool, saying I was still on file and would be brought in when they had the right spot. I don't think they realized the same guy had been hired by WCW. But there were still a few bumps in the road before that happened.

New Delhi, 1992, versus Baljit Singh, nephew of the great Dara Singh.

5

A Passage to India, a Close Shave in Egypt and the Big Break

I might have impressed World Wrestling Federation, but I still had to pay the bills. So I went back to work for Brian Dixon. Then my second bite at the apple presented itself, in the shape of a phone call from Oric Williams. "WCW are coming on tour. Would you like to work for them for a week?" I told him I'd love to.

The tour started at Earl's Court in London – two nights there, one at Sheffield and one at the Point in Dublin over in Ireland. On my first night I wrestled Michael Hayes, who's now a WWE writer and agent, and the next night I wrestled Giant Haystacks. They wanted a look at this huge monster and, since he and I had wrestled together so many times, we were able to put on our usual solid match.

That was also my first night speaking on a microphone in the ring. You just didn't do it in England, or any of the countries I'd visited. The only times I had ever talked on television had been at a press conference, when you would be sitting down and wearing a suit, like the boxers do it. I wasn't used to talking on a mic like the Americans do – or doing promos, as we call them. At the time Paul Heyman was working for WCW as a manager called Paul E. Dangerously and he did an interview segment called the Dangerous Zone. He asked the agent Grizzly Smith, who was Jake the Snake's dad, if he could do a live segment in the ring with me. We did it and it was okay. If I watched it now I'd probably think it was rotten, but everyone thought it was fine and I was grateful to Paul for giving me the chance.

There were some great guys on that tour, who all spoke up for me. Scott Hall, whom I knew from Germany; Arn Anderson, who has become a good friend; Larry Zbyszko and the Steiner brothers. Grizzly said he would talk to management when he got back to the States about bringing me in. Great news. I was going to join whoever offered me the first deal; because America, without a doubt, was the place to be. In England and several of the other countries we visited around that time, World Wrestling Federation and WCW were being broadcast on TV. World Wrestling Federation was on the Sky network in the UK while WCW was on ITV – late at night, true, but still there. Once people were used to their brands, I thought, they wouldn't want to see the local stuff.

And that's exactly what has happened. The local scenes have dried up around the world. I was lucky to get my chance at the right time. I came to America in 1993 and by 1995 or 1996 work in England had withered away. If I'd stayed I would have had to get a regular job – a horrendous prospect.

In 1992, though, Brian Dixon still had plenty going. Dave Taylor and Fit Finlay were chasing each other round the buildings of England over the British Heavyweight Championship and business was good. We worked six or seven nights a week and double shots as well. All this while my car was out of order – if my mate Glen hadn't driven me to shows I would have been properly stuffed.

And back then the foreign trips were still worthwhile. That year I went to India for three weeks and the trip turned into one of the most amazing experiences of my life. Good money for me in those days, too – £800 a week. On March 1 I went from a double shot in Oldham and Bolton to Heathrow airport and then straight into the biggest culture shock anyone could have. I'd asked Dave Taylor, who'd been twelve times, and several other people what India was like and they all said the same thing – you cannot put it into words. And that's the truth. I saw some of the most beautiful and some of the worst sights I have ever seen. The poverty is dreadful. It's terrible to see the people having to live and suffer in those conditions.

I was lucky to get my chance at the right time. I came to America in 1993 and by 1995 or 1996 work in England had withered away. If I'd stayed I would have had to get a regular job – a horrendous prospect.

Wrestling is a national sport in India, second only to cricket. Wrestlers are treated like gods. We were wrestling at a soccer stadium in New Delhi – although you could hardly call it a stadium: a pitch with lots of chairs around it would be a more accurate description. All over the city I was dumbstruck to see 15-foot-high handpainted pictures of me, announcing that I was going to appear. There were lifesize pictures of me on the sides of the scooters and rickshaws they used as cabs. Whenever I walked down a street, everyone wanted to touch me. No exaggeration – I'd turn around and there would be literally a hundred people following. A lot of them were kids. They would run up, touch me and then run off. And the Indian wrestlers are even bigger heroes. Many of them are film stars too so they are a massive deal, their faces recognized everywhere.

The matches were on Wednesday and Saturday nights. The hotel was fairly decent, but we were warned not to leave it on our own after dark, which meant there wasn't a lot to do except sit in the hotel restaurant and eat. The wrestling was very different too. I had to put on very long matches with their local wrestlers.

One night I wrestled a guy who was not only a policeman in New Delhi, but also a silver medal winner in the Los Angeles Olympics, so you can imagine just how big a local hero he was. I beat him in the eighth round by kicking him in the bollocks – it was the only way I could beat him. I half-expected a riot that night.

India was fascinating and overwhelming in equal measures. Outside the hotel you would be surrounded by beggars, many of them with no legs, propelling themselves on skateboards. But it was a country of great opportunities. There was a tailor underneath the hotel and I took him two pairs of my trousers and asked him to run up some copies. I asked him for five pairs and he quoted a ridiculously small price, something like £12 for the lot. He dropped to his knees and started kissing my hand for asking him to do the work. He can't have earned very much if that was what my commission meant to him. So I had some shirts made, some leather jackets for me and Chris and some clothes for the kids.

I was joined on the trip by Skull Murphy, who came from Plymouth in the south-west, but had lived up in Manchester for years and was, to put it mildly, something of a character. One Sunday the money man behind the trip had his son drive us to the Taj Mahal. Of all the things I've seen in my life, that was the most unforgettable. It was fantastic, absolutely stunning. We were given a full tour and it remains a treasured memory. But once we'd seen the sights, we were getting somewhat restless back in our hotel, so I said to the money guy: "Look, I'm bored to death here. Can't you take us out to a show or something?" "Sure," he said. "I'll come and pick you up at seven o'clock tonight."

Indian time means nothing. When someone says he'll pick you up at a certain time, you soon learned to expect him four or five hours later or even the following week. But this guy eventually turned up at the hotel with a friend in tow and clutching a bottle of whisky. I didn't drink at that time but Skull certainly did, so Skull, the money man and his friend sat around polishing off the booze until nearly midnight. I was bored to tears. I was just about to go to bed when the money man said: "Right, we're going out now."

"At this time of night?" I asked.

"Yes," he replied. "We're taking you to a cabaret."

That meant an Indian car ride, which is a hair-raising experience. Their attitude is that it is only by the grace of God that they don't die in a car crash, so until then, anything goes. They don't care which side of the road they drive on and they beep their horns constantly, whether there's anything coming or not. They screech around corners with no thought to whether something is coming the other way. They go straight through intersections. An added bonus is the large number of scrawny cows wandering around

Soaking up the scenery at the Taj Mahal with Skull Murphy.

everywhere. Because cows are sacred in India they are quite content to stroll across main roads, knowing the traffic will screech to a halt rather than hit them. It's hard to convey just how terrifying the whole thing is.

This particular ride took us further and further out of town until Skull and I were beginning to wonder what was going on. In the middle of nowhere, the car pulled up outside a large, featureless concrete building. "Come on," said the money guy. "Get out – this is the cabaret."

We followed him round to one side of this concrete block, where he banged on a door. A little hole in the door opened and, evidently having satisfied himself that we were harmless, whoever was on the other side let us in. We walked into a darkened room illuminated only by a feeble string of Christmas lights around the walls. At one side was an old wooden stage on which a desperate three-piece band was plugging away. For the whole time we were there, the only number they played was "Devil Woman" by Cliff Richard – over and over again, and badly, at that.

Skull and I were the only non-Indian faces in the place and we sat there, wondering what on earth would happen next. We were asked if we wanted a drink, whereupon Skull called for a beer, only to be swiftly informed that no alcohol was allowed. The choice was simple – Coke or water. Since we didn't trust the water, we went for two Cokes. They also brought us some pieces of dodgy-looking cheese – at least I thought it was cheese – which looked as though eating it would mean a month-long holiday on the toilet and an arse like a chewed orange.

That was when the cabaret started. A woman who must have been the wrong side of fifty walked on to the stage, dressed in nothing but a bikini and an old brown cardigan. Without further ado she tossed her cardigan to one side and started dancing – or, to be strictly accurate, shuffling from one foot to the other and flopping her arms around. She must have been about fifteen stone (210 pounds) – she looked like a badly made bed. Skull and I just stared at one another, wishing she hadn't taken off the cardigan. But the rest of the audience were going absolutely mental. They were whooping the place up and crawling up the walls – including our money man and his friend.

It was stinking hot in there, which added to the *Twilight Zone* atmosphere. Suddenly I noticed a bit of intrigue in the act. For some reason, the dancer had got the right needle with the bass player in the band. As she shuffled to and fro she would turn around, give him what sounded like a serious bollocking in an aggrieved tone of voice and then turn back to the crowd with a big smile. She had gaps in her teeth – when she smiled it was like a graveyard looking at you.

We followed him round to one side of this concrete block, where he banged on a door. A little hole in the door opened and, evidently having satisfied himself that we were harmless, whoever was on the other side let us in. We walked into a darkened room illuminated only by a feeble string of Christmas lights around the walls. At one side was an old wooden stage on which a desperate three-piece band was plugging away. For the whole time we were there, the only number they played was "Devil Woman" by Cliff Richard – over and over again, and badly, at that.

Finally the dancer whipped her bikini top off and her bristols fell out. They looked like a pair of slatelayers' nailbags. Now we had these things hanging down and flopping about in front of us, too. It was terrible. But the room was going even barmier. Most of these blokes would probably have had a stroke in a proper strip club. The shuffling dancer came to a stop and a moment later her bristols stopped moving, too. She picked up her cardigan, put it on and strolled to the side of the stage where she sat down by the bass player and continued to harangue him.

Then the second girl came on. She looked about thirty and when the punters saw her they started flipping out. By the time she whipped her top off they were doing back somersaults, and when her knickers came off you would have thought that World War Three had begun. The only one who wasn't delighted was the old woman at the side of the stage, who was sitting looking daggers at her rival.

A third girl came on who was younger again. Within five minutes she had all her gear off and to be honest she didn't look too bad. She grabbed hold of this lad in the crowd and pulled him up on stage, where she made him lie down and began to dance all over him. The poor fellow looked like he was about to have a heart attack on the spot.

The crowd was throwing money at the third girl in appreciation – note after note. That made the old woman even more annoyed. She'd been growling away in the corner – where she was *still* slagging off the bass player – to the strains of "Devil Woman". When she saw the money, she climbed back on stage and whipped her cardy off for a second time, in the hope that a few pennies would be thrown at her. But the audience had settled down by then; their earlier frenzy had tired them out. The two guys with us had worn themselves out, too, with all the whooping and clapping. And the excitement had nearly killed the granny. She was shuffling about without even as much swing as before.

> **By the time she whipped her top off they were doing back somersaults, and when her knickers came off you would have thought that World War Three had begun.**

> **By now Skull had the right hump. He turned to me and, in his West Country accent, said: "If this old slapper was on in a club in Manchester, they'd set fire to her." I just exploded with laughter.**

He was deadly serious, but I thought it was one of the funniest sights I'd ever seen. We told our hosts we were ready to go. And so ended one of the more unusual nights of my life.

Most of our trips had something unorthodox about them. This was wrestling, after all. Shortly before Easter 1992 Anne Relwyskow organized a tour of British army bases in Germany. We went for ten days doing a different base every day – me, Dave

Taylor, Klondyke Kate, Drew Macdonald, Johnny South, Barry Douglas and his girlfriend Debbie, who was wrestling Kate.

We knew the army boys wouldn't want to watch the wrestling, they would want to sit there and take the mick. So Johnny South and I would go out first and knock the living hell out of each other. And every time, by the second or third round we had them – they were buying it. So they should have, because we were killing each other, wrestling really hard. That's how we got them, every night, and it meant they would enjoy the rest of the show. The girls would come on and do their performance and everything would go over well.

At one base one of the army lads told us: "You blokes have done well. We get all kinds of acts here – comedy, bands, all sorts. And you've lasted the longest of anybody. Usually after ten minutes we can them off – throw cans at them. It doesn't matter who they are, we normally can them off. You've managed to do your whole show without it happening to you."

A hell of a compliment, in its way.

I got back from Germany on Easter Sunday and did a show that day at Maggie May's on Blackpool Central Pier for Bobby Baron. The next morning I got a 7 a.m. taxi ride to Manchester and flew to South Africa for a month. This time we stayed in Cape Town, which was absolutely beautiful, a magical setting. We did shows in Cape Town, Durban, Johannesburg and Port Elizabeth. A couple of weeks after that tour, I went to Egypt with Geoff Kay, a fine wrestler in his time who still referees today.

It was a good crew again – me, Tony St Clair, Franz Schumann, Dave Taylor, Ian McGregor and a few others. It was a nice little five-day trip. We stayed in Cairo and wrestled three times at the police academy there.

Within a few months I'd seen the Taj Mahal, caught the sun on South African beaches, and now here I was, going to see the Pyramids. We went inside one too, although that was underwhelming. We crawled through these tiny passageways until finally we reached the middle of the thing, and all that was there was a big room. If I'd read up on it before I went I might have got more out of it, but I expected more than an empty room – followed by another cramped journey to get out.

It wasn't much better when Dave Taylor and Tony St Clair suggested we took a camel ride. I've never been much good on motorbikes or horses, let alone camels. I climbed up on this animal and it kept turning round, trying to bite me. As it got up a head of speed, I'd had enough. I shouted to the camel boy, "I'll give you all the money I've got, just get me off this thing."

But the camel ride was a walk in the park compared to my trip home. Back then, in my early twenties, on occasion I took steroids. I'll be completely honest about it, as I am trying to be with everything in this book. But as with everything else, I will only talk about my own business. I don't get involved in what other people do.

I did steroids because I wanted to get a better body for wrestling. In gyms you meet a lot of bodybuilding types who are very into it, but I was never very interested in bodybuilding. I first took them when I was nineteen after which I took them on and off for a while.

That first time I took them for eight weeks and put on a lot of weight. Then the year after I read up on it and took them for a month before I went to Germany for the first time and then for the six weeks I was there. I stopped when I came back because I couldn't really afford them. For the next two years I took them for a month before going to Hamburg and then while I was there. The first time, I took tablets – four a day. Next it was a drug called Dianabol, before I went to Hamburg. The following year I did an injectable drug called Deca Durabolin and also Parabolan. I would take five Dianabol a day. That worked well for me and I got very muscular and strong.

I never suffered any side effects because I never took very many and not for very long either. Anabolic steroids enable you to recover better from your workouts. You absorb more protein into the muscle. When you train and break your muscle down, it will repair it quicker and put more into it so it gets bigger. When I took them they never made me feel like Superman, I just felt stronger and was able to train harder.

It's when you are training that you feel the difference. You'll look good no matter what you eat. It changes your body composition – more muscle and less fat. I always trained but I was always naturally heavy. The steroids used to lean me up and take away a lot

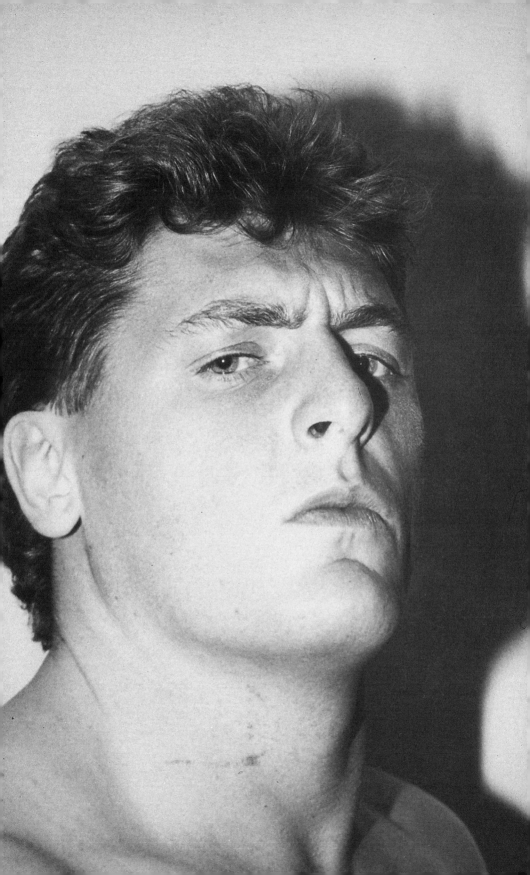

of my body fat. When you see pictures of me from that time, you can tell when I was on them and when I was not. I didn't need them in England for shows where I was earning £20 or £30 a night and people didn't expect you to look like a bodybuilder. They didn't necessarily in Germany either, but I'll be honest – I liked looking good. When I was on steroids I would get my publicity photos done and send them around the world. If a job ever came up where I needed to look like that, I could get back on the steroids. But the choice was always mine. In my whole career, no one has ever told me I had to take steroids to work for them.

Anyway, it was my last day in Egypt and I had heard that you could buy cheap steroids from any pharmacy there for literally pennies. So I went out and bought a fair amount – enough to last me for a while. I packed them in the top of my case and thought no more of it. I wasn't breaking the law. I had bought them legally. I was taking them back into England, where they were legal then. And as long as you had a receipt and had bought no more than about £200 worth, it was legal to bring them back into the country.

I got to the airport with the guy who had been looking after us all week. We were just about to go through security when they stopped a fellow in front of me, opened his bag and pulled out all these drugs, which later turned out to be insulin. He was instantly surrounded by police. They knocked hell out of him with their sticks and dragged him off.

I asked my guide: "What's going on here?"

He said: "People come over here and buy stuff from pharmacies because it is a lot cheaper than in their home countries."

"So why are they arresting him?"

"Well," he explained patiently, "It's cheap here because the government subsidize it so the poor here can afford it. So when people buy it and take it out of the country they are effectively stealing from the Egyptian government."

All the colour drained from my face. Here I was with a bag full of steroids. I kept telling myself to look as calm as I could. But as soon as my bag went through the X-Ray machine they spotted something unusual in it – all the phials of stuff in there.

They opened my case and I was immediately surrounded by

policemen with machine guns, all screaming at me. I was trying to act cool but my bottle was well gone – you couldn't get a nail up my arsehole. I thought I was looking at twenty years in some Egyptian hellhole, eating rats and cockroaches to survive. The fellow with me was distraught. "What have you done?" he demanded.

"I didn't know," I feebly explained. "I just bought this stuff. I didn't know it was illegal to take out of the country."

Then the Cairo chief of police arrived and started screaming and shouting at me. My tour guide started talking to him in Egyptian. They went back and forth for ten minutes while a cold sweat started going down my back. He came back and said, "The chief of police would like a present."

"He can have one," I agreed, eagerly.

"How much cash have you got?"

I had about £90 in Egyptian money. The guide said: "Give it to me."

I gave it to him, he took it to the chief of police who said: "Send him through." I sealed up my bag, went straight through, got on the plane and melted into my seat. And so ended my brief career as an international drugs smuggler. Holidays are long enough as it is, I decided. I didn't get stopped at Heathrow, got home, went straight to a DIY store to buy a crowbar to prise my buttocks apart, and that was that.

I was working in England when I got a call from the German promoter Otto Wanz. He wanted me to join his long German tour, the one which lasted six-and-a-half months. Steve Wright, an English wrestler who was living out there, had got involved in an accident, which meant that they needed a replacement.

I travelled over with my mate Dave Taylor and his caravan. After a few spot shows in Hanover and elsewhere in Germany, we were

Chris, Daniel and Dane in our Vienna apartment.

on our way to Graz in Austria. Dave and I drove the 700 miles, towing his caravan all the while. We stayed at a scenic campsite at the foot of some mountains for three weeks, working every night and enjoying every minute of it, until Dave developed a hernia and had to return to England for an operation.

I went on without him to Vienna – an incredible city. I loved it there. I had the run of a little apartment and Chris and the kids came out to spend four weeks with me. It was perfect. Staying in the same place all the time is always a blessed relief for a wrestler. We went to a beautiful park every day which had a gym in the middle of it where I could train. We had a swimming pool, too and we ate out every day and walked around the city. It was idyllic; a real change.

The wrestling was outdoors in a tennis stadium right in the middle of Vienna. We had Mondays off and also we didn't have to work if it rained, when we'd get half-pay. Luckily that only happened on the penultimate night in the whole seven weeks we were there.

Working all the time like that does put strains on the body.
I was having a lot of trouble with my back, which had been killing me for quite a while. I was getting shooting pains down my legs as well. So after Vienna, while the tour did three days in a holiday resort called Seeboden, I went home to Blackpool to see what my physio friend Dave Rogers could do to put me right.

Whatever he did it succeded, because I was able to rejoin the tour and do the whole nine weeks in Hanover, where we wrestled in a giant circus tent. That was a lot of fun, too – I lived in a caravan parked behind the tent and would go to the gym, eat, sleep in the afternoon, leave the caravan at 6:50 to be in the tent by seven before wrestling at eight and going out for the night.

Among the usual faces there was an American called Rip Rogers. After Hanover he came back to the UK with me to do a few shows before we went out to Brehmen for the five weeks leading up to Christmas.

Rip did me a big favour while we were out in Germany: he asked me if I'd heard anything from WCW. I hadn't. I'd been sending them postcards from wherever I was working, saying who I was, how I'd tried out for them and letting them know where I was working now. It was good business sense, something Dave Taylor had taught me years before, because when you look busy, people always want you.

But Rip had news. A guy called Bill Watts had taken over at WCW. Rip had worked for Bill and knew what he liked to hear. So he said he'd dictate a letter I could send to Bill which would get on his right side. It said how many years I had been wrestling, where I'd worked, how I'd trained. Bill liked to hear that people had "trained diligently" – so that's exactly what the letter said.

A week after sending it, I called home and Chris said WCW had been in touch. She had a number they wanted me to ring straight away. I dialled in and spoke to Bill Watts' secretary.

"When can you start?" she wanted to know.

I was booked in Germany until Christmas, I told her.

"Can you start in January?" she asked.

You bet I could. She said to send my passport details and everything would be sorted out. My whole world was turning upside down – and very quickly too.

From Brehmen, I went home for Christmas, and after a brief delay as WCW dealt with the red tape, I flew to America on January 23, 1993. My last show in England was fitting – for Bobby Baron in the Winter Gardens in Blackpool in his traditional show two days after Christmas. I started wrestling for WCW in America on January 25, 1993. I'm still here.

6

The Kiss of Death Belt

Like most Brits, all I knew of America I learned from watching movies. When I landed in Atlanta, the reality was a shock. There were no bright lights, no yellow taxis, and no obvious glamour. No pavements either, which was weird. I was surprised there was no one from WCW at the airport to greet me. I would learn that as far as WCW organization went, that wasn't unusual. I booked myself into the Ramada hotel near the airport, which would become my home for quite a while.

On my first night there I met Bill Dundee,

one of the agents, and we struck up an instant relationship. He was a Scotsman who had left Scotland when he was sixteen and had had a good career as Jerry Lawler's rival in Memphis. The pair of them sold out the Memphis Coliseum more times than anyone else.

They'd asked me to be a straightforward wrestler. But even after the first few weeks of TV it was obvious to everyone that this wasn't working. It wasn't what people were used to. When you want to wrestle, it helps to have people who know your style. And putting people into holds takes time to tell a story – just doing a couple of minutes' worth is not going to do anyone any favours. It was rotten.

> As soon as I got here I realized I needed to know how to talk. That'll sound crazy to a lot of people. But being able to give a good interview is one of the key skills in this business. It's not as easy as it looks.

It was a different story on the house shows, something that would become a theme. I had more time when the TV cameras weren't around and so I was able to build a match and tell a story wrestling in my style. So the people in charge could see that I knew my stuff. But it wasn't right for TV.

I knew I had to learn other skills – and quickly. As soon as I got here I realized I needed to know how to talk. That'll sound crazy to a lot of people. But being able to give a good interview is one of the key skills in this business. It's not as easy as it looks. Years before in the late eighties in England, I'd met a wrestler called Pat Barrett. He was an American who worked for Brian Dixon. He'd been big in the WWWF, run by Vince McMahon's father. Pat had been around a bit and I met him when we were in Hastings on the south coast when I was nineteen. Pat told me, "You're going to go to America one day. You need to learn how to talk."

He'd always been a great talker and his advice was simple. "Get yourself in front of a mirror and practise." Which was what I did – and I tell people starting out to do it today. I'd read things out of books, or memorize passages and speak them into the mirror, working on my voice. Yet I'd never spent as much time on it as I should have – I'd always felt that seeing yourself in a mirror and on a TV screen were two very different things.

The WCW studios and office were in the CNN Center in Atlanta and they were all owned by Ted Turner. So I talked to them and soon, on my days off, they would set up a camera for me and I would go into the WCW studio at CNN in Atlanta and talk into it for hours. I would talk about anything, practising my timing. A twenty-second promo, a thirty-second promo, a minute promo. All day long.

I got very good very rapidly, but I was still using my own voice. I soon realized that if I was going to do good promos, I had to sound posher than I am in real life. It wasn't difficult. Growing up in Codsall Wood there were two types of people – the ones who were born there and the ones who'd moved there. The town was getting gentrified, and becoming quite an upmarket little place – it even had a country house nearby called Chillington Hall. A lot of families had lived around there for generations, working the area, but plenty of new money was moving in, so I had been around these posh people and could easily slip in and out of the way they talked.

A lot of my values were picked up from my granddad – good, working-class values I suppose you would call them. My granddad would never swear around women and I won't either – though perhaps I do around Chris now and again.

There were a few examples of cultural confusion when I got to the States. I wasn't used to being called by my last name only. You very rarely did that in England. The way my granddad had brought me up, calling someone by their last name was a put-down. It was something the upper classes did to put the working classes in their place. If a teacher ever called me Matthews at school, I'd completely ignore them. So when I got here and people started calling me Regal, I got the right hump. I've got used to it now but it's taken a long time.

A lot of my values were picked up from my granddad – good, working-class values I suppose you would call them. My granddad would never swear around women and I won't either – though perhaps I do around Chris now and again.

Learning how to talk would stand me in good stead in the long run but in those days, I was still struggling on TV. Then in

March, a hammer blow fell. Bill Watts got fired. I wasn't aware of all the politics going on that caused it. But Bill was a wild and woolly character, not the sort of man who would be understood in Ted Turner's big TV empire.

I liked Bill, and not just because he had brought me here. He was very abrupt, but his whole idea of wrestling was to make it all as believable as possible. He enforced the kayfabe rules very strictly. That meant good guys or babyfaces and bad guys or heels were not allowed to travel together. Bill thought that if the fans saw them hanging out, having a good time together, it would ruin the idea that they hated each other when they saw them get in the ring.

There's nothing wrong with that. People may know it that wrestling is smoke and mirrors but they don't actually want to see the smoke and the mirrors – we shouldn't rub it in their faces. We shouldn't pretend it's 100 per cent real because that is insulting to people's intelligence. But we should make it as easy as possible for fans to suspend their disbelief. A lot of other guys will talk about their matches in front of non-wrestlers but I refuse. I think it should be like working with a magician, when you have to sign a contract promising not to expose his act. Magicians don't talk about how they do their tricks and in my opinion wrestlers should be the same.

Bill had the same attitude and I liked him for that. I also liked his son Erik, someone who never really got a fair shake in this business. He got a bad reputation simply because he was his father's son. A lot of people didn't like his dad, and when Bill pushed Erik – as any father would – it got up people's noses. He was pushed a bit too strong at the beginning but he was a nice kid who had talent. That early push went against him later on. Erik is one of the few people who has taken the time to call me and thank me for the help I had given him early on. He should have had a good career in wrestling, but it never worked out for him.

The same scenario played out with Ole Anderson. He was at WCW when I arrived and he ran the company for a while. He hated Eric Bischoff and Eric hated him. Ole asked me to train his son Brian, another good lad with talent. But as soon as Eric got the power he got rid of Brian. It was wrong. Brian worked hard and ended up without a job because of politics. He grew sick of wrestling and ended up as a teacher.

As soon as Bill went, I thought I would be the next one straight out of the door. As in any other business so in wrestling, the new man in charge would bring in his own guys and get rid of the fellows associated with the old regime. I thought that would happen to me and, if I'm honest, I wasn't too upset at the prospect. Yes, I was earning $1,500 a week. But I had to pay for the hotel I was living in, and for rental cars too. I had to save forty per cent to pay my tax bill at the end of the year and had to send money home to pay my bills in England. I'd actually been better off the year before, working for people who'd pay your tax and your hotels and I'd come home from a trip abroad with a chunk of money.

But good or bad, I was quite convinced that this was the end of my little American adventure, almost before it had got started. I spoke to Bill Dundee about my worries. The only way I could succeed in America, I told him, was to work as a heel, a villain.

I'd always worked as a babyface in England but I had done a lot of over-the-top comedy matches and knew a lot of that material would fit in with being a heel. I could take stuff I'd seen from people like Kevin Connelly, Pedro the Gipsy, Catweazle, Steve Peacock, Mal Sanders and Cyanide Sid Cooper. I knew I could nick a lot of Sid's mannerisms. And with my wrestling style I knew I could make my opponents look good by putting them in and out of holds.

I knew I could mix it all together and create the English heel character I wanted to be. I kept on at Bill that this was what I wanted to do. For something like that to happen, you often have to let the people in charge come round to think that it was their idea in the first place.

Sure enough, after a couple of weeks Dusty Rhodes came up to me and said: "We've got a great idea for you. We're turning you heel and you're going to be called Lord Steven Regal." I didn't care whose idea it had been. It was going to happen, and that was all I cared about.

In that first year WCW announcer Tony Schiavone, with whom I always got on well, had popped his head in a few times to see me practising my interviews at CNN. Tony put the word out that I'd be good at commentary, and sure enough that's what happened. When WCW was shown in England, I would do the commentary with Gordon Solie. He was one of the great announcers in our business and I was privileged to work with him. Gordon loved wrestling. He knew what I did and respected it so we got on fine. It was another great learning experience that might come in handy in the future.

At the end of March 1993, Chris arrived for her first look at America. The plan was for her to spend three months out here and help me find an apartment. I was wrestling a young Rob Van Dam, appearing as Robbie V, in the North Georgia mountains. Real *Deliverance* country – it was where they'd made the film.

I picked Chris up at the airport and we drove up to the high school gym or wherever the show was taking place. As we neared the building it started to snow. When we got there and got out of the car there was already an inch of snow on the ground. Rob and I were on first and I decided we should get going early as we had to be somewhere else a few hundred miles away the next day. But

Gordon Solie taught me plenty about the art of commentating.

when we got out of the building the inch of snow had turned into a foot. After driving just a few miles we couldn't go any further. The weather had closed right in and the winding roads across the top of the mountains had become impassable.

In that first year WCW announcer Tony Schiavone, with whom I always got on well, had popped his head in a few times to see me practising my interviews at CNN. Tony put the word out that I'd be good at commentary, and sure enough that's what happened. When WCW was shown in England, I would do the commentary with Gordon Solie. He was one of the great announcers in our business and I was privileged to work with him. Gordon loved wrestling. He knew what I did and respected it so we got on fine. It was another great learning experience that might come in handy in the future.

So we pulled over at the first motel we could see and, without a word of exaggeration, it was just like the Bates Motel. The old woman behind the desk started bawling her eyes out as soon as she saw me. When she settled down, she said it was because I reminded her of her grandson who'd been killed horribly. Not a particularly good start. But there was no choice, we had to book in for the night.

The room was about as grand as we'd expected and as soon as we got in there the electricity cut out. That caused the water to go off too. There was no heat, no water and you couldn't even flush the toilet. We went down to see the woman, who burst into tears again as soon as I approached her. The only creature comfort she could provide was a battery-powered radio, so we took it back to the room and tried to make the best of the situation. We huddled up together and thought that at least we'd be able to get out of there in the morning.

No such luck. Next morning I couldn't even see the car – it was completely covered over with snow. We trudged across the street to a Hardy's burger joint. The only reason it was still open was because some of the staff hadn't been able to get home before the snow came down. They were cooking what food they had left so we got some crusty old crap and went back to the hotel and gave some of it to the old lady.

I couldn't tell if this cheered her up, since at the first sight of me she began crying again. By now a few more stragglers had come down from the mountains but they were as stuck there as we were – no one could go anywhere. As we got through that Saturday, Chris was wondering what on earth she had gotten herself into.

The only thing I could think about was that I was going to miss a show for the first time in my life. I couldn't get in touch with anyone to tell them what had happened. You've no idea what it meant to me to be forced to miss that show. To me it's one of the unwritten rules – no matter what happens, you have to make the show. Of course I found out later that everyone else was caught up in the snow too. But at the time, all I could think was that because I was the new boy, I'd get fired for not turning up to do the show.

The only thing I could think about was that I was going to miss a show for the first time in my life. I couldn't get in touch with anyone to tell them what had happened. You've no idea what it meant to me to be forced to miss that show. To me it's one of the unwritten rules – no matter what happens, you have to make the show. Of course I found out later that everyone else was caught up in the snow too. But at the time, all I could think was that because I was the new boy, I'd get fired for not turning up to do the show.

That night the batteries ran out on the radio. When I woke up on the Sunday morning, Chris was crying in a heap on the floor. She'd left the kids with my dad and stepmum in Codsall, and she was convinced that we'd never see them again.

By now we were ravenous – and so was the old lady. Not long beforehand I'd seen the film *Alive*, about a plane crash in the Andes where the survivors had to eat the dead in order to stay alive. I joked to Chris that I'd start off with her arm or leg, but she wasn't in the mood to see the funny side. The old lady told us there was a hospital a mile up the road, so Chris and I wrapped ourselves in all the clothes we had and set off to see if they had any food to spare.

We took it one step at a time through three feet of snow and when we got there we found the hospital was full of stranded people. It was one of those times when you're made to realize that you might have all the credit cards and money in the world but they don't matter in the least when you can't do anything with them. The hospital staff were able to give us some peanut butter sandwiches and some milk, so we set off with our meagre provisions. We had to look after the old lady now. She was starving, and she had wept so much I began to wonder whether she wasn't dehydrating too.

> Chris honestly thought she was being kidnapped. I had to stand there watching as this stranger drove away with my wife. Chris later told me the guy never said a word to her as they disappeared from my sight. He stopped a mile or so up the road, turned to her and said, "I just wanted to turn the engine over."

At last the odd snowplough started to get through and eventually, at four or five o'clock on Sunday, the police came and dragged the car out. Chris was in the passenger's seat while a fellow who was working with the police drove it out of the snowdrift – and then carried on driving off up the road.

Chris honestly thought she was being kidnapped. I had to stand there watching as this stranger drove away with my wife. Chris later told me the guy never said a word to her as they disappeared from my sight. He stopped a mile or so up the road, turned to her and said, "I just wanted to turn the engine over." When he came back with my wife and car, we loaded our bags and Chris and I and a hitchhiker who wanted a lift to Atlanta got in and off we went.

I'd missed all my shows and was off until the following Friday. And it was Chris's last week. So from North Georgia we drove all the way to Atlanta, where we dropped our hitchhiker off and then carried straight on driving to Florida. We stayed the night on the Florida border and then called my godparents who happened to be staying in Inverness, near Orlando. We spent a couple of much-needed days with them, trying to get the chill out of our bones and the horror out of our minds.

We had, however, managed to find an apartment to live in. Chris went back to England and I went back briefly to the Ramada, which I'd had quite enough of by now. It was a madhouse. All the wrestlers stayed there when they were in town. Life revolved around the hotel bar – and at that time I didn't drink. It was a crazy place. We nicknamed it the Dungeon.

The woman who ran it was a raging, drunken lunatic – marvellous qualifications to be a manageress. I've no idea how she contrived to run the place. She had a fondness for getting inebriated and calling me in my room with the news that I was a "limey cocksucker". Well worth $1,200 a month for the privilege.

I wasn't interested in any of this madness. I wanted to do my work, go back to the hotel and not be bothered by anyone. I had to be booked in there permanently – I needed a base for my gear when I was on the road, paying for hotels out there too. Needing the rental car seven days a week was another big financial drain. So hotel life got real old real quick and when we saw some apartments in Marietta on the north side of Atlanta, that seemed like a good way out.

At the hotel I'd been sharing a room with Maxx Payne, another WCW wrestler I'd known from the year before in Germany. We both moved into the Marietta apartment until Chris returned, when Maxx moved out. A few of the lads moved into other apartments – Sid Vicious; Rob Fuller, who appeared as Colonel Rob Parker; Tex Slazenger; Shanghai Pierce. It was a nice set-up. Sting's gym was only across the road, which was handy for all of us. And soon Chris and the kids would be out for the summer, for the three months they were allowed under the rules.

The plans were set for Lord Steven Regal. I was going to be off people's TV screens for a while so I could come back in as this new character. In the meantime I got to know and learn from some of the great wrestlers this business has seen. I struck up a good friendship with Steve Austin. I travelled with Bill Dundee at the time and Steve travelled with Brian Pillman, but Steve and I hit it off instantly.

I soon got to know Brian too, once I understood his sense of humour. I also got on well with Cactus Jack – Mick Foley. I learned so much from watching these guys in action. Anyone in this business who has a genuine love for it watches everyone else's matches. I do. I want to know what's going on. This is my job, and when I get to the building I have to use everything I have at my disposal. That means learning and improving all the time – and that includes watching other people because you'll always learn from it, whether they're doing something well or badly.

Not everyone shares my attitude. Some of the younger guys in the business today are there for the fame and the glory. When I started there was precious little of either. I did it because I liked being a wrestler, and I loved wrestling. Yes, it was more glamorous than working in a factory. But there wasn't too much glamour about touring the country, wrestling in fairgrounds and holiday camps.

Triple H has the same outlook. The first time I met him I liked him straight away because he always watched the other matches. Bill Watts had a rule that no one could leave before the main event. A lot of the guys used to moan about it, but that was because they didn't get why he made the rule in the first place. If you wanted to be in the main event one day, first you had to learn how to do it.

You've also got to condition yourself to peak at that time of night and be ready to work then. There's a hell of a difference between being in the opening match at 7.30 p.m. and wrestling in the main event at half past ten. My philosophy is always to be ready, because you never know what might happen. You can get thrown in the main event out of the blue. That's why you have to watch everybody – you need to know what moves they do, what they do well, what they do badly and how it would fit in with what you do.

So I used to watch Cactus. When I first got to WCW he was in a feud with Paul Orndoff. I'd been a big fan of Paul's ever since the 1980s because he was so intense and aggressive. He always used to tell me my wrestling had to be more intense – I had to attack more. I thought I was plenty aggressive but Paul was right – I wasn't intense like he was. I am now.

He was doing this stuff with Cactus and there was something about Cactus that intrigued me. When he walked through the curtain every night he had a presence about him. It's difficult to put your finger on, but he had that certain something. He'd shuffle along with his whole body sloped to one side and that crazy grin on his face, but he radiated presence. Having that is more important than knowing all the wrestling moves under the sun.

Some people just have it. Like Tommy Cooper, the comedian, one of my heroes. When someone asked the great actress Thora Hird whether Tommy was a great comedian, she said: "No, he was a comic presence." He was. And Cactus was a presence too.

I watched everybody. I was lucky to be in WCW at the same time as Ricky Steamboat, who was so good at what he did. Pillman and Austin were tremendous too as a tag team called the Hollywood Blondes. They used to have phenomenal matches against Steamboat and Shane Douglas. There was Bobby Eaton and Arn Anderson too, people I'd loved watching back in Blackpool when my mate Peter used to get videos of 1980s NWA. I'd met Arn in England and clicked with Bobby as soon as I met him. Bobby is one of those rare characters in wrestling – someone about whom absolutely no one has a bad word to say.

I also got to know Davey Boy Smith. He'd been signed in January and he was staying along with the rest of us in the Ramada. He was very funny and we had a lot in common. We'd done a lot of the same things when we were younger and knew a lot of the same people. There was a great deal of good wrestling in WCW then. Since I was off TV I did a lot of house shows instead, working against Chris Benoit for weeks at a time or Too Cold Scorpio. Benoit and I always had great matches and Too Cold Scorpio was excellent too, which meant I was loving the house shows.

We worked in Georgia, Alabama, Florida and the Carolinas in

front of people who grew up watching wrestling from the NWA and Florida Promotions. That meant they liked my style of wrestling. All of it was the opposite of the company at the time where everything was very gimmicky and all the wrestlers were cartoon characters. By contrast, we used to have 25- or 30-minute matches every night and the fans loved it. I loved it too – it was a great time for me. Yet all the time I knew I had the real challenge ahead of me. I was going back on TV.

Lord Steven Regal debuted on TV at the end of May. Virtually everyone who had ever come from England had played lords or toffs, and I would be no different. They wanted me to have a manager.

Originally Dusty was going to put Larry Zbyszko with me. Larry's real surname was Whistler and for some reason Dusty thought that was a very English-sounding name. But Bill Dundee saw his chance to get on TV so he got the job instead. He played my butler and was called Sir William. Pretty daft when you think of it – why would a butler have a knighthood? But it worked well for American audiences.

On my first night on TV I came out and did a promo and it just clicked. It worked great from day one. After a month to six weeks off TV, I was back and being used plenty. My debut came on the WCW Saturday Night show at 6 p.m. on TBS, which had been running for about seventeen years at the time. The following Wednesday or Thursday was one of their TV specials, a *Clash of the Champions*. I beat Buff Bagwell and everything fell into place. I couldn't do anything wrong.

I find the interviews difficult to watch now because they seem so old-fashioned, all tea and crumpets. But they were effective at the time. I was using my posh voice and a lot of Terry-Thomas. I'd been watching British comedy all my life and it became a mine of material I could adapt and borrow from whenever I needed. Films, shows and comedians I'd watched all became great ammunition.

Soon I was working a programme against Ricky Steamboat. There's never been anyone like him and I don't think there ever will be. I've been lucky enough to wrestle a lot of great opponents over the years. For me, the absolute best was Fit Finlay. Benoit, Terry Rudge and Ray Steele would be on the list too. But when I came over to America, there was something about Steamboat that made him awesome.

In September we did a big Pay-Per-View show, *Fall Brawl* in Houston, Texas, and I beat Ricky to lift the television title for the first time.

I was holding the belt in my hands backstage, walking on air, when Arn Anderson saw me and started laughing.

"What are you laughing for, Arn?" I asked.

He said: "That's the Kiss of Death belt."

I soon learned what he meant. It earned the name because whoever was given it kept the thing for a long time. They would have to be very talented because they would have to work with everybody – and work a lot. You would be on every single show because it was the TV title, defended on every TV show. And sometimes they would tape three TV shows in one night, which meant wrestling three times in same evening. With run-ins and interviews, your nights on TV would be non-stop.

We'd tape the Saturday night shows at Center Stage in Atlanta and tape the Sunday night shows, called *The Main Event*, at other places in Alabama and Georgia. This was before the days of *Monday Night Nitro*. There was the syndicated worldwide show which was taped at Disney in Orlando, when we would do a batch of them in one week.

When I had the title I worked twelve out of thirteen shows, three a day. And the matches were tough, too. The gimmick with the TV title was that the matches had a ten or fifteen minute time limit. The TV champion would very rarely beat anyone. But he would do just enough to scrape by, escaping to stay unbeaten until the time limit to keep the title was up. They were never what we call enhancement matches, when you go out and beat a guy very quickly.

That's why it was called the Kiss of Death belt. It was great to be TV champion when it meant you got to work with great guys. But the TV champion worked with everybody. A lot of the wrestlers – most of them, in fact – weren't particularly talented. You would have to do ten-minute matches with people who couldn't do much more than lace their boots up. Ten minutes might not sound very long, but having to drag someone through a match for that length of time makes it feel like an age. Having to put people in and out of holds, trying to make them look good meant having to work twice as hard as just worrying about yourself.

I was following some illustrious names as TV champion. Arn Anderson, Bobby Eaton and Steve Austin all had it before me. And for all the hassles, being TV champion meant a great run for me. I loved the Kiss of Death belt.

I loved that
TV Title belt.

7

Big in Japan

That October I had my first trip back to Britain as a bona fide WCW star. The lord gimmick had clicked and things could not be going better. I knew by now I was going to stay and Eric Bischoff, who took over from Bill Watts, sorted it so the family and I all got green cards. I had been on a one-year visa, but now it meant Chris and the kids could come out for good from the start of the new year.

I was looking forward to the UK tour, particularly as my first match, in Cardiff, would be against Ric Flair. He was one of the guys I'd always loved to watch; I thought he was tremendous – and I still do. He was an incredible wrestler, so talented in the ring and someone who has done so much for this business. It was nerve-wracking to wrestle him, but a big honour, too.

I'd rented a car, so after the Cardiff show I drove up to Blackpool and spent the day there with my wife and kids, walking along the promenade and doing all the things I loved to do whenever I was home. When I turned up at the next show, in Blackburn, I discovered that all hell had broken out the night before. The crew were travelling in two buses, A bus and B bus. B bus was supposed to be all the villains, and certainly earned a villainous reputation by the end of the trip. They'd got caught up in horrendous traffic, thanks to an accident which blocked the motorway for several hours. Everyone had been drinking and there had already been some mayhem on the bus before they arrived at the hotel at three or four in the morning.

I try to not to get involved in other people's business and the incident was nothing to do with me. But it set the tone for the rest of the tour.

I don't know exactly what happened next because I wasn't there, but it was all over the national newspapers the next day. It appeared that Sid Vicious and Arn Andersen had got into a fight and ended up stabbing each other with a pair of scissors. When I got to Blackburn the following day the police were there. Although he was playing my manager, Bill Dundee was still one of the agents and he had to sort the whole mess out. I try to not to get involved in other people's business and the incident was nothing to do with me. But it set the tone for the rest of the tour.

At the Blackburn show I wrestled Dustin Rhodes, Dusty's son, who went on to become Goldust in WWE. We then did a double shot at the Albert Hall in London, afternoon and evening, before we went straight to Germany for a week of shows. I had to abandon the car and join the bus with the rest of them. Chief protagonists on the bus – which rapidly became the bus from hell – were the Nasty Boys; Brian Knobbs and Jerry Sags. I always got on well with them because they made me laugh. But they were loud, obnoxious nuisances on this completely insane bus.

The Nasty Boys –
Brian Knobbs and
Jerry Sags – were
a permanent riot
on tour.

All the trips in Germany were long ones taking several hours but now it felt like they were going on forever. People were flipping out, cracking up, all kinds. Ole Andersen, one of the WCW higher-ups at the time, couldn't handle trying to keep order on the bus so he just upped and left. I just sat there quietly amused by it all. It was such a mad tour, having started out with the double stabbing and gone downhill from there.

The night Sid had his fight with Arn, Sid had managed to cram himself into the tiny toilet they had on the bus, when one of the Nasty Boys followed him in and peed all over him. There were benches at the back of the bus where Maxx Payne and Nick Patrick, a WWE referee these days, both had electric guitars and amps set up and blasted out music. The Nasty Boys kept running up and down the bus naked and Sags spent the whole trip showing his arse to everybody.

When we got back from Germany they printed up T-shirts for us all with a picture of a bus, which had Sag's arse hanging out of one window and a hand coming out of another holding a pair of scissors, and the slogan "I survived the B bus".

It was mental. A few headlines came out of a plane ride home from a WWE European tour we had recently, but that was absolutely nothing by comparison.

It was on that trip – and on that bus – that I first started drinking a few beers. I wasn't drinking a great deal, but back then it didn't take a lot to get me drunk. I had never really been a drinker. I might have had a pint or two of Guinness once a year. In truth, I'd been turned off it by my mum and my stepdad, who were both heavy drinkers. I'd spent time with them and seen too much of the consequences. But every night on that tour we'd have a six- or seven-hour bus ride after the show to get to a hotel at five or six in the morning. It was on those bus rides that my love affair with booze began.

Bill Dundee on his best behaviour as my butler, Sir William. That's Dory Funk on the left.

The night we got to Hamburg, one of my old haunts, at four in the morning, I wanted to hit the town. It was impossible to sleep having been on the bus with all those lunatics. I took Steve Austin and Bill Dundee to a bar and restaurant run by a friend of mine. I'd always got on fine with Bill, but his only problem was that if he got even so much as a sniff of whisky, he thought he was ten feet tall and bullet-proof, and rapidly became a pain in the arse. Plenty of people didn't get on with him at all but I liked him because he had been good to me. Yet I could not be around him when he'd had a drink because he became a nightmare.

Before we went into the bar I tried to explain the protocol to Bill. It was my friend's place, I told him, and he'd always give you a particular Yugoslavian spirit to drink to begin with. But being Bill, he had to create a scene, shouting that he didn't want this strange drink and demanding whisky instead. That was embarrassing enough to begin with.

As we walked back along the Reeperbahn I tried to tell Bill it wasn't a place in which to mess about, especially late at night. It was full of drug addicts and pimps who could kill you. But Bill got louder and louder and more of a liability so at five in the morning, Austin and I left him and went back to the hotel. Bill had no idea where he was or where the hotel was and was blind drunk by then, but he managed to get back all the same – I've no idea how.

Because of that incident and one or two others, I decided to start travelling with Austin when I got back to the States. I couldn't handle travelling with Bill any more. On the road, you spend more time with your travelling partner than you do with your own family. I've only found a handful of partners I'm comfortable with all the time. Steve Austin is one. Triple H is another and there are very few in between.

> As we walked back along the Reeperbahn I tried to tell Bill it wasn't a place in which to mess about, especially late at night. It was full of drug addicts and pimps who could kill you.

Sometimes you stick together, other times you travel with someone for a while and then go your separate ways. You share everything with your travelling partner. They see you at your worst and at your best. You eat together, you stay at the same hotels, you go to the gym together. You share your problems. We're away 200 days a year. Ideally, you find someone who likes doing the same things as you at the same time and laughs at the same things too. Austin and I were like that.

We had some fun trips too. At Easter in 1994 we went to St Martin in the Caribbean for Ric Flair, who had a gym there. He treated us well and we only had to wrestle once on the five-day trip. I wrestled Ricky Steamboat, which was always a great privilege.

I shared a room with Bobby Eaton, and over those five days got to know him a lot better. Everybody loves Bobby. He's funny, kind and generous and just a great guy to be around. He's famous for carrying the biggest bags in wrestling. It doesn't matter what you needed at any time of the day when you're on the road, Bobby could supply it. If you needed shirts he had them. If you had holes in any of your gear he had the sewing kit to sew them up. If you needed

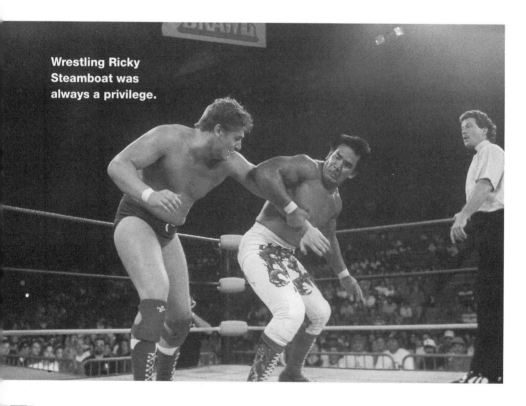

Wrestling Ricky Steamboat was always a privilege.

some small part for your car . . . You name it, he had it in those big bags he'd lug around all day, sweating furiously as he did so. I truly think the world of Bobby. You can't help but like him.

We had a grand time in St Martin, combining a little bit of wrestling with a lot of jet skiing and general enjoyment, then went back for a short stint in America before another trip to the Bahamas. We flew into the Bahamas on a Saturday, did a show on Saturday night and the next day flew to Fort Lauderdale in Florida ahead of a Monday night show. It was an outdoor show in front of a sparse crowd, and I wrestled Cactus Jack.

On this trip Cactus, Steve Austin and I were travelling together. We'd stayed somewhere pretty expensive in the Bahamas which wasn't as good as it should have been for the price, so we decided to change our tickets and fly back on the Sunday. This time we were paying for everything ourselves, except our flights. That's generally how it is in wrestling. Can you imagine someone like David Beckham picking up his own hotel bill?

So we flew into Fort Lauderdale. Mick Foley has told this story in his own book, but this is how I remember it:

We got a cheap small car between the three of us. I've never been one for being cheap with myself but Mick has built a career on it. He's so mean that I think he only breathes in. He doesn't waste anything – as tight as a duck's arsehole.

We drove along the beach and spotted an Econolodge – a very cheap hotel. Since we were only there for a few days and would be out on the beach for most of the time, we decided we could split the one room three ways. Steve and I had a double bed each and Cactus had a rollaway bed to sleep on. We dropped our bags and went out. After a while by the hotel pool, we strolled down to the beach across the road. As soon as we got there, Cactus stripped off his clothes and dived into the sea. Seeing Jack in the water was the strangest thing. He laid on his back motionless but somehow floated. I'd never seen anyone able to do that. It was as if he was on a lilo.

It was at that point that Steve and I began to realize that there weren't many women knocking about on the beach. There was one bloke with his arm around another and a few fellows wearing pink and yellow G-strings, putting oil on each other's backs. "What's going on here?" I thought. The penny dropped. "They're all shirtlifters." Steve and I looked like we fitted in, too. He had long blond hair and was wearing a tank top and pink shorts. I was blond too, and wearing a polo shirt and a pair of shorts.

But the amazing floating Jack was still happily oblivious to what was going on. Steve and I beat a hasty retreat back to the hotel pool. We could still see Jack, blissfully floating around in the sea. Eventually he got out and started drying himself off. You could see him looking around to see if there were any girls about or whether anyone was eyeing him up. Then you could see the penny drop for Jack too, as he spotted these fellows on the beach. He panicked and bolted. Steve and I nearly wet ourselves laughing.

We spent the rest of the day by the pool. Steve indulged in one of his favourite pastimes, drinking a few cocktails, while I had a few beers. Jack wasn't drinking. Then we went to the movies, where the only picture we were in time to see was a Michael Keaton flick called *The Paper*. It was rubbish. Jack and I were trying to watch it, but Steve started laughing as loud as he could; a phoney horse laugh. It was something he and Pillman did whenever they thought something was crap. He'd bellow out at all the wrong times in the film and people were getting up and walking out.

After we got out of there we went for a walk along the promenade. It was night time with a perfect gentle sea breeze blowing through the palm trees but there were all these fellows walking around hand in hand. We were right in the middle of the gay section of town. So Steve and I put Jack in the middle of us so at least no one would think that we two blonds were a couple.

We found an open-air restaurant to get a bite to eat. A scruffy-

After we got out of there we went for a walk along the promenade. It was night time with a perfect gentle sea breeze blowing through the palm trees but there were all these fellows walking around hand in hand. We were right in the middle of the gay section of town. So Steve and I put Jack in the middle of us so at least no one would think that we two blonds were a couple.

looking waitress came over with the menu. We ordered, but before long she came back with bad news. "I'm sorry, there's no food, but I can get you a sandwich. The chef's drunk and he can't do anything." We said we'd just have a drink instead. The tablecloth was covered in debris. Someone had eaten chips and salsa before we got there and left most of it smeared on the table. Jack asked the waitress if she could clean it up. She put her hand on the table, scooped all the garbage off and then licked her fingers clean. We were gobsmacked.

"Were they expensive?" I asked.

"What?" she said.

"The lessons at the charm school," I replied.

That year I did a very enjoyable angle with Larry Zbyszko.
He was known as The Living Legend because he'd had a steel cage match with Bruno Sammartino for the WWWF which had drawn a huge attendance at Shea Stadium and was his claim to fame. Larry was still a wrestler but at the time was also announcing for WCW. The angle came about because I would go out and do my Lord Steven Regal schtick with Sir William alongside me and cut down the interviewer, Tony Schiavone.

So as part of the storyline, Tony refused to interview us. Larry stepped in do the interviews instead and I began having little jabs at him until it got to the point where we wrestled each other. We had a match on Memorial Day weekend for the TV championship. He beat me and it got the highest TV rating they'd ever had up until then for that weekend. I believe the Nielsen rating was a 3.2 – that's how they measure these things – and the bosses were ecstatic. They thought it was incredible. We had a follow-up match at the next big show, a *Clash of the Champions* in Charleston, South Carolina, when I won the title back.

We had a match on Memorial Day weekend for the TV championship. He beat me and it got the highest TV rating they'd ever had up until then for that weekend. I believe the Nielsen rating was a 3.2 – that's how they measure these things – and the bosses were ecstatic. They thought it was incredible.

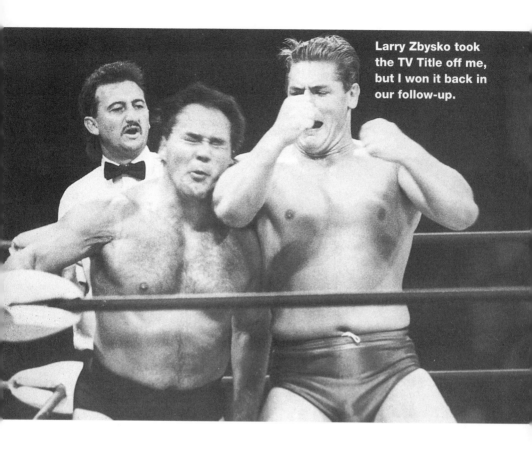

Larry Zbysko took the TV Title off me, but I won it back in our follow-up.

I made my first trip to Japan that year. It was a marvellous opening in itself, but had come about because of an even greater opportunity – a chance to wrestle Antonio Inoki. WCW were trying to set up a talent-swapping deal with Inoki's company, New Japan Pro Wrestling. As I remember it, part of the deal was that Inoki wanted to come to America and beat one of WCW's stars – and he chose me.

That was a massive honour. Inoki is one of the most famous men in Japan. Originally Brazilian, he had made himself into Japanese wrestling's biggest-ever name. His most famous match was against Muhammad Ali which, while the match itself was horrid, made headlines all over the world. By this time Inoki had become a senator. Bobby Heenan put it best on commentary when we did eventually wrestle: "It's like Regal wrestling Ted Kennedy." And, in a way, it was.

So to build me up for the match, I went to Japan for the first time, on a ten-day trip. The idea was for me to become a threat to Inoki in the eyes of Japanese fans with a few wins over there. On the tour were the Nasty Boys again, Too Cold Scorpio, and Eddie Guerrero and his tag partner Art Barr, who wrestled together as Los Gringos Locos. It was the first time I had met them and I got on with them straight away. They were the top heel tag team for AAA in Mexico, back in that company's heyday when they were doing phenomenal business.

They were incredibly good at what they did. I'm a huge fan of Eddie's – you won't find anybody better at what we do. Eddie can do every aspect of this business perfectly. He can wrestle any style in the world, he can entertain, he's got the lot. From promos, to entertainment, to pure wrestling ability, Eddie is probably the best all-rounder in the world.

I fell in love with Japan straight away. I met a guy called Victor Marr who wrestled over there as Black Cat. He was Mexican but had lived in Japan for twenty years and was the head trainer at the New Japan dojo, their training centre. He'd trained Chris Benoit when Chris lived out there for a year. Black Cat had a great reputation, was a wonderful fellow and looked after me well.

My first match there was a tag. I can't remember who my partner was but I was wrestling Kido and Fujinami, two very well-respected Japanese performers. They wanted me to do a submission move in the match, but I didn't have one. So on the dressing room floor, just before the match, the three of us tried out different things and came up with the Regal Stretch.

Virtually all the submission moves you see in pro wrestling are real – if they're applied with full pressure, the victim would have no choice but to tap out. That's true of the Regal Stretch, too. To apply it, you cross the left ankle in behind the right knee joint and bring the right knee forward so it's in a figure four crossbow position, putting pressure on the right knee joint.

You are also leaning against the right ankle which stretches that out, so the knee and the ankle are stretched out. Then you lean forward, slide your left arm underneath the right shoulder, feed it around to the left side of the face and pull back. That means the arm is straightened out against the joint, the shoulder is stretched as far as it will go, and my forearm is tight against my opponent's cheekbone – the most vulnerable part of the face.

With any kind of submission move on the face you try to put your wristbone on their cheekbone because that's what will hurt the most. Then you just pull back and every part of the body is tied up. If it was put on very tight it could be very painful. We came up with that in the dressing room and twenty minutes later I was doing it in the match. We invented it, went straight out and did it and that was my finish from then onwards.

Thanks to the fact I was set to wrestle Inoki a few weeks later, I was made to look like Superman on that tour. I beat everybody. In Japan, the wrestling style is very hard-hitting and physical. You hit everyone as hard as you possibly can and they do the same right back to you. In a sense it's harder than fighting for real – real fights wouldn't last as long. When you've had a match over there you feel like you've come through a war. It was right up my street. I had some great matches over there and loved every one of them.

I'd travelled a lot of the world in my career but had never come across anywhere so completely different from anywhere else as Japan. In most other places, even if you don't speak the language you can get by. Not in Japan. All you can do is point. The trouble is that in Japan it's considered very bad manners to say no to someone, so whatever you're after people just smile and nod until your head starts going in circles.

Anywhere else, after a few days you can start making out the odd word in the newspaper. In Japan you can't even do that. So you're totally reliant on the people looking after you – which was why Black Cat was such a godsend. He'd take me out every night, usually with Eddie and Art too. He would have sponsors in every town. They'd want you to come to eat in their restaurants. They would take you out and pay for everything. The food took a while to get used to, and eating and living is very expensive over there. Everything in Japan seems very small, too. Outside the main cities like Tokyo or Osaka they would put you up in the best hotels they could find but some of the rooms were still only five feet wide with a 3-foot-wide bed.

While I was there I had a fantastic time. The Nasty Boys were their usual boisterous, loud, obnoxious selves, still making me laugh as much as ever. They were very interested when Art started talking about a hair versus hair match he and Eddie had lined up for AAA when they got back from Japan. The loser would have his head shaved but be compensated with a large pay day. Art had longish hair and was talking about how much he was going to get for losing it after this match.

One night, Art passed out after drinking a beer. I don't know for

Thanks to the fact I was set to wrestle Inoki a few weeks later, I was made to look like Superman on that tour. I beat everybody. In Japan, the wrestling style is very hard-hitting and physical. You hit everyone as hard as you possibly can and they do the same right back to you. In a sense it's harder than fighting for real – real fights wouldn't last as long. When you've had a match over there you feel like you've come through a war. It was right up my street. I had some great matches over there and loved every one of them.

sure, but I wouldn't be surprised if someone had dropped something in one of his drinks. When he woke up the next morning, he was horrified to find he had a bald head – and no eyebrows either. When we got on the tour bus, Art was fuming mad. He went to his usual seat to find a bag full of his hair with a five dollar bill sitting on top of it. Luckily Art didn't miss out on his pay day in the end. He still had some tufts of hair left and had extensions put in to be shaved off after his hair match.

After that trip, Art and I used to speak regularly on the phone. I liked him a lot, but sadly he died not long afterwards.

The legendary
Antonio Inoki.

We were in Japan for the Fourth of July. Not only is that Independence Day, it was also the birthday of Jerry Sags of the Nasty Boys. Jerry wasn't about to miss that opportunity for a party. We were in a little hotel in a little town somewhere, occupying every tiny room on one little hallway. Jerry sent some of the young Japanese wrestlers out to get a load of fireworks and a load of beer.

That wasn't enough to make it a special night though, so Jerry decided it was going to be a toga party. We went up to the roof of the hotel all wearing sheets like a bunch of silly fools as we drank beer and let off fireworks. The manager came and told us to stop it – not surprisingly. So we trooped back to our hallway and started running in and out of each other's rooms. I was sat on a bed having a chat to someone when I saw a flash go past the door, followed by a huge explosion. Knobbs and Sags were at the end of the hallway, shooting rockets out of bottles at the elevator at the other end. It turned into a total mess when the police arrived.

August 28, 1994. At the Five Seasons Center in Cedar Rapids, Iowa, I wrestled Antonio Inoki at *Clash of the Champions*. It was something like number seven in his final ten matches counting down to retirement. I went to his hotel room earlier in the day to discuss how the match should go. He told me to beat him up throughout. "Okay," I thought.

The only trouble was I did it a bit too well. Right at the beginning of the match I kneed him in the side of the ribs, knocking all the wind out of him. That killed the match more or less because it meant he couldn't do a lot. On the outside it might have looked like not much was happening. But I was beating him up, just like he'd asked me. I hit him hard, kicked him and just generally pounded the hell out of him. Of course, he won in the end. A lot of people didn't get that match – plenty of wrestling fans thought it was the worst match of all time. But Inoki loved it – and that's all that mattered to me. It wasn't his show but I knew what the whole thing was all about.

Shortly afterwards WCW signed a contract with New Japan for a huge amount of money to swap talent. I knew our match had played a part in that happening. It was a real coup for WCW. Back then, New Japan was the biggest and most profitable wrestling company in the world. Inoki was one of the main shareholders and his being in the Japanese senate certainly didn't hurt.

That match was great for my future career. It meant that whenever I went to Japan, Inoki always took care of me. And whenever I went to Japan I loved it. Until much later, anyway.

The Blue Blood
With us is New
Japan referee
Tayama.

8

Triple H and the Blue Bloods

I met Paul Levesque when he first came into WCW – and I liked him from the start. I didn't know then he would become Triple H, one of the biggest stars this business has ever seen, but it was obvious he was going to do well. His attitude set him apart straight away. He had a real desire to get on and a love for this business. I like anyone who has that. I don't meet too many people like that these days, but they're the ones who succeed.

We used to train together at the Power Plant, WCW's training facility in Atlanta. He

Paul Levesque – Triple H – in his WCW days.

hadn't had a great deal of ring experience and was quite raw, but you could see so much talent in him. He'd only worked independent shows in New England then, the area he's from. At that time, in 1994, WCW weren't running many untelevised or "house" shows because house shows cost them money – so they concentrated on TV. That meant Paul was getting most of his ring time only at the Power Plant. We'd lock up there and I taught him everything I knew. He can do pretty much everything I can – and it didn't take him long to learn either.

In October Ric Flair, who was WCW's head booker in those days – meaning he was the matchmaker – said he wanted the two of us to become a tag team. Paul had started off with the ring name Terra Ryzing and they wanted to change that. Because his name was Paul Levesque, they thought they'd call him Jean-Paul Levesque and make him a French aristocrat. He went out, bought lots of new gear and did it well. So it made sense for him and me, the French and British aristos, to team up. We were excited at the prospect – but we knew we needed advice. We spoke to Arn Anderson and Bobby Eaton about it, but the guy we knew could really help us was down at the Power Plant – head trainer Jody Hamilton.

> *At that time, in 1994, WCW weren't running many untelevised or "house" shows because house shows cost them money – so they concentrated on TV. That meant Paul was getting most of his ring time only at the Power Plant. We'd lock up there and I taught him everything I knew. He can do pretty much everything I can – and it didn't take him long to learn either.*

Jody is known in this business for being one of the greatest tag wrestlers of all time. The father of WWE referee Nick Patrick, he spent his whole career in a masked team called The Assassins. He was one of those guys who had incredible ring psychology – the art of making people believe in what you're doing and getting the greatest reaction out of them you can. The craft of knowing what to do and when to do it. Jody may have been wearing a mask but he still made people feel his every emotion without them ever seeing his face. Every tiny little bit of body language was used to tell the audience what he was feeling. So Jody was the best guide we could have.

He started teaching us the rules of being a good tag team. They're hardly followed by anyone any more but they're very important, especially if you're a heel tag team. You cut the ring in half. When you throw your opponent into a rope, it must never be the rope where his teammate is. Otherwise his partner would be able to tag him and when he didn't, it would make no sense to anyone watching. It's little details like that which have to make sense if fans are going to believe in what you are doing in the ring. Jody spent a lot of time with us, showing us all this.

We debuted on Saturday night TV. Both of us stood in front of a mirror before we went out, admiring our posh new outfits. Neither of us are shy in the nasal department, as Arn Anderson noted when he walked by. "You two look like a pair of fucking woodpeckers," was his assessment.

We had a few enhancement matches – in other words, quick wins. One match which sticks in the memory was against the Armstrongs, Scott and Brad. They were a cracking tag team from a massive wrestling family. There was their dad Bob; Brad, Steve, Scott and Brian, known to WWE fans as Road Dogg. They all know exactly what they're doing. In our match with Scott and Brad things just clicked. We both knew we were going to be a top tag team. If we had stuck together, we could have been one of the great teams of the 1990s.

> We debuted on Saturday night TV. Both of us stood in front of a mirror before we went out, admiring our posh new outfits. Neither of us are shy in the nasal department, as Arn Anderson noted when he walked by. "You two look like a pair of fucking woodpeckers," was his assessment.

But it wasn't to be. Paul's contract was up. He'd come in for a pretty low offer and a one-year deal. Now it was up, they didn't want to offer him much of a raise. World Wrestling Federation had been in contact with Paul and I believe they were interested in bringing us in as a tag team. But I had a guaranteed contract with WCW, something the company didn't offer at the time. It meant nice security for me – I would not have to worry about providing for my family, the schedule wasn't too demanding and it meant I could go to Japan too.

But Paul needed the experience. If he went to work for them it would be a tough schedule with long tours, lots of house shows and more overseas touring. It was precisely the opportunity he needed. He was getting better by the day and you could see the potential in him, but he needed that ring time. A select few people get good at our job straight away. Kurt Angle, who's one in a million, was one and so was Danny Boy Collins in the UK. Steve Austin was another, who in just a short time looked like he'd been doing it for years. People like me took a long time to get proficient at it.

When you do TV, you're not performing for the crowd – you're performing for the cameras. But it's only by listening to crowd reactions that you learn how to perform. You can put things in your act, take others out and work out what works for you. You need to listen, to know if the crowd aren't buying what you're doing and how to change it.

Paul needed to perform in front of a crowd to improve. You learn that on house shows rather than on TV. When you do TV, you're not performing for the crowd – you're performing for the cameras. But it's only by listening to crowd reactions that you learn how to perform. You can put things in your act, take others out and work out what works for you. You need to listen, to know if the crowd aren't buying what you're doing and how to change it.

That was exactly what Paul had to learn. So when he came to me and asked for advice, I urged him to take the chance that he'd been offered. "Go," I told him. "They'll make you a star."

That Christmas I went home to try something new – I was going to become a wrestling promoter for the first time. In the spring of 1994, my friend Peter in England had told me Bobby Baron had been ill. I called Bobby's house and his wife told me he'd died recently. He was only in his early fifties, but he had suffered from a bad heart ever since I'd known him. In 1983 when I first met him, it wasn't long after he had needed open-heart surgery. There was a family history of heart trouble too. In fact he'd never had the best of luck with his health. Once upon a time Bobby Baron had been due to be a member of the British Olympic amateur wrestling team. But one day he was in a public swimming baths when someone dived off a diving board, landed on Bobby and broke his neck, ending his Olympic dream.

His death was a big blow. I'm where I am today thanks to Bobby Baron. He gave me my break into the wrestling business, he looked after me and treated me like one of his sons. We thought the world of one another.

I flew back for Bobby's funeral and everyone who cared about him was there. One of his claims to fame was having the worst wrestling rings in the business. All English rings are bad but Bobby had the worst of the worst. They were always falling to pieces; there were big holes in the mats, broken boards and fraying ropes. So there we were at the crematorium, all very sad. Dave Taylor was there, along with his dad and his brother Steve. We went to look at the floral tributes outside. Bobby and I had a mutual friend, Jack, who'd sent a big ring made out of flowers. It was beautiful – three feet square, made from red and white flowers with "Beautiful Bobby Baron" written across it.

And Steve Taylor said: "It's the best ring he's ever had." That set us off. It was one of those occasions when you shouldn't laugh but you can't help it – which of course only made us laugh all the more.

Every year, Bobby had run a show on December 27 in Blackpool Tower Circus. He reasoned that plenty of people would come to Blackpool for Christmas and at that time of year there wasn't always that much for them to do. A pantomime at the Grand Theatre or a show on at the Opera House and that would be about it. So this year, once Bobby had passed away, I decided to have a go myself. I ran it with Oric Williams, the Welsh promoter, and told him who to book so all my friends would be there. Those shows never relied on advance sales, they'd be down to walk-up sales with people who were sitting around, wondering what to do and turning up on the night. It only held around 400 people so we were pretty confident we'd fill it on the night.

We were relying on tourists. People who live in Blackpool don't go to wrestling – they tend to work in the entertainment industry so they don't want to watch it themselves in their free time. But people knew me locally and from seeing WCW on TV, plus my friend Tony Francis had been plugging it on the radio and we'd plastered the town in posters. We hadn't been able to book the Tower Circus itself for our show because the Moscow State Circus was on there. And the night before my show – Boxing Day – there'd been 150 people watching their performance when one of the trapeze artists fell and killed themselves.

It was the death knell for my show, too. People love a tragedy so the circus was packed the next night while only 120 came to my show – not quite what I wanted. Dave Taylor was there and Drew McDonald; and I put myself on with Tony St Clair. I didn't mind about the poor house – I was only upset that Oric had neglected to book Robbie Brookside and Doc Dean, so not all my friends were there. I paid everyone and ended up £700 out of pocket but I wasn't bothered. It had been worth it just to have a night with my friends, see them all and have a laugh.

On my first day back after that Christmas, at a TV taping at Center Stage, Ric Flair came up to me in a hell of a state.

"Levesque's gone! He's gone! He just left us! I don't know what to do!"

I'd been one of the few who had known that Paul had been plotting his escape. Ric was panicking, though. "You two were going to be tag team champions!" Ric said they'd had big plans for us because they liked what we did. They were going to put Sherri Martel with us. I wasn't selfish about it – I thought it was good that Paul. And time has proved him right, since he's gone on to be one of the best ever as Triple H. For myself, I was happy to stay in WCW with the guaranteed money. But Ric was desperate. "What are we going to do?" he asked me.

I looked up and spotted Bobby Eaton, sitting in the seats across from the ring. An idea came to me in a flash. I laid it out to Ric. "Why don't you put Bobby with me? We can do the *My Fair Lady* thing, where I'll turn Bobby from an Alabama redneck into a nobleman."

Gimmicky stuff I know, but I thought it was a good idea. Ric thought so too – and that's exactly what we set out to do. They sent us out with a film camera. We went to Disney's Epcot Center in Orlando, where they have a British section. We filmed these vignettes where we turned Bobby from a redneck into a moody nobleman. He eventually became Earl Robert of Eaton and we became the Blue Bloods – one of the names we'd thrown around for myself and Paul but never actually used.

Bobby and I had a great run. We worked with lots of talented people – the Armstrongs, the Fantastics. The main WCW tag teams then were the Nasty Boys, Harlem Heat – Booker T and his brother Stevie Ray – and Bunkhouse Buck and Dick Slater who worked with Robert Fuller as their manager Colonel Parker. The only trouble was that apart from the Nasty Boys, the rest of us were all heels. And out of those four teams, we were the only one who didn't end up with the tag titles at any point. I don't want to blame anybody but I don't know why – we were the carrying force in that group of guys. We worked with everybody – and worked well, too. The titles aren't the be-all and end-all, but it would have been nice as recognition for what we were doing.

Our partnership started with this little angle where Bobby kept coming out and saying he wanted to be my partner. But I of course wanted nothing to do with this filthy dirty redneck. He challenged me to a match and, being the cocky, no-good bastard that I am, I said if he beat me he could become my partner. We got in the ring and he knocked me from pillar to post. After a minute of that beating, I bailed out of the ring and went straight up to Tony Schiavone, who had the microphone, and said: "I think he'll be a great partner. What a wonderful idea."

In our first vignettes I took Bobby to a tailor to get him dressed; to a manicurist to get his nails done and to an elocution teacher to get him speaking properly. Bobby would repeat "How now brown cow" as though his mouth was full of marbles – which really was

Bobby and I make a fine pair of aristocrats.

the way he talked. The last vignette showed Bobby being knighted, supposedly by the Queen. I was standing behind him crying, saying I could remember when it happened to me. I failed to get the tears flowing, even resorting to poking myself in the eyes, but nothing would work until I threw Sprite into my eyes to make them look moist. It was double moody. When I watch those vignettes now, they look so corny and don't really stand the test of time because of the production values, but they weren't bad for their day.

They were great fun to do, too. They'd send us out with a film crew and we would come up with the ideas between ourselves. The bosses began to trust us and they'd let us go out with our only instruction being to come back with something, because they knew we'd come up with something good. For the *Bash At The Beach* in 1995, which was held outside on the beach in Huntington,

California, they wanted us to do a long vignette to put at the beginning of the home video. So we went out and about in Los Angeles. We came up with a few ideas and the production people chipped in too. We had a scream as we drove around Los Angeles in a limousine all day.

We started off at the place where Hugh Grant had recently been caught being given a blowjob by a prostitute. I stood right on the spot where it happened, talking about "this dirty filthy philanderer". Then we went to the Viper Room where River Phoenix had died. I said: "This is the Viper Room, where River Phoenix died, and I've not stopped tossing, turning and worrying about it since." With that I spat on the floor, said: "Dirty scruffy bastard!" and walked off.

Everyone was shocked, saying: "You can't do that!" But I'd said I was going to, so I did. Next up was OJ Simpson's house. We were standing there with the house behind a big hedge in the background while I talked to the camera. Bobby was behind me, seemingly oblivious to all that was going on. I began: "This is the scene of the shocking OJ Simpson case, a terrible one indeed. It's an awful shame – and look at those people driving past, gawping."

The people who were driving past were heckling us, shouting, "Leave them alone!" While I was doing my spiel, Bobby was still behind me, looking completely bemused. Then he spotted something hidden in the hedge, dived in and came out holding a twelve-inch blade. Over my shoulder you could see Bobby look closely at the knife, shrug his shoulders and throw it away. At the end of the skit, Bobby came up to me and I asked: "Is there anything here of interest?"

"Absolutely nothing," said Bobby, and that was that.

9

On the Way to Hell

I had every reason to be happy. Work was good and my family were settling in to the American way of life. But for various reasons, I wasn't. And soon I'd start on the journey that would make everyone around me more miserable than anyone deserves.

I was wrestling Chris Benoit in Japan in 1995 when I had a bad accident. Someone had spilled water on one of the mats outside the ring. We were going at it on the mats when I slipped on the water and felt my knee go. I knew straight away it was in very bad shape. We finished the match – a

Chris Benoit and I had some spectacular matches whenever we got the chance.

really good one too – but in the dressing room afterwards, the knee had swollen up like a balloon. We only had one match left on the tour and I was happy to strap it up and get on with it. That was the way I'd been brought up in the business. But Inoki wouldn't let me. They said they had plenty of other guys and there was no need.

I had time to rest when I got back to America as there was a break before I had any WCW commitments – but the knee was hurting bad. I went to see a doctor, who prescribed some pain killers. Hydrocodone, ten milligrams a pill. That wasn't the start either. I'd already been taking Valium for quite a while. Originally it had been prescribed to help me fight sleepless nights, something I've struggled with for years. But now I wasn't only taking them to sleep. I was taking them in the day when I had nothing to do.

I found they took the edge off life, which was a good thing. I was downing myself out a lot of the time – and drinking a lot more, too. I started drinking a lot of wine at home. I was telling myself that red wine was good for your health. Cobblers, of course – complete nonsense. One glass a day might be good for your heart. But I was drinking a gallon a day – and taking downers with it too.

> I started drinking a lot of wine at home. I was telling myself that red wine was good for your health. Cobblers, of course – complete nonsense. One glass a day might be good for your heart. But I was drinking a gallon a day – and taking downers with it too.

Relations were starting to be strained at home because of my behaviour. For a long time, I believe, Chris thought it was just a phase I was going through. She'd heard me say so often that drugs were not for me. But she had no idea how bad things would get before they got better.

This was what was going on when I took my first pain pill. It took the pain away straight off. And what's more, it made me feel like Superman. After taking that one pill, leaping a tall building in a single bound would have been no problem whatsoever.

But soon I had the same problems with pain pills that I'd faced with Valium and other downers. Inside a day, one at a time was no good. Within a week I was taking four or five at a time. And just a week after that it seemed that no matter how many I took they didn't have any effect at all. Sure, there was no pain in my knee – but there was no buzz either. And it wasn't really about the knee after the first day anyway.

When it comes to pain, unless it is chronic you can get by on anti-inflammatories. They reduce inflammation and that reduces pain. But I was taking pills all the time to feel good. I did it because I enjoyed it. It was nothing to do with me being injured any more – I'd strapped my knee up and got on with wrestling weeks ago. Two weeks after doing the injury I went back to Japan for one match, against the Great Muta. I've seen it on tape recently and, wrestling with my knee strapped up, it was a decent match. Not outstanding, but good enough.

I put up with the knee injury. I don't consider myself a tough guy in the fighting sense, but I did consider myself a tough guy in terms of dealing with injuries. Slap a bit of Deep Heat on it and it'll be okay was my philosophy. Which is why it's obvious those pills weren't for the knee at all. They weren't to abuse either. I gone beyond abusing drugs. I was addicted to them already.

There's a big difference between addiction and abuse, as I eventually learned. Addiction is about a chemical reaction in the brain where you become physically and mentally hooked. Some people can abuse drugs without getting addicted. They can drink gallons, take a load of drugs and then not do it for a while.

That's not me at all. Everyone has a level somewhere where they cross that line from abuse to addiction. Imagine a picture of a human body. For some people – like me – the crossover line is somewhere down by their ankles. For others, the line might be up around their forehead. Some people would have to abuse themselves as much as I did for twenty years before they crossed that line.

As soon as you do cross the line from abuse into addiction it becomes a completely different ball game. I'll tell you what I did then to try to make it clear why I did it – that's the difficult part to explain. Once you cross the line, your mind tells you constantly that you need those drugs so you can function; so you can take that edge off the day. And you often think you cannot function without

As soon as you do cross the line from abuse into addiction it becomes a completely different ball game. I'll tell you what I did then to try to make it clear why I did it – that's the difficult part to explain. Once you cross the line, your mind tells you constantly that you need those drugs so you can function; so you can take that edge off the day. And you often think you cannot function without taking that edge off. You become slightly insane. There's the physical side too – your body reacts and if you stop taking the drugs, it makes you ill. I found that out the hard way. Early on, there were times when I knew I was getting too heavily into the drugs and would try to stop. But all you get for your efforts is the worst case of flu you've ever had. The symptoms come on very quickly and last for a long period of time. It makes you feel like death. You can fight through it. But when you're on the treadmill I was on then, in a job like mine which depends on you feeling decent half the time, battling through those symptoms becomes very unattractive.

taking that edge off. You become slightly insane. There's the physical side too – your body reacts and if you stop taking the drugs, it makes you ill.

I found that out the hard way. Early on, there were times when I knew I was getting too heavily into the drugs and would try to stop. But all you get for your efforts is the worst case of flu you've ever had. The symptoms come on very quickly and last for a long period of time. It makes you feel like death. You can fight through it. But when you're on the treadmill I was on then, in a job like mine which depends on you feeling decent half the time, battling through those symptoms becomes very unattractive.

Unlike many people, I'm not blaming the job. I did what I did. Many other wrestlers, who work just as hard, don't. It's just the way my mind was working at the time. The only thing that made me feel good – or normal, more to the point – was taking those pills.

In fact it wasn't normal at all – but that's how I thought then. Most people don't fight through the side effects. You think you don't have the time. Or if you do fight through it, you miss the way the drugs used to make you feel. You forget all the bad times and all the shit. All you remember is the five minutes when it made you feel good.

Having a low threshold before I crossed from abuse to addiction wasn't the only driving force. The other was that I developed a high tolerance for the drugs I was taking. Within a short period of time – probably a matter of weeks, and certainly not much more than a month – the pain pills were having no effect. I'd heard that taking pain pills along with a muscle relaxant known as soma would make them kick in. They're two separate drugs but when you mix them together it makes a completely different drug. I tried it. And it was like rocket fuel. I felt I could take on the world.

On the first occasion I did it, I took a couple and it was the best feeling I have ever had in my life. Much better than pain pills. But of course I didn't stop at just a couple. Within two weeks I was taking two pain pills and two somas at a time. That would make me feel good for twenty or thirty minutes. But then thirty minutes later I'd take another two and two.

It built up very quickly. But at that point, it wasn't affecting my work. I didn't take them all the time, and I never took them before

I got in the ring. I'd take two and two, then I'd take no more for a while if I knew I had to get on and do something. Then I'd take another two and two at night, after I'd worked; or earlier in the day if I wasn't working.

Throughout this period, I was still taking downers to get me to sleep at night. I was taking three different drugs a day and sometimes more. If I couldn't get Valium I'd take Xanax, or if I couldn't get that I'd find some other sleeping pills, or just somas on their own. Somas are a muscle relaxant so they will knock you out at night. I had to mix and match because I couldn't always get the drugs I wanted. But I could always get the pain pills. That's what my drug of choice became – pain pills and somas mixed together.

And I could get somas most times too. Which meant that from mid-1995 onwards, my drug consumption went through the roof. Eventually, when it was at its worst, it got to the point where I was taking thirty pain pills and thirty somas a day. From the moment I woke up in the morning I'd take five of each, six times a day. But that was still in the future.

When I went out drinking, I was drinking properly now, too. It wasn't a few beers or the odd pint of Guinness any more. It was shots of vodka. Mixing all these pills with alcohol was obviously a stupid combination. I drank to get drunk. I took pills to get high. I took downers to down myself out. All day long, it was constant. Anything to stop me having time just looking at myself, realizing what a mess I was making of my life.

There were a few things which had started me off on this destructive course. I wasn't very happy in America. In fact I was very homesick. It hit me when I went back to England for that Christmas in 1994. I had friends in America and got on well with most of the people I met there but I missed Blackpool; I missed all my old mates and I missed the English sense of humour. You can have a laugh over here but it's not the same humour I grew up with. When I watch TV over here I usually stick with the History Channel and animal programmes – the comedies leave me cold.

But on that trip home, I began to learn that people didn't always treat me like they had before. That wasn't true with my real close friends – Peter, Glen, Alan, Stuart and Dennis the New Zealander we call Joe. And they're the same to this day. But others would start trying to bait me, as if I was big-headed. All of a sudden I wasn't just Darren the wrestler they'd always known me as. Now some people treated me like I was a big TV star. At the gym or out at clubs with people, someone would pipe up: "He's the big star, the one with all the money – he'll pay for it."

> When I went out drinking, I was drinking properly now, too. It wasn't a few beers or the odd pint of Guinness any more. It was shots of vodka. Mixing all these pills with alcohol was obviously a stupid combination. I drank to get drunk. I took pills to get high. I took downers to down myself out. All day long, it was constant. Anything to stop me having time just looking at myself, realizing what a mess I was making of my life.

So now not only did I feel I didn't belong in America, I didn't belong back home in Blackpool either. And the homesickness got worse. In 1995, we moved from Marietta to the town where I live now and within the first day in the new house, I felt homesick for Marietta – somewhere I hadn't particularly cared about one way or the other when I lived there.

The homesickness was really about harking after the security of the past. I was obsessed with how happy I'd been working at the Pleasure Beach, or when I was doing Butlins. Every day I wished I was back working with Robbie Brookside, travelling around Britain. Or working back in Germany, which had been great.

I had got further than I'd ever thought I would. I'd never expected to get the success I had as Lord Steven Regal. For the last two years I'd had a real good run on my own and then tagging with Bobby. I was twenty-seven and I didn't know what on earth I would do next.

Chris Benoit and
Ric Flair are two
of my favourite
opponents.

Courtesy *Pro Wrestling Illustrated*.

© 2002 World Wrestling

Chris Jericho and I both heading for the mat.

Flying the flag with Lance Storm.

GOODWILL AMBASSADOR
WILLIAM REGAL

had some memorable highs . . .

. . . and some painful lows.

I felt there was nothing more to achieve. Wrestling was as big as I'd ever seen it and as far as I was concerned, it couldn't ever get any bigger.

I came up with plenty of reasons to feel miserable. Steve Austin, my travelling buddy, was injured and I really missed him. We'd got on so well together and, as my travel partner, he'd been closer to me than anyone except my wife. It's hard for me to look back on all this now, when I have absolutely no time for self-pity. But that's how I felt then. It wasn't that I was sorry for Steve, I was sorry for myself – I didn't have my great mate Steve on the road with me any more. A real contrast with my altruistic attitude when Paul had told me he wanted to quit WCW.

There were all these silly feelings rattling around in my head and that meant I took more drugs and more drink to blot them out. Before I knew it, my normal routine was to get up and take pills all day long, drink through the evening and then take downers before I went to bed. After a while, the downers didn't really work either. So instead of falling asleep, it meant I was staggering around the place, doing stupid stuff around the house with no idea of what I was doing.

Still Chris believed I would kick out of it, thinking it was just a bad patch I was going through. Some nights I would be downstairs, decide I wanted something to eat and would put some food in the oven and not turn it on. On other occasions I'd leave the oven on. I could have burned the house down with the kids in it. I talked a little bit to Chris about these things – but I never properly sat down and talked to her about how I was feeling. I didn't discuss it with Bobby, my new travelling partner, either.

At work, Bobby, Ric Flair and Arn Anderson became my new mates. And being a drunk and a drug addict wasn't all doom and gloom. Yes, I took pills every day, but when I went out drinking at night, I was happy. It was only later on, when I was drinking and taking pills together, that I became a sloppy mess who fell all over the place.

There were some genuinely good times as a happy drunk. One tour started off on a Friday night at the Red Rocks amphitheater in Arizona. The next night saw us in Las Vegas, then it was the Sunday

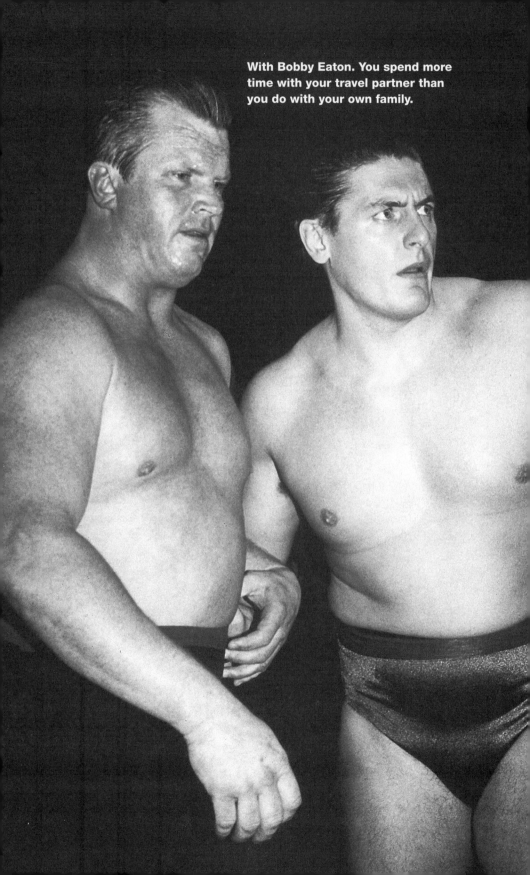

With Bobby Eaton. You spend more time with your travel partner than you do with your own family.

off before a show in Lancaster, California on the Monday. We could have got a Sunday flight to Los Angeles and driven back to Lancaster, but we thought it would be fun to drive from Vegas to Lancaster, up in the Californian mountains. Having performed there the year before, I knew the show was in a rodeo arena. It was the hometown of someone who worked for WCW and organized this annual fair as the local hero.

Arn, Ric, Bobby and I got to Vegas and after we wrestled we drank and we drank and we drank and we drank. Sunday afternoon was spent around the pool at the Mirage hotel. I paid the bar bill for an afternoon three-hour session for the four of us. It came to just over $400. We were hitting the frozen drinks, which you can drink all day, trying one of each kind. We hammered it hard and it was a lot of fun.

After a Monday morning training session at Gold's Gym we set off on the drive. Looking at the map – never my strongest suit – it looked like just a couple of hours through the desert. I'd tried to warn Ric not to dress in his usual immaculate way for this show. It was an outside show, it would be hot and there would be dust and red clay blowing around everywhere. And we'd be getting changed in a tent, with no showers afterwards, which meant we couldn't get changed again after the show until we got to the hotel. But appearances were very important to Ric so there he was, dressed up to the nines as usual.

Arn, Ric, Bobby and I got to Vegas and after we wrestled we drank and we drank and we drank and we drank. Sunday afternoon was spent around the pool at the Mirage hotel. I paid the bar bill for an afternoon three-hour session for the four of us. It came to just over $400. We were hitting the frozen drinks, which you can drink all day, trying one of each kind. We hammered it hard and it was a lot of fun.

Before we got going we stopped at a Subway, a sandwich place. Ric and Arn got their food and while I was waiting for mine, I listened to the news on the radio. A bulletin announced that St Martin's had been flattened by a hurricane – St Martin's where Ric had his Gold's Gym. I crammed into the little Ford we'd hired with the three other guys and all our bags. It had been the only car we could get and was a climbdown for Ric, who usually preferred booking himself a Cadillac. I told him the bad news: "Hey Ric, a hurricane just went through St Martin's."

He looked at me in the driver's mirror and his face dropped. "Oh no, brother. I've got no insurance on my gym."

When a lot of people are completely wiped out, the slightest thing can make them flip. When I crack, I start giggling. Not a bad way to crack and certainly better than trashing hotel rooms. I can go on for hours and laugh so much I make myself ill.

I'd tried to warn Ric not to dress in his usual immaculate way for this show. It was an outside show, it would be hot and there would be dust and red clay blowing around everywhere. And we'd be getting changed in a tent, with no showers afterwards, which meant we couldn't get changed again after the show until we got to the hotel. But appearances were very important to Ric so there he was, dressed up to the nines as usual.

That's what happened when I saw Ric's face. I started to giggle. Then I started to laugh. I'd already had a mouthful of my sandwich and now bits of it were coming down my nose. Tears were streaming down my face. I was getting hysterical and I set Bobby off. He didn't really know why I was laughing so hard, but it didn't matter – he'd caught the bug. Soon Arn was off too. We were all laughing except for Ric, who was driving towards the desert with a face like thunder.

Every time I got my composure back, I caught sight of Ric's face, and his look of total distress set me off again. Arn got us to pull over at the worst truckstop you ever saw in the middle of the desert and came out with a bag of greasy onion rings and fries. That stunk up the car and we couldn't open the windows to ease it because it was baking hot outside and we had the air conditioning blasting.

The stink made Ric furious, which made me start laughing again.

Every time I looked at him, I laughed. Every time I laughed, Bobby laughed. Ric looked at me in his mirror and said:

"I'm Ric Flair. I'm used to flying in Lear jets and driving in limousines. And I'm stuck in the desert with three drunk lunatics and the gila monsters."

His pained expression made me laugh even more. When we'd calmed down, Bobby – who always used to call me Lord – said: "Talking about gila monsters, Lord keeps lizards."

Against his better judgement, Ric fell for it and asked me what I'd got. I went off on a long list of the lizards and snakes I kept at the time. Ric looked me in the mirror, deadly serious, and asked: "Are they alive?"

Arn Anderson shot straight back: "No, they're nailed to a board in his house." That set us off again. And put Ric in a worse mood than ever.

All this time we'd been driving along this straight road through the desert. Ric asked me to have a look at the map to make sure we were going the right way. I had a look and read exactly what I saw: "We're in the Mo-jave desert," fully pronouncing the J. Ric looked at me as if to say "you silly bastard" and that started me laughing yet again.

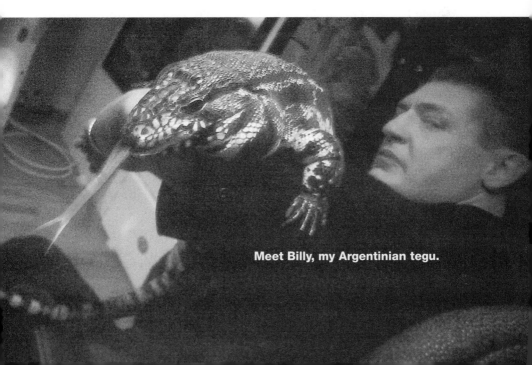

Meet Billy, my Argentinian tegu.

After five hours of this, we reached our destination. I'd calmed down at last and was aching from so much laughter. Everyone else was the same – except for Ric, who was fuming harder than ever. He got out, slammed the car door and a big wave of red dust rose up and covered him from top to toe.

That was the place – and it may even have been the year – where Steve Austin wrestled Steamboat in a match which ended Steamboat's career. He went up to the second rope to superplex Austin, Steve pushed him off and he just fell back and landed oddly. It broke his back. It shows up all those people who say wrestlers never get hurt because they know how to fall. Here was one of the greatest the business had ever seen breaking his back on a simple back bump.

It's impossible to fall correctly in a wrestling match because you're in motion the whole time. You tend to land on one side or the other. Even if you do land correctly, you take the brunt of the fall by whacking your arms – or your feet come down first. All that shock goes into your ankles, your knees, your hips, your hands and your elbows, and eventually it ends up in your neck.

Doing that time after time is bound to wear the body down. The human body isn't built for it. So even if you escape injury, you slowly wear your joints out.

I think Ricky Steamboat worked a few times after that, but that was the injury which finished him. It was a great loss to the wrestling business because there was never anyone quite like him and there never will be again. You meet a lot of nice people in this industry but very few real gentlemen, and Ricky "The Dragon" Steamboat was one.

It wasn't long before wrestling took its toll of me too. We were in Vegas again, Caesar's Palace, at the start of 1996 for a *Clash of the Champions*. Bobby and I were in a tag match against Sting and Lex Luger. Chris Benoit was due to wrestle a dark match – one for the live crowd before the TV cameras come on. But he had no partner, so I volunteered for extra duty.

My knee was still strapped up but I love wrestling against Chris and always take any chance I get. We went out and the exact same

thing happened as in my previous match with him. He threw me outside the ring and came through the ropes to get me. I took a step back, slipped and twisted my knee again. It was the second time and the same knee, too – and both times Chris hadn't touched me. This time I knew it was properly done in. I'd had it strapped for six months but now I knew there was no going back.

I got through my tag match, but that night Eric Bischoff ruled enough was enough. He wouldn't let me work any more until I got it fixed. I went back to Atlanta, where a doctor told me I had a torn

ACL and PCL; I needed a lot doing to it and would be out for nine months. Deep down, I knew it wasn't quite as bad as he made out. I went to another doctor to get a second opinion. He did all the same tests, an MRI scan and everything, and said: "You don't need all that surgery. You just need it scoped – you'll be back in three weeks."

The whole episode made me wonder about doctors, especially in the US. When they see anyone with health insurance, I think they cut you open at the drop of a hat because they know they'll get paid a lot of money for it.

When it came time for my scope, they tried to give me an epidural, but it wouldn't take and I could still feel everything. Clearly, with all the painkillers I'd been taking I'd built up a huge resistance. Dave Taylor was with me and the doctors took him to one side, wanting to know if I was on anything. Trying to protect me, he said no – even though he knew that wasn't close to the truth. So they put me under a general anaesthetic for the op. I vividly remember coming round afterwards. As soon as there was no one in the room, I got my little bag of pain pills out so I could swallow them. That's how screwed up I was.

My knee was still strapped up but I love wrestling against Chris and always take any chance I get. We went out and the exact same thing happened as in my previous match with him. He threw me outside the ring and came through the ropes to get me. I took a step back, slipped and twisted my knee again. It was the second time and the same knee, too – and both times Chris hadn't touched me. This time I knew it was properly done in. I'd had it strapped for six months but now I knew there was no going back.

Dave had come over from England the previous November for a Pay-Per-View called *When Worlds Collide*, which had a three-ring battle royal. There were twenty in each ring and when ten had been thrown out of each they moved into one ring. It might have looked good on paper but it was an absolute disaster of a match. But it meant a job for Dave, since Eric Bischoff told me he wanted him to come over and work after that.

At the turn of the year, the office had started talking about me going back into singles, which left an ideal spot for Dave to come in and join Bobby in a tag team. He wasn't the only one of my pals who came into WCW then, either – they also brought in Fit Finlay and Giant Haystacks.

It was sadly too late for Haystacks. Both his knees and his back were bad by then and, though I don't think he knew it at the time, he was already ailing. His spell in WCW didn't last long. He went back to England when his wife fell ill. It was desperately sad to see him as he became near the end of his life. I barely recognized him in the last pictures I saw of him taken shortly before his death: he looked very sick, and his hair and his beard had gone. He wasn't the man I'd known.

Fit, on the other hand, was ready to tear the place up. He and I were about to have the most brutal match American wrestling had seen at that time. We did a little angle where Fit beat me up at Center Stage and I disappeared for three weeks to have my knee operation. Then I came back and we built up to a match at *Uncensored* in March 1996.

The plan was to wrestle a thirty-minute draw. But things got out of hand. We went out and got stuck into each other so much that Finlay hit me in the face with one punch which gave me twelve stitches over my eye, a broken nose and a fractured cheekbone. There was blood everywhere – and WCW still had a strong anti-blood policy.

There was panic backstage. They pulled the cameras back off us as much as they could. Dave Taylor and Bobby Eaton were there in their suits, ready to do something after our match ended. But suddenly they were needed out there right away.

"Get out there now and stop them!" they were told. Dave and Bobby were sent down to beat Finlay up. But the adrenaline was flowing through the Belfast Bruiser and he just attacked them. If you ever see the match on tape, you can see Dave running for his life as Fit attacks him. But the match was a great success for the two of us. It made a name for us both. They'd never seen anything like it in

America before. That sort of brutality hadn't been done outside of Japan. We battered each other – hard.

We had a rip-roaring feud going for a while and people were sitting up and taking notice. Fit was only in America for a few months before he went back to Germany to wrestle for Otto Wanz, so it was decided we should finish it in style. Our final match was a parking lot brawl on *Nitro*. The show was taped but there was nothing edited whatsoever in our match. When we were told this was going to happen, we said okay and went out to the car park.

There were four cars surrounded by metal barriers.
"Which are the gimmicked cars?" we asked.
"What do you mean, gimmicked?" came the reply.
They were 100 per cent real.

Bloody but unbowed. I've clearly been in the wars, while Fit looks fresh as a daisy.

Fit and I walked around, looking at the set-up. The only thing we did was to loosen one of the car bumpers. There was nothing else that could be fixed. All we could do was run into stuff hard and break it. The only exception was the loosened bumper. That fell off when we ran into it, upon which Fit thought it would be a good idea to pick it up and hammer me over the head with it.

We killed each other in that match. Fit's head went through a side window, and there was nothing gimmicked about that. Glass was everywhere – we were covered in it too. We hit each other as hard as we could, ground each other's head into the concrete, banged each other, slammed each other on cars and it ended when I gave Fit a piledriver on top of a car. And after all that, we didn't need a single stitch between us. We just had small cuts everywhere.

It was amazing – I don't know how we got away with it. Roddy Piper and Goldust had done a similar one at *WrestleMania* that year but theirs was edited together. No knock on them – theirs was good. But ours was live, as you saw it. Eric Bischoff was commentating and he kept shouting to pull the cameras back as far as they could. For months later, Fit kept finding little fragments of glass under the skin on his legs and he'd have to pick it out.

Brutal matches never scared me. In WCW matches with Chris Benoit, we used to compete to see who could headbutt each other the hardest. Whoever bled first lost. I'd always lose. I think Chris must pickle his head in vinegar. A few years later, wrestling Chris at the Brian Pillman memorial show, I got a long scar on my head from a Benoit headbutt.

Once Fit left, and Dave and Bobby were tagging together, those in power had to decide what to do with me next. Kevin Sullivan was booker by then and he liked me, so I went up as high as I'd ever gone in WCW. At the *Great American Bash* I wrestled Sting in the third biggest match on the card. In the build-up, I put down Sting by calling him "sunshine" – an expression I'd nicked from the comedian Eric Morecambe. In one skit I ended up backhanding him across the face as hard as I could. Because I'd hit him so hard he swore for real. They left it in and bleeped the swear word – something they'd never done before.

But within a couple of days of our big match, they told me: "We don't really know what to do with you. We're thinking of giving you the TV title back." I wasn't in a position to sniff at it – in fact, I was happy to do anything. And I came up with an idea. I thought I should go on a world tour as television champion. I had a few trips to Japan coming up, all in a six-week period. I could work a few shows in England and in Germany, where Peter Williams was running Hanover.

They liked it – it was something different, so they told me to go and do it. Chris was pregnant with Bailey at the time and going away and leaving her was the wrong thing to do. But I did it anyway.

I went to England and worked for Brian. I wrestled Robbie Brookside in Croydon, and even did Butlins again. I went to Germany and wrestled Tony St Clair. Fit hit the ring on me for the finale. WCW was on a five-day tour of Japan and I met up with them over there. I had a championship match in Tokyo with Hashimoto, our second match together. It was a great match; he won in the end but made me look like a king in the process. I kicked out of all the big moves with which he beat other people. He did me a massive favour there and at that point I could have been given the ball to run with in Japan. Within six months, though, thanks to my drug problems, I'd screwed that up royally.

The only problem with the world tour was an old enemy – WCW organization. They hadn't lined up any film crews or anything. The only one who made an effort was Colin Bowman, a Scot who lived in America and ran WCW's magazine – he came to Croydon to see me wrestle Robbie. But no one else did anything. It meant a good idea had gone to waste.

And if I'm honest, the world tour idea was a selfish one. I was still harking back to the past, nostalgic for former glories back home that I wanted to relive. I was trying to recapture what I felt was missing in my life. But in reality you can never go back. That was then, this is now, and it's just not the same.

When this hit home, it became another excuse to take more drugs. I took a lot of drugs with me on that trip. I wasn't out of control, though. I could still function. The only exception was late

Wrestling Sting at the *Great American Bash.*

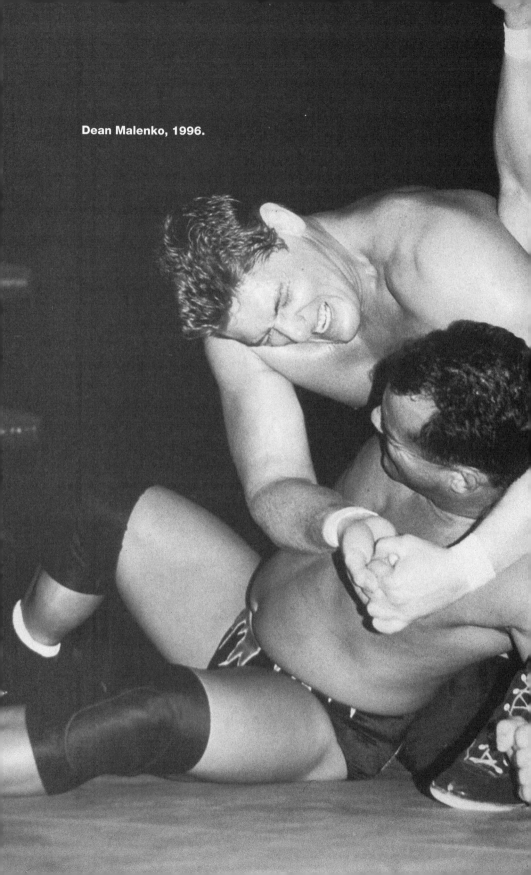

Dean Malenko, 1996.

at night when sometimes I passed out if I'd been taking stuff and drinking on top.

The drugs weren't yet affecting my work. I had a lot of good matches in 1996 as TV champion. Some were with Benoit and Dean Malenko. There was one before Christmas with Psicosis, a high-flying *lucha libre* guy from Pensecola, Florida, which I remember as being exceptional. I had several memorable matches with him and Rey Mysterio. They were smart lads and between us we worked out how to mix their high-flying moves with what I did.

They weren't one-dimensional either – they knew how to wrestle. I clicked with Psicosis – he didn't speak much English so we never used to lay anything out beforehand. We'd just go in and wrestle – and it would always work.

Bailey was due to be born on Christmas Day, 1996. He was late and eventually turned up on December 30 – just in time for New Year. I was heavily into my drugs by then but I made a special effort to stay clean that day – it was a tremendous feeling to become a dad again.

Back at work, I was having serious problems with my neck. All the treatment in the world didn't help.

> **I went to Japan in early 1997 but my neck was still giving me trouble when I returned. I came back on the day of the *Spring Stampede* Pay-Per-View. I got in my truck to drive from Atlanta to Tupelo, Mississippi. And soon I was caught up in a lot more drama.**

10

Crossing the Line

I picked up Chris Benoit and Nancy, who would later become his wife. She sat in the back. We had stopped at an intersection when, without warning, a car rammed into us from behind. He hit us square on but the car flipped over three times.

I had no idea what was happening. Our car came to rest on its roof and, sitting upside down, I could see the other car. An old fellow climbed out of the driver's side, went round to the passenger's side and got in while his passenger, a young lad, slid over to the driver's seat. I looked over at

Chris and thought he was dead. His neck was to one side and his eyes were shut. A few moments later, he came round. We were all done in, good style. I managed to kick the windscreen out and got us out.

Shortly after that the police turned up and I told them the kid wasn't driving the car which hit us, the old fellow was. We soon learned the reason behind their quick switch. The fellow was steaming drunk, even though it was only 10 a.m. The kid was under age and they had no licence or insurance between them. People driving the other way who'd seen the smash later confirmed it was completely this guy's fault. But the police didn't charge them with anything, and we heard no more about it.

> I can't remember anything about the rest of the day. People said they saw me walking around and talking to myself. My memories of the next day or so are in and out.

A more immediate concern was that my truck was completely wrecked. The police put us in a car but, being wrestlers, all we could think about was getting to the show on time. Since it was a Pay-Per-View we were supposed to be there by 1 p.m. So we told them not to take us to the hospital. Instead we went straight from the crash to the hotel, picked our bags up and went straight to the venue.

Nancy was shaken up, Chris was done in with a great big gash on his hand and I was completely out of it – gone. I'd obviously suffered a serious concussion. I've since watched the match I had that night with Prince Iaukea but I can't remember it at all. I was on autopilot, just going through the motions of my basic routine. I can't remember anything about the rest of the day. People said they saw me walking around and talking to myself. My memories of the next day or so are in and out. All I do remember is coming to in a limo on the way back to Atlanta with some people I didn't normally travel with, who were saying they'd drop me home.

I was sat in a chair in my house the next morning when Chris came in – and absolutely flipped out. She thought the crash had happened because I was drunk or on drugs – I can't say I blame her for thinking that either. She battered the hell out of me. I could hardly move so I let her get on with it to get her frustration out. She was screaming at the top of her lungs, punching and kicking lumps out of me.

The whole episode had shaken me up and I made a conscious effort to stop taking drugs. It wasn't going to be easy, either. Up until Bailey was born I had been taking a lot of drugs and drinking a lot – but I hadn't completely lost it. But my consumption skyrocketed from January until April, when I had the accident. The crash woke me up: I was feeling terrible; my wife was at her wit's end; and I had a new baby. I sat at home in my chair and thought: "This has got to stop."

I tried. And it lasted eight weeks. For the first four weeks I honestly felt I was dying. I couldn't believe how sick I was. I had withdrawal symptoms bad. Shaking. Constant diarrhoea. Throwing up all the time. No ability to eat anything. No sleep whatsoever. Horror stories.

After a month I was still sticking with it but in a lot of pain. Diamond Dallas Page suggested I go to see Dr Kenneth West, an applied kinesiologist, who fixed me up pretty well. He's an advanced chiropractor, a muscle specialist who does a lot of weird stuff which works. I went to see him a few times but I didn't keep it up. And I didn't tell him anything about the drugs. I still thought of myself as just Darren. Yes, I did my pills, but I wasn't going to admit to being a drug addict. I didn't think I was one. Nothing wrong with Darren.

For the first time since turning eighteen, I'd stopped training. Initially I stopped because of my neck trouble – but I could have trained through it. I didn't. I started putting on a lot of weight really quickly. I took more and more drugs. And I stopped doing the things I'd always done to look after myself. I stopped drinking a gallon of water a day. That meant I had all this poison in my system and wasn't sweating it out or pushing it out with water.

Up until then I'd still been able to function – and have all those good matches in 1996 – because I had kept up the training. Yes, my neck was still bothering me. But that wasn't the real reason I started to let myself go. The problem was that I'd given up on everything. I was very unhappy – though I had no reason to be. I had a great job and a great family, but I didn't see it that way at the time. And after the car wreck, I started putting on weight even faster. I was always a big heavy lad but one who trained and was always in good ring condition. Before January I had been 255 or 260 pounds. In May I was 265 or 270.

All I did was eat. I was a slob, basically. I was off the drugs but fat, not training and not feeling good. So one day the little voice started up again. "You feel like crap. You know what used to make you feel good, don't you? Those pain pills and those Somas. You used to feel great on them, didn't you? If you took just one of each – no, better make it two of each – you'd feel fantastic. Remember how it used to make you feel?"

It made perfect sense at the time. So I got myself a prescription, got myself some pills and took them. And that was all it took – I was away again.

> **One day the little voice started up again. "You feel like crap. You know what used to make you feel good, don't you? Those pain pills and those Somas. You used to feel great on them, didn't you? If you took just one of each – no, better make it two of each – you'd feel fantastic. Remember how it used to make you feel?"**

Before this, I'd been taking ten pain pills and ten Somas a day. It was now that my consumption began to climb up rapidly to thirty and thirty a day. On top of that, I was still taking downers come night time – any Valium I could get my hands on. Plus I was drinking. It all added up to me becoming an enormous lump of lard.

I was getting fatter and fatter and life meant nothing to me at all. And here's the truth: it doesn't matter how much you are earning or how famous you are. None of it is worth anything if you are not happy. I know it sounds like crap, but it's true. Right then I would have given away everything I had for a glimpse of happiness.

I thought drugs would provide that. I was about as wrong as you could be. But it wasn't until much later that I realised how

I was getting fatter and fatter and life meant nothing to me at all. And here's the truth: it doesn't matter how much you are earning or how famous you are. None of it is worth anything if you are not happy. I know it sounds like crap, but it's true. Right then I would have given away everything I had for a glimpse of happiness. I thought drugs would provide that. I was about as wrong as you could be. But it wasn't until much later that I realised how wrong-headed I was. And unfortunately many people who make the mistakes that I made don't come out the other side.

wrong-headed I was. And unfortunately many people who make the mistakes that I made don't come out the other side.

What I've told you so far has just been the starters – the garlic bread, if you like. Now we come to the really interesting stuff. The meat and potatoes. While I was completely out of shape, I could still just about get by in the ring. Anyone who is competent at their job can coast along on autopilot for a certain amount of time – and that's what I did.

Some people were bothered by my lack of effort. Some weren't. And I could always justify my behaviour to myself. "I'm a villain anyway. People are supposed to hate me. Won't they hate me even more if they can see I'm out of shape and still getting away with it?"

> Some people were bothered by my lack of effort. Some weren't. And I could always justify my behaviour to myself. "I'm a villain anyway. People are supposed to hate me. Won't they hate me even more if they can see I'm out of shape and still getting away with it?"

I could still do it. I never blew up, meaning running out of wind in the ring. I did get the odd talking to: "Can't you cut down on the drugs a little bit? Start training a little bit? Get yourself a bit of a tan?" I was as white as a milk bottle back then. But most of the time I could get through. I thought I was okay.

In truth, I wasn't okay at all. But because of the state I was in, I was never put in any position which meant anything, anywhere where I would be exposed. That's how I coasted through. I did lower-card matches on TV. Once every three months we went down to Disney to tape worldwide matches which got shown at 3 a.m. in Bolivia and places like that, and I'd do those. Actually, it's probably true that more people saw those matches than any of my others because they were shown all over the world. I was a big star among Bolivian insomniacs. And that was exactly how I used to joke about my diminished status.

Within a week of going back on the drugs I was taking those thirty Somas, those thirty pain pills, anything else I could get and the booze as well. I screwed up more and more often. Passing out in hotel bars. Falling asleep in restaurants. It's hard to think back to that time now, but I'd become a complete and utter wreck. A waste of time. I find it hard to believe now that I managed to get myself into that state. I know what I was like before it all happened and I know what I'm like now. The bit in between I find hard to face.

It was a few weeks before a three-day trip to Japan when the drugs started to dry up. I cut down on them not through choice, but because they became increasingly hard to get. Most of my time became a constant quest to find drugs. I knew a few doctors I could call up who would instantly write me a prescription. Some had to be visited in person. But it was getting harder and harder. The docs who were a bit bent started to get pulled in, sometimes by the FBI, for writing too many prescriptions. Some of them were cutting me off.

Within a week of going back on the drugs I was taking those thirty Somas, those thirty pain pills, anything else I could get and the booze as well. I screwed up more and more often. Passing out in hotel bars. Falling asleep in restaurants. It's hard to think back to that time now, but I'd become a complete and utter wreck. A waste of time. I find it hard to believe now that I managed to get myself into that state. I know what I was like before it all happened and I know what I'm like now. The bit in between I find hard to face.

So, having to cut down on pills, I made up for it with more alcohol. I drank anything I could get my hands on. Guinness. Cheap wine by the bottle. Vodka. Anything at all – it wasn't important.

I got to Japan for a three-day tournament at Tokyo's Sumo Palace without any pills whatsoever. It hardly helped. They soon realized I wasn't the wrestler I had been. Back in 1996 Hashimoto had made me look like a champ. Now they discovered I wasn't the person they thought I was, although I was still treated well and shown respect. I had a good match with a lad called Kojima who's turned into one of the greats. He's recently defected to All Japan. I had another match with Hiro Saito and ended up in a tag match. But then it was time to come home – and prove to everyone just how big a screw-up I'd become.

It all started when I acquired some strange muscle relaxants off somebody. I had no idea what they were, didn't even know their name. But I didn't care. I took three or four on each of the first and second nights I was in Japan. Each time I was out like a light and slept all night. When it was time to fly home I had a few beers and took a couple of these pills before I got on the plane. We were due to arrive in Detroit to do *Nitro* on the same day. Once we were airborne I carried on drinking.

The next thing I remember was being asked to get off the plane. I didn't have a clue what was going on. But everyone was very insistent. "Please get off the plane."

I walked down the stairs onto the tarmac in a daze. I had no idea where we were, or what was going on. The next thing I knew a policeman had handcuffed me and taken the little case I carry my gear in when I'm travelling. I vaguely remember being thrown into the back of a van. The rest is a blank.

When I woke and looked around me I was in a 15-foot by 15-foot jail cell with bars all around. I wasn't alone either. My new buddies were all wearing gang colours – and staring straight at me. Looking down, I found I was wearing an orange jump suit about three sizes too small and a pair of flip flops. I couldn't remember donning this strange garb.

After a while I plucked up the courage to ask one of them, "Where am I?"

"In jail," came the predictable answer.

"I know that," I persisted, "But where am I?"

"Anchorage."

"What? Anchorage where?"

"Anchorage, Alaska."

I thought my informant was winding me up and started getting the hump with him. "Don't fuck about," I demanded, "Where am I?"

The whole cell erupted in laughter and confirmed he was indeed telling the truth. Anchorage, Alaska? What the hell was I doing there? A screw arrived, telling me to go with him. That I did, shuffling along after him though I was still in a daze. He handcuffed me to a row of twenty other people – women and men together. They put us in a big truck and started driving.

Now I was really baffled. Where were we going? But no one I asked felt like answering me. Soon we were in a courtroom, and the guy next to me struck up a conversation. To my astonishment, he was English.

"This is bad, innit?" he said.

"It might be if I knew what it was," I told him.

Then the judge entered. "All rise."

We did. She went along the line, telling people what they were charged with. It took a while to get to me in the back row.

"Darren Matthews," said a clerk.

"Yes," I answered.

"Causing a disturbance on an airplane. Urinating on the airplane and urinating on the foot of a flight attendant."

I was right through the looking glass now, I thought. *Alice in Wonderland* time. No way I'd have done that. They must have got it wrong. Don't say anything, I thought to myself. Best keep your gob shut.

"You are hereby fined ten thousand dollars."

A bit strong, I thought. Then they turned to the English guy next to me, who it turned out had been on the same plane. A long list of charges began: "For hitting three of the flight attendants . . ."

What sort of flight had I been on, I wondered? Soon I was back in jail. But I was still absolutely gobsmacked. Someone must have messed up somewhere. I couldn't have done what they said.

Just like in the movies, I was given the right to one phone call. I didn't know who to ring. They gave me a phone number. I rang it but nobody answered. Then, in the late afternoon, two FBI fellows arrived and started questioning me. I told them my story, which was unconvincing to say the least.

"To be honest," I told them, "I don't know what happened."

I lied and told them I hadn't taken any drugs. But I admitted drinking some beer and told them that the next thing I knew I had woken up in jail. They said it would take $1,000 bail money to get me out. I had no money, I told them – the policeman at the airport had taken my bag with all my cash in it. They gave me the number for a bail bondsman. The idea was he'd go to the airport and pick up my stuff so I could post bail and get out. I rang him and he didn't want to know. It doesn't matter who you are or what you earn. When you're in a situation like that you are truly helpless.

What sort of flight had I been on, I wondered? Soon I was back in jail. But I was still absolutely gobsmacked. Someone must have messed up somewhere. I couldn't have done what they said.

I tried the bondsman again and managed to talk him round. The FBI guys had obviously run a check on me and learned I'd never been had up for anything in my life because they were happy to let me go. I got my money, got out and got to the airport to find a flight leaving at midnight with a connection in Denver which would get me home.

But this is how sick it is. After going through all that, I got to the airport bar, had a few beers and started rummaging through my pockets. Almost without realizing it, I was looking for a pill which would knock me out on that plane. Luckily there wasn't one to be found – but it shows how screwed up I was.

When the plane landed in Atlanta, I was half-frightened there'd be a phalanx of press people to greet me as I got off the plane. I was happy that wasn't the case. Chris wasn't there – another lucky break, I thought. She was in England with the kids and wouldn't be back for another two days. So I went home – but not without stopping at the supermarket to get myself some beer, of course.

When I called WCW I learned I'd been suspended without pay. A couple of others who had been on the plane with me had also got up to mischief, but fortunately for them they hadn't got arrested, so they were in the clear.

Months later, after I got my belongings back and my bail money, I discovered exactly what had happened during the flight. Drunk and pilled up, I had gone to the bathroom. I had staggered in but dragged one foot behind me, so the door had failed to shut. I was having a pee when one of the stewardesses came along and tapped me on the shoulder. I turned around and, befuddled as I was, peed on one of her shoes.

When I called WCW I learned I'd been suspended without pay. A couple of others who had been on the plane with me had also got up to mischief, but fortunately for them they hadn't got arrested, so they were in the clear.

After she had cooled down she had realized that it hadn't been deliberate. But I'm not seeking to belittle my actions. I had still been drunk on that plane. I'd still caused it to come down out of the sky. Two years later I received a letter from the Federal Aviation Administration saying that because I had caused a disturbance, I was fined $2,500. I paid and got on with my life. I know that others were being pressured to go back to Alaska to sort it out. I wasn't the only one who caused that plane to

Months later, after I got my belongings back and my bail money, I discovered exactly what had happened during the flight. Drunk and pilled up, I had gone to the bathroom. I had staggered in but dragged one foot behind me, so the door had failed to shut. I was having a pee when one of the stewardesses came along and tapped me on the shoulder. I turned around and, befuddled as I was, peed on one of her shoes.
After she had cooled down she had realized that it hadn't been deliberate. But I'm not seeking to belittle my actions. I had still been drunk on that plane. I'd still caused it to come down out of the sky.

land so abruptly – there was the man handcuffed next to me in the courtroom, for a start.

The most difficult part was confessing it to Chris. When she came home, I told her what I'd done. I had to wait for her return because we hadn't been speaking on the phone. Considering my general state at that time, I don't blame her one bit. I picked her up from the airport and, driving home, I broached the embarrassing news. She went predictably berserk. She wanted to go straight back to the airport and home to England again.

For the next seven weeks, I sat at home in a major slump, feeling sorrier for myself than ever before. When I could sneak out, I did so to get drugs. When I could sneak it in, I got some booze. They were bad times. Terrible. We were staring divorce in the face. And it was all my doing. I had three children, no money coming in, a wife who wasn't speaking to me, and I was a serious drug addict and an alcoholic.

I didn't think life could get any worse.
Wrong again.

11

My New Friend

On my first night back at work after seven weeks out, I got to the arena to be told I was wrestling Bill Goldberg. It was early in his massive win streak but it was obvious he was on his way to becoming a major superstar. Up until then he'd beaten everyone on the WCW roster in a minute or less. His longest match must have been no more than a minute and a half. Everyone has their own version of what happened next – this is mine. I remember it all clearly because for once I went to work without taking any drugs beforehand. I weighed about 280 pounds by now: I looked like a badly-made bed.

Anyway, these were my orders for the match – to go out and have a competitive six-minute match with him. He was to win in the end. We laid out this match in front of the people in charge. I got into the ring, did one or two moves on him and he did nothing back. I did one or two more with the same comeback from Goldberg – nothing. That's how it went on. I had to keep attacking him to keep the match going. I was opening myself up for him to retaliate and he wasn't taking the openings. I was even telling him to do this or that and he just wasn't doing it. I don't know what his excuses were for the match. All I know is that he's blamed me publicly for it.

> I had to keep attacking him to keep the match going. I was opening myself up for him to retaliate and he wasn't taking the openings.

When we eventually got through the match and got to the back, straightaway Bill apologized to me – something else he seemed to forget about later when he retold the story. "I'm sorry," he said. "I just didn't know what to do out there."

We had a chat, shook hands and everything was fine. Then Eric came in and started chewing Bill out, which I took as my cue to leave. Then I was called into the office in front of Eric and the people who had laid out the match. Eric was screaming, going absolutely berserk. I told him: "Eric, I can't hit myself. It's not my fault. How can you expect someone who has never wrestled for more than a minute and a half to go out and do six minutes? He won't know what to do."

That was the truth of it. It wasn't Bill's fault. I'd always liked Bill because he was always nice to me. Ever since that match, every time I've seen him he's gone out of his way to shake my hand and even hug me. Always. But I haven't seen him since he wrote about the match in his book and slagged me off for it. I thought he was more of a man than that.

If he had a problem with that match he could have come and fronted me up about it any time. We must have met 100 times since it happened and he's said nothing to me about it – not until he printed it in his book.

The incident earned me a right bollocking off Eric Bischoff.
I've always got on well with Eric but now I know that he had got sick of me by then. He was right, too. He knew what I could do and saw me wasting my talent and not doing it. Eric was always straight with me. If he didn't like something he'd tell me, and I was the same with him. When *Monday Night Nitro* started he was a very busy fellow but he was never too busy to come and shake my hand if he saw me at a show – even if I was at the other end of the arena. Eric knew I wasn't living up to my potential. I didn't look good enough to be put in a position to perform. Eric did the right thing and I've no gripes with him for doing it.

For the rest of that year I just got deeper and deeper into my drugs and further and further into my life as a slob. Somas and Hydrocodone. Percocet and Percodan when I couldn't get anything else. Those two didn't even do anything to me. But I took them anyway because they were drugs. That's how stupid I was.

Just before Christmas 1997 we were in Buffalo, New York to do some Saturday night TV tapings. I flew up with Dave Taylor and Fit, who shared a room while I split one with Steve Armstrong. The next morning I woke up, coughed and blood came out of my mouth.

> I felt like I was going to die. I could hardly breathe. I was in a shocking state. So shocking that for the first time in my life I could not go to the show. I couldn't even get out of bed and crawl to the door.

Every time I coughed, blood poured out of me and onto the pillows until they were soaked. It still wasn't enough to be the wake-up call I needed. "I'll be okay," I told everyone. "Leave me here today and I'll be fine tomorrow."

On the plane back to Atlanta they put me on oxygen. When I got home Chris took me to the local hospital. After a couple of tests they announced I had pneumonia. It might have had something to do with the flight, because a couple of other fellows on the plane ended up with walking pneumonia. But because all the drugs had run down my immune system so badly, it hit me strong.

An ambulance took me to the big hospital in Atlanta where, for the next week, my lungs were eighty per cent filled with blood. I was on oxygen constantly and they thought I was going to die. That's how I felt, too – as though every breath would be my last. I was also worried because I was supposed to be flying to England in a few days' time. Chris came to see me in hospital and I broke down. I lost it: "I'm so sorry for all the things I've put you through. I'm so sorry for all the drugs."

Chris told me I would be okay. Maybe she still believed that. I really felt like I'd had enough. It was one of those moments of clarity. I was contrite. Yet I still didn't ask for help to get off the drugs. They released me with the warning that a flight across the Atlantic wouldn't be sensible. But that wasn't going to stop me so they gave me inhalers and antibiotics to take while I was in England.

For the rest of that year I just got deeper and deeper into my drugs and further and further into my life as a slob. Somas and Hydrocodone. Percocet and Percodan when I couldn't get anything else. Those two didn't even do anything to me. But I took them anyway because they were drugs. That's how stupid I was.

We flew back and the first thing I did was to ditch the antibiotics. I wasn't going to take any of them – they'd stop me going out drinking with my mates. And as soon as I got to Blackpool, meeting up with them for a drink was the first thing that I did. I went back to my old gym too. Not to train but to find someone I knew who could get me some drugs.

He delivered in spades, by giving me some GHB. Of all the things that I've taken, GHB has caused me the worst problems. It's a horrible drug and anyone who tells you different is a prick for saying so. People in bodybuilding magazines will write that it's misrepresented. It isn't. It has no benefits whatsoever.

All sorts of extraordinary claims are made for this stuff. It is supposed to boost your body's growth hormone output and burn body fat. All it does is screw you up and ruin your life.

It is a very strange drug. Its supporters make it sound like a wonder drug. And if you don't abuse it, maybe it is. The trouble is lots of people do get hooked on it. It is said that if you take it you will instantly go into deep sleep and you wake up feeling wonderful. You can get the benefits of eight hours of sleep in four hours. Your body rests better. It makes more growth hormones, your skin improves. It is supposed to do all these things.

But very few people take it in the way they should. That's because if you don't take enough of it to go to sleep, it gets you high. You get a euphoric feeling. Then when you get used to GHB it doesn't make you sleep but you speed on it instead. And if you take a little too much it acts as a muscle relaxant and you pass out. Either that or you black out, when you can do some really weird things and have no memory of them afterwards. Half the time I would have no idea what I was doing. That used to happen to me a lot.

Right before Christmas, at my mother-in-law's house in Blackpool, I took some GHB. I was still deathly ill, and the next thing I remember is waking up in the Victoria Hospital in Blackpool. I got a cab back to my mother-in-law's to find no one was speaking to me. It gradually became clear why. I had taken the GHB, flipped out and threatened to hit my father-in-law. I'd threatened any-one else who had come near me as well. I had stopped breathing several times, so they'd called me an ambulance, which was why I'd woken up in the hospital. Now they didn't want me in the house. Quite right too.

> You can do some really weird things and have no memory of them afterwards. Half the time I would have no idea what I was doing. That used to happen to me a lot.

GHB wasn't the only drug I was taking on that trip. I didn't have any pain pills so I got some Nubain instead. It's an injectable painkiller which was a big thing in England at that time, and is unfortunately a big thing in other countries now; although it's been discontinued in the UK as of December 2004. It was popular with bodybuilders. Again it is supposed to have all sorts of beneficial effects but really it is just another morphine-based drug which gets you high.

I would inject a couple of ccs of Nubain into my shoulder. Never straight into my veins, because my twisted logic said that was what junkies did, and I was no junkie. Doing it into your muscles is okay, I told myself. I was too stupid to realise that anyone addicted to drugs is a junkie. That's what the word means.

So it's no surprise that I can't remember much of what I did on that trip. All I know is that I took every chance I got to get drunk or drugged-up. People who knew me of old could not believe this staggering, stumbling figure was me. On my first night of madness I'd even threatened my mother-in-law – whom I have always treated as my own mum. She'd known me since I was seventeen and now she had to put up with this.

We spent New Year with some friends in Kidderminster. I proceeded to drink as though I could never get enough. Chris couldn't hide her disgust any more and went to bed. But I stayed up to drink a couple of pints of vodka and a bottle of wine. I'd gone so mad that the next day, when I was supposed to go and visit some of my wife's family I couldn't even get out of bed.

You can imagine how strained my relationship with Chris had become. It was all my doing, but of course I thought Chris was the problem. She was a nag, I told myself. She didn't understand me. The same old words you hear from blokes the world over who don't want to look too closely at themselves in the mirror.

As 1998 rolled around, things were getting worse at home. I found it increasingly hard to get pain pills so I wasn't doing thirties and thirties any more. But I had become such a slob by now that it didn't matter. If I couldn't get pills, I would drink. I had always promised myself that I would never drink and drive, but even that rule went out of the window.

Late at night, I would get into the car, drive to the local supermarket and buy a cheap bottle of wine. Then I'd pull up near my house and guzzle it down before putting the bottle in the bin at the end of the path, as if that meant Chris wouldn't know what I was doing. I would then go inside and pass out on a chair and wake up an hour later feeling like absolute death. That was normal living to me at the time – anything to get a buzz. If I was out and someone offered me ecstasy, I would take it. Cocaine too. The only thing that stopped me taking more cocaine was my dodgy nose. Because I'd broken it a few times, cocaine would start a nose bleed which would last for days.

The only reason I never did crack or heroin during that period was because I was lucky – no one ever offered me any. I can't say I would have turned them down. I'm sure I would have given it a go because I'd have taken anything I could to get a buzz.

In March I got a phone call from Dave Taylor to say he'd been let go by WCW. I couldn't believe it, and didn't know what to say to him. A few minutes later my phone rang again. It was my turn. It was JJ Dillon from WCW on the line. His news shouldn't have been surprising: "I'm very, very sorry to tell you this Steve, but we've got to let you go."

I demanded an explanation. I honestly couldn't see why this was happening. It was the only time in my career that my ego got the better of me. Chris recently explained my attitude at the time. For years I had been this wrestler who had accepted all the accolades for his work. But I never bragged about it. The only time I went on

With Dave Taylor in our WCW days.

about how good I was, she said, was when I became a piece of shit. I was convinced that it was everyone else who was wrong.

"I'm good," I'd tell myself and anyone else who would listen. "Everyone says I'm good. I've been in work all my life. I've travelled all over the world."

I find that attitude one of the hardest things to grasp when I look back because that really is not me. I know my strengths and weaknesses. Good at talking, good on house shows. Not so good at short TV matches when I can't work off the crowd. I don't go round thinking I'm God's gift.

Straight away I went into action. If WCW couldn't see how good I was then it was time to give World Wrestling Federation a try. I rang Bobby Eaton for the number of Jim Cornette, who was working for the company then. They called me back instantly, Bruce Prichard and then Jim Ross saying yes, I could have a job. I'm embarrassed now to think back about it, but I thought I deserved a big job. WCW didn't understand, so I'd go into World Wresting Federation and turn the world on its head.

I still felt rotten. It takes a long time to get over pneumonia and obviously my lifestyle wasn't helping. There was another obstacle to overcome before I got to work for the company though. My WCW contract had a no-compete clause, which meant I couldn't work for anybody else for four months after they let me go. I never understood how they had the right to stop you making a living for your family. But I live in Georgia, a right-to-work state, which meant that clause was void, so the company got their lawyers onto it straight away. They spent money and went to court to sort it out.

> I'm embarrassed now to think back about it, but I thought I deserved a big job. WCW didn't understand, so I'd go into World Wresting Federation and turn the world on its head.

So I started on the payroll, another great opportunity for me. But no sooner had I signed the contract, than I woke up one April morning and coughed up blood again. Back to the same hospital; then to a different hospital in Atlanta. This time I was double creamed. Well and truly done in, worse than before. Not only did I have pneumonia, I also had a viral infection and a big pocket of fluid around my heart. My lungs were full of blood and I was really bad. I lay in hospital for another full week. I received a beautiful bunch of flowers from the company. I was very sick and it was all my doing.

I didn't think it was my fault then. "Poor me," I'd moan. "I can't get a break." What a complete pillock.

When I got out I was really done in. I wasn't taking any pills, both because I couldn't get any and because I knew I was really sick and shouldn't take any. It was what is called white-knuckling it – I craved those pills desperately. Taking pills was all I could think about, night and day.

But I knew I was seriously ill. There was a bit of clarity too – I knew I had a job with World Wrestling Federation and I had to try to get in shape. The two companies were head to head. WCW's business at that time was the best it ever got. The rivalry between the two had made wrestling bigger than ever.

I could be a part of that – if only I could get in shape. I forced myself back onto my Stairmaster and it was really hard. I kept at it, though and after a couple of weeks I started to get a bit of wind back. Through my sickness I'd lost thirty pounds but I still looked terrible. I was still grey and my face was swollen up.

One day Jim Ross called me up from Madison Square Garden while I happened to be on the Stairmaster. I asked him how Austin was. The next thing, Austin called me, saying he was looking forward to me coming to work. "Yes," I said. "Can't wait."

In the first week of May I was flown up to New York and driven to Stamford to Titan Towers, the company's offices. I was going to meet Vince McMahon, Jim Ross and everybody. What happened next is a shocking thing to have to own up to but it is true. I'd managed to get some pills from somewhere and I've only reconstructed what went on from what people have told me since – I can't remember a thing about it.

> I'd managed to get some pills from somewhere and I've only reconstructed what went on from what people have told me since – I can't remember a thing about it.

I met Jim Ross and was ushered in to meet Vince – the most powerful man in wrestling. And I passed out in his office. I can remember coming to and Vince smiling at me, saying something like: "Being sick must have really knocked you about."

"Yeah," I agreed, not knowing I'd passed out. Jim Ross has never spoken to me about it but I know he's told others it was one of his most embarrassing moments in the business. Steve Austin had spoken up for me, Jim had gone out on a limb to bring me in and this was how I'd repaid them. Then Jim took me for a meeting with the creative team. I rabbited on, talking nonsense. They were looking at me, wondering what on earth this prick was doing there. My first time in Titan Towers and it was all a blur.

Three days later was May 10, my birthday, and it wasn't one of my happiest. I got up, sat on the edge of my bed, coughed and covered the wall four feet away from me with blood.

By now I was getting used to the routine. Into the ambulance, off to the first hospital and then to the other hospital in Atlanta. Another week wired up to monitors, giving blood samples all the time and feeling terrible. I was double done in like you would not believe.

After a week I came out and couldn't walk up the stairs without stopping halfway in order to get my breath. Every single part of me felt like it was going to fall to pieces. I couldn't breathe. I had no energy. I was white-knuckling it for drugs, which I couldn't get. I couldn't even get out of the house to try to find any and I wasn't happy about that either.

So on top of the physical sickness was the mental sickness. I WANTED THOSE DRUGS.

And I soon found how to get some.

I discovered a place that would send me boxes of the stuff in two-pint bottles. It was the only stuff I could get which would give me a buzz. It took the edge off, so after a while I was drinking a bottle a day.

GHB had been banned; but someone had altered the formula slightly so it could be sold legally as a product called Renutrient. It was available everywhere in the

United States and had exactly the same effects as GHB. When I found out about it I started getting it shipped to the house. I discovered a place that would send me boxes of the stuff in two-pint bottles. It was the only stuff I could get which would give me a buzz. It took the edge off, so after a while I was drinking a bottle a day.

I spent all of my time in the bedroom because it was too much effort to go downstairs. If I wanted to go downstairs I'd have to sit halfway down. That meant I wasn't spending any time with my kids. I had always thought of myself as a good dad. I loved my kids to bits. I'd never hit them, and I would kill anyone else who laid a hand on them. But when you're lying in bed all day, that's not being a good dad. At best, I was half a dad. They would come into my room for a couple of minutes maybe and that was all. It was a part of my life where I let everybody down, and them especially. I wasn't there for them. And I wasn't any sort of a husband either. Chris and I never talked now.

It might seem incredible looking back but I had just signed a lucrative three-year contract. Whatever state I was in, Vince didn't fire me. At the time I had no idea what any of them thought of me. Vince isn't the kind to tell you. We'll find out later on just how good he was to me. I think now he realized I was a good person with a bad problem. I wasn't a bad lot through and through and I think they were hoping I'd pull through.

I was flown up to *King of the Ring* in Pittsburgh but I was in no shape to do anything. I was still desperately ill but I was doing my best to put a brave face on it. I still wanted drugs although I wasn't taking any at the time. I hadn't gotten deep into the Renutrient by then either. I was sober enough to realize I had to do something or I would lose my job – this great opportunity which had been handed to me.

It was the night of the second Hell in a Cell match, the famous one when Mick Foley, wrestling as Mankind, went off the top of the cage twice. Cactus always used to worry me. I knew his wife and children, who were wonderful, and I'd worry at the risks he took – but that was his style. I was in shock that night, watching him take all those bumps. It was a classic piece of wrestling history and an incredible performance by Cactus and Undertaker. They showed total dedication to their art form.

When I first came to America I used to watch Cactus and would see him do the most amazing things. I remember him wrestling Paul Orndorff when Paul suplexed him and the middle of his back landed on the guard rail. His whole body bent completely the wrong way and sprang back with a sickening thud on to the concrete. I thought he must have been instantly paralysed, there was no way he could walk away. But it was just a regular part of a Mick Foley match. It's just how he was. That mad look would come over his face and you'd worry about what he'd dreamed up to do next.

When I first came to America I used to watch Cactus and would see him do the most amazing things. I remember him wrestling Paul Orndorff when Paul suplexed him and the middle of his back landed on the guard rail. His whole body bent completely the wrong way and sprang back with a sickening thud on to the concrete. I thought he must have been instantly paralysed, there was no way he could walk away. But it was just a regular part of a Mick Foley match. It's just how he was. That mad look would come over his face and you'd worry about what he'd dreamed up to do next.

I was badly worried about him that night at *King of the Ring*. I said to his old mate Terry Funk: "Terry, he's got to stop this." But Terry knew the truth. "It was something he had to do," he said. I didn't understand it then, but I do now. Do you want to go through life reading about other people's achievements or do you want to achieve something for yourself? The only regrets you should have are not for the things you've done but for the things you haven't.

The next night saw my first match on *Raw*. I went into the ring with Darren Drozdov and I looked like a bag of shit. I got the win but it was just a match. The next night I wrestled a horrible match against Tiger Ali Singh at Penn State in Pennsylvania. When I got home I received a phone call, telling me to go to the company training camp to try to get in shape.

The camps were run every month by Dory Funk Jr at the production studios in Stamford. Ever since I'd been in America I'd been friendly with Dory, one of my favourite wrestlers. For the week I was there I was trying to get in shape while the company took a look at some young prospects. Rhyno was there, who got hired a long time after. Test – Andrew Martin – was there, as was Christian. There was also Teddy Annis, one of the Hart family and a very talented young man. And among all this young talent there I was, getting through a fair amount of Renutrient every day. I don't know how I managed it but I struggled through the training.

My abiding memory is of lying in bed, feeling deathly ill. One day I couldn't even get up to go to the camp. I had to come, I was told – but I couldn't. I was a disgrace. On the last day everyone had matches and mine was with Rhyno. Somehow I twisted my ankle slightly. It wasn't too serious but it left the ankle weak and loose and I had to hobble to the dressing room.

I went back home. By now I was a complete hermit who did nothing but sit in his bedroom and drink Renutrient. I was out of my head on it all the time, to such an extent that Chris and I were living separate lives. Out of my head, I staggered into the bathroom. I put my weight on my damaged ankle, it went to the side and as I went down I felt something in my leg pop. I'd managed to break both the ankle and my leg. The ankle had been weak already from the training. Because I'd been so doped up, I might have broken it in the match without knowing.

Slowly my ankle turned black and blue. Chris didn't want anything to do with this latest horror. She had moved into the spare room a long time ago. So I called Dave Taylor, who turned up and took me to hospital. They X-rayed the leg and put a temporary cast on it that night before I went to Atlanta the next day for an operation where they screwed the ankle back together and put my leg in a cast. All I cared about was getting myself on a morphine drip with a clicker so you could administer yourself a dose whenever you felt like it. I thought that was marvellous.

I came out of hospital and, if you can believe it, it was from this point on that things got really bad. Before that, though, I had a strange burst of normality. I got home and went up to my bedroom. The kids came in, and I told them to ask their mother if she wanted to go to Florida. From where we live it's an easy 450-mile drive to Orlando. So amid all this madness, we went to Florida and had an idyllic ten-day family holiday. I got an electric wheelchair to get about in; the four of us went round all the parks, spent a lot of money and had a really good time.

Chris and I made the most of it, if only so the kids could enjoy themselves. Reality only intruded towards the end when Chris went down to the pool on the last day. I ordered a load of those frozen drinks and tried to cover my tracks by hiding all the glasses in a cupboard in the hotel room. Chris found them and there was a scene.

When we got back I shut myself up in my bedroom with my new friend, Renutrient. And I went insane.

12

Black Hookers and Crack

I was back up in my bedroom and all I did from now on was get boxes of Renutrient shipped to my house and drink it. This is how sick my mind was and how stupid things got. I would drink the stuff, throw up instantly and then panic because I had wasted it, so I'd drink more immediately. This is what I did all day long. I hardly ever ate. I'd turned into a recluse. I was a lunatic. I was completely gone. I cleaned myself or shaved very rarely. I showered about every third day. I lay in the bedroom and drank Renutrient all day long. I'd turned into Howard Hughes.

It got to the point where I could not sleep – and that went on for the next two or three months. I only ever passed out for twenty or thirty minutes at a time. Most of the time I lay in bed, speeding. Sweat poured out of me as though a tap had been turned on. I'd pass out. Then when I came to I was racing again. Then drink more and pass out again. That was my life. Twenty-four hours a day.

While I was doing this, I actually lost my mind. I used to sit there with a writing pad. In between drinking Renutrient, passing out and waking up, sometimes an idea popped into my head and I wrote it down. I scribbled pages and pages. One time, I thought I had solved all the world's problems. I had pages and pages of stuff and I kept scribbling and crossing stuff out until I ended up with one simple, little equation. Whatever your problem was you could put it into one side of this four or five-figure equation and it would come out solved the other side. Having solved the world's problems, I drank some more and passed out. When I woke up I looked at my discovery. It was complete nonsense. There were pages and pages of this shit lying all over the room. It was all total gibberish. But it had made complete sense to me when I had written it.

I spent a couple of months in that state. The only time I went downstairs was late at night when everybody was asleep and I would raid the fridge for something to eat. I'd have the TV on. There's one show on Nickleodeon with two black kids in it. Whenever I see it now it makes me shiver because I can remember sitting and watching it then. I watched this show as I passed in and out of consciousness, drinking Renutrient and throwing up.

Another time I was on my hands and knees in my room when my arms gave way and I fell on a cupboard, breaking my nose all across my face. I remember Fit Finlay coming round – Chris must have had a word with him. I remember him pleading with me. "We all love you and we want you to get out of this." But I wasn't having any of it. "There's nothing wrong with me. Leave me alone."

My cast eventually came off but I was still staying in the bedroom. Then one day Vince McMahon called, saying they had an idea for me. Was I ready to get back to work?

While I was doing this, I actually lost my mind. I used to sit there with a writing pad. In between drinking Renutrient, passing out and waking up, sometimes an idea popped into my head and I wrote it down. I scribbled pages and pages. One time, I thought I had solved all the world's problems. I had pages and pages of stuff and I kept scribbling and crossing stuff out until I ended up with one simple, little equation. Whatever your problem was you could put it into one side of this four or five-figure equation and it would come out solved the other side. Having solved the world's problems, I drank some more and passed out. When I woke up I looked at my discovery. It was complete nonsense. There were pages and pages of this shit lying all over the room. It was all total gibberish. But it had made complete sense to me when I had written it.

"Yes," I told him.

It was a lie. I wasn't ready to go back to work. I shouldn't have been allowed within a thousand miles of a wrestling ring. I had done no rehab on my leg and in fact never did have any physio on it, though it's fine today.

"We've got this idea for you," said Vince. "You're going to be called the Man's Man. It's Vince Russo's idea."

"Yes, Vince, whatever you want." I apologized to him for everything that had happened.

"You've just had a bit of bad luck, that's all," said Vince. That was just what I wanted to hear. "Vince understands me," I thought. "What a nice fellow. He knows what I'm going through."

I was told to go and get stuff like checked shirts and cut-off jeans. I was to go to Stamford where we'd make some vignettes to introduce this character. We went to the house of one of the producers somewhere in Connecticut with woods behind it for the filming. I chopped down trees. I squeezed oranges into a glass. I shaved myself with a cut-throat razor. Then I was taken to TV and all I can remember is the first time the Man's Man was on TV. X-Pac was the European Champ at the time and I hit the ring on him.

This Man's Man gimmick was something I really hated doing. I was willing to do it because I wanted to keep my job. I thought that no one gets the right gimmick the first time. Steve Austin started out as the Ringmaster before hitting the big time as Stone Cold Steve Austin. I thought I'd be the Man's Man for a bit and then do something else. It was a truly ridiculous gimmick, but it was all I was worthy of at the time. I wasn't even worthy of that. And if you think about it, there's no reason why a Man's Man might not be good, if it was given to the right person. But the fact was I didn't want to do it.

All it did achieve was to make me feel more sorry for myself, which made me drink more Renutrient, which made me more useless, which made me take more pills when I could get them. I was a complete and utter mess. I'd given up on life. Chris was ready to leave. Everything was a nightmare. All of it was my doing but I thought it was her fault. Everyone was to blame but me.

I'm a lumberjack and I'm certainly not okay . . . The Man's Man.

Another problem I had was that I could not sleep. I've never been a good sleeper and the Renutrient only made it a lot worse. So I paid to go to a clinic to get a sleep study done. It was a strange night. On my way to the place in Atlanta I took some pills – downers, I think. They put wax in my hair and attached wires to my head. Then they put me in a completely silent, black room and I lay down and went to sleep.

I woke up a few hours later needing a pee. I stood up in the darkness and started groping around. Then a deep voice came over the loudspeaker: "There's a pot by the side of your bed." I grabbed it and did what needed to be done, still with all these wires on me. The next morning I came out of the room and saw a fellow sat there in front of several computers and TV screens.

"Were you watching me sleep last night?" I asked him.

"Yeah," he said.

"And you went to college just so you could watch me sleep and piss? That was money well spent, wasn't it?"

"There's no need to be like that," he huffed.

They sent a report to my doctor – who'd referred me there in the first place – and he gave me some sleeping pills. Since I was accustomed to taking handfuls of strong stuff such as Valium and Xanax, these were absolutely worthless.

Then he put me on a drug called Clonopin, which certainly did have an effect on me. It meant I couldn't talk. It didn't make me go to sleep at night but mixing it with somas meant that when I opened my mouth, only gibberish came out. That was the reason I could no longer hide my drug taking. I'd been messing up at work – but now I couldn't even talk to people.

One night I was given a microphone and was slurring my words on live TV. I believe I was wrestling Goldust and he helped me through the match. The memories are hazy and I refuse to watch anything I did back then.

I was the Man's Man for about five or six weeks, I think. Life meant nothing to me and I didn't care about anything. I was thirty years old, looked like death and might not have been that far away from it. It might have taken just one more disease for my whole system to shut down. And, though I've been asked the question time and time again, I never once contemplated suicide. It just never entered my head. But I wasn't right, wasn't anywhere close to being so; and I wasn't going to be because I wasn't doing any of the things I needed to in order to get myself right.

The powers that be knew it, too. Jim Ross and Gerry Brisco pulled me into the office because they could see how bad I was. I told them I was so messed up because I hadn't been able to sleep for months. It was actually the truth but I didn't tell them the reason for it – that I was guzzling Renutrient all the time. They were still willing to believe me. My wife was ready to leave and take the kids, I told them. I told them about all the bad things that were happening to me. All those things *were* happening to me. I just didn't think they were my fault.

> I was thirty years old, looked like death and might not have been that far away from it. It might have taken just one more disease for my whole system to shut down.

I was told to report to the Talbot Recovery Center in Atlanta to talk to someone to see if I had a problem. I went in and bluffed my way through it. Not too hard, I thought. I told them the answers I thought they wanted to hear. I had a ready excuse for everything. I took pills because I had a bad back and getting hurt was my living. I took downers because I couldn't sleep. Addicts always have an excuse and as long as you have one, you're going to carry on with your drugs or your drinking. I left the centre and thought no more about it.

But it hadn't been forgotten by everyone else. When I turned up at the dressing room in San Diego, California, Jack Lanza, one of the agents, said I had to call Bruce Prichard right away. I did and Bruce told me what I didn't want to hear. "Listen. People don't want to work with you. You're a danger to them and a danger to yourself. You've got to go into rehab."

I flew back to Atlanta right before Thanksgiving to check into the

TRC for a four-day evaluation. Next to the TRC is a place called the Anchor Hospital, which is half drying-out ward and half psych ward for people with depression and the like.

I was locked in at the Anchor for four days. I couldn't get out. It was a horrible, old-looking place straight out of *One Flew Over The Cuckoo's Nest*. The drying-out itself could have been worse. Luckily I was off the pain pills at the time because I hadn't been able to get any. They give you really bad withdrawal symptoms because Hydrocodone is an opiate. Somas and downers, which I'd been taking a lot of, don't give you many withdrawals. So I didn't feel deathly ill.

They did have to wean me off the Clonopin. It's a drug which you must reduce gradually – if you stop taking it cold you can have seizures and all kinds of problems. The only problem was I couldn't sleep. I spent every night pacing up and down my room, which I shared with a fellow who snored. The food was diabolical – fair enough I suppose, seeing as you're in there to dry out and not for the *haute cuisine*. But it certainly wound me up because I still didn't think I needed to be in there.

All day long I went to see different doctors, filled out a lot of tests and went to groups with a lot of people just like me. None of us thought we should be in there. We had to go to Alcoholics Anonymous groups with the twelve-step programme. It was totally foreign to me. What, start talking about my problems with all these strangers? No bleeding chance. I came out, glad only that my four days were up. But one of the doctors told me: "No, four days isn't going to be enough. You need to be here for at least a couple of weeks."

A couple of weeks? I was furious. I got Bruce Prichard and Gerry Brisco on the phone, swearing up and down that they had to get me out of there. There was nothing wrong with me. It had all been a big mistake. I called Chris with the same message. I was surrounded by nutters and shouldn't be in there.

The next thing I was told was that they were moving me to TRC, the place next door. "What's that?" I asked. "This is just the drying-out place," I was told. "For rehab you need to go there."

I was just there for an evaluation to find out what was really wrong with me.

This was the Wednesday, the day before Thanksgiving. I was met by a couple of people, and all I could see were all these people bustling around with folders and things, looking very busy. I demanded to know what was going on. This was the last meeting before Thanksgiving, I was told. There were a hundred people together in a room who would all be going home afterwards. But not me. I was told I had to stay in until the Monday when I'd start my programme.

"But I don't need to be in here!" I shouted. "Why can't I go home and come back on Monday?"

They were insistent. "You need to stay here. We're going to observe you."

I was introduced to a fellow who was going to show me round. He was an anaesthesiologist, he explained, whose own addictions were black hookers and crack cocaine. He worked in a hospital and so had access to all the drugs he could want, but black hookers and crack was what turned him on. His thing was to disappear into the night, get a blow job and smoke some crack. And he was my tour guide!

> He was an anaesthesiologist, he explained, whose own addictions were black hookers and crack cocaine. He worked in a hospital and so had access to all the drugs he could want, but black hookers and crack was what turned him on. His thing was to disappear into the night, get a blow job and smoke some crack. And he was my tour guide!

I soon learned the form. We had to live together in these little apartments and there were so many rules to follow. It was totally alien to me. Since I'd been a kid I had followed my own rules. I'd lived on my own since I was sixteen and bought my own house when I was eighteen. I considered myself pretty savvy, and yet here were people telling me everything I could and couldn't do.

We had four days together in our apartment – myself, a Greek Orthodox priest who knew who I was, the hookers-and-crack fellow and one other. You were only allowed out in threes. You had to be back by a certain time. You had to go to meetings – either in the centre or anywhere there was an AA or Narcotics Anonymous meeting. They're pretty similar because if you're an alcoholic you're a drug addict and vice versa. I didn't like sharing an apartment with these other fellows. I'm pretty choosy about people to whom I open up. I know thousands of people but I'll only open up to a very few. That was even truer then.

I was at TRC for two weeks. Straight away I was put in two groups – primary care with a guy called Jim Weigel and a process group with another guy called Cliff. Between them, these two fellows were the only reason I didn't leave. I didn't want to be there, but Jim and Cliff made a lot of sense to me from the start. I liked what they had to say, I could talk to them and got on with them. They were the only two I connected with in there.

I was at TRC for two weeks. Straight away I was put in two groups – primary care with a guy called Jim Weigel and a process group with another guy called Cliff. Between them, these two fellows were the only reason I didn't leave. I didn't want to be there, but Jim and Cliff made a lot of sense to me from the start. I liked what they had to say, I could talk to them and got on with them. They were the only two I connected with in there.

I sat in groups all day. Everybody had a story. TRC was the place they sent anyone in the medical profession who'd screwed up. Doctors, dentists, surgeons, anaesthesiologists, the lot. There were also a number of lawyers and other white collar types – it was an expensive place. I felt I had nothing in common with any of them. Not only was I English and had never felt like I'd fitted in across the Atlantic anyway, but the fact that everyone else was a professional person felt like another reason I stood out. I was still polite with everyone, quiet and kept my manners.

After another week or so the guy addicted to black hookers and crack got caught out. He was allowed out every Friday to go to see a doctor in Atlanta. He could go out on his own and get a train into town. So he had saved up the pocket money his wife used to send him and would leave early so he could go and get a hooker and a bag of crack. He'd smoke the crack, get a blow job, go and see the doctor and be back at the centre in the afternoon.

This had been his Friday routine for nine months before he got caught. When anyone arrived at the centre they'd be given a colour. Mine was yellow. Every day they put up a different colour on a board. And if it's your colour, you do a drugs test. Different drugs spend a different amount of time in your system. Crack lasts three days – which meant this guy would only test positive on a Monday. By the Tuesday he would be clear. The only reason he had never been caught was just that his colour had never come up on a Monday. So his insurance company had been spending all this money on him while he'd been getting his regular Friday fix. He only got caught because he came back one Friday afternoon and fell asleep in a group. If that ever happened they took it very seriously and were immediately suspicious. After nine months that was the only way he got caught. And that was my introduction to rehab.

He only got caught because he came back one Friday afternoon and fell asleep in a group. If that ever happened they took it very seriously and were immediately suspicious. After nine months that was the only way he got caught. And that was my introduction to rehab.

After two weeks I'd made up my mind that I wasn't going to do any pills or drink any more. I couldn't stand being in the place. I was obviously taking too many pills but there was nothing really wrong with me. That's what I thought then, anyway. It was just a bad habit I'd gotten into. Then the doctor told me he'd recommend to the company that I take their full fourteen-week course.

I couldn't believe it. As far as I was concerned I was only supposed to be there for four days. The company wasn't going to agree to that, I thought. They needed me back at work. I couldn't see them paying only to keep me away for that long.

In fact the company was doing all it could to help me but I just couldn't see it. The doctor wanted me to stay in from that moment and continue with the therapy. But I had already booked to go back to England for two weeks and just wanted out. They said okay – but they warned me they'd be in touch with World Wrestling Federation. Then I was allowed to leave.

When I got home after my two weeks of evaluation, my mind was made up. I wasn't going to do any drugs. I wasn't going to drink. But it wasn't as easy as that. One night I was sat at home and my mind started again. "You know what you need? Some of that Renutrient. That's all right. It's not a drug, is it? You can buy it in a health food store. They wouldn't sell it in health food stores if it was a drug."

Never mind that I'd spent months locked in my bedroom on this stuff, scribbling out textbooks to stop world hunger. That was all forgotten about. "Helps you sleep, it does. Burns body fat, you know. Oh, it's so good for you. It's a wonder drug." So I went to the health store, bought myself a bottle and started drinking it in the car on the way home. I drank Renutrient all the time until we went to England.

> It wasn't long after we arrived at my mother-in-law's house that I drove to meet a drug dealer I knew and collected a bag of goodies. Valium, Nubain and another drug called Hypnoval – an injectable drug which puts you to sleep instantly. You inject it just under your skin and boom, you're out. Sounded like wonderful stuff to me. Go to sleep straight away? Oh, I needed that – I did.

It wasn't long after we arrived at my mother-in-law's house that I drove to meet a drug dealer I knew and collected a bag of goodies. Valium, Nubain and another drug called Hypnoval – an injectable drug which puts you to sleep instantly. You inject it just under your skin and boom, you're out. Sounded like wonderful stuff to me. Go to sleep straight away? Oh, I needed that – I did.

In the two weeks I was home I bought 500 10mg Valium and by the time I boarded the plane back to Atlanta all but a handful were gone. I'd swallowed the lot – an average of forty a day.

That was when the shit really hit the fan.

A couple of days before leaving for England, I'd had agent Gerry Brisco on the phone.

"Steve, you have got to go back into rehab."

"I don't need to go."

"Yes you do. You've got to. These doctors are professional people and they know what they're talking about. We paid for you to do this evaluation and now you can't keep your job with us unless you go into rehab for fourteen weeks."

"I can't do that, Gerry."

I would have signed my life away right then if I could have. Absolutely sworn that I'd never take another drug in my life.

"That's all over with, Gerry," I insisted. "I'm not going to do that any more. It was just a stage I was going through."

"Steve, you've got to go in. You're a drug addict and an alcoholic."

There was no arguing with him. They wanted me to go on December 28 but I wasn't having that. I wouldn't be back from England until January 2, so they said I had to go in on the fourth. I knew rehab was there when I went back, but I can't say my behaviour on that trip was one last determined blow-out. It's more that this was how I lived my life then, the normal thing to do. It was there and I had to do it – it was what I did every day.

At night I shot Hypnoval into myself to get sporadic sleep. Then Nubain all day and Valium on top. A handful of ten Valium before I could consider getting out of bed in the morning. A lot of staggering round the place. I'm not describing these amounts to show how tough I was. It should be clear to any reader by now that drugs are a mug's game. Anyone who tells you different is a mug too. If you use drugs recreationally then that's your business. But if you're addicted to drugs, if your life revolves around nothing but drugs and how to get them, then you're going to wind up dead.

I'm not bragging about what I took – I just want to show how sick I was. I hope it reads as a warning to others.

When I was conscious on this trip and staggering around like a monster, my wife would have nothing to do with me. She was sleeping downstairs, on a pull-out bed. No one else was speaking to me either – and for my part I was content to ignore them. I wandered aimlessly around Blackpool, bumping into old mates like Peter, Stuart and Glen. They've all told me since how shocked they were by the sight of me. When I went out drinking, people were horrified to see the state I was in.

Glen sat me down in a pub one night, demanding to know what was wrong with me. I told him I was screwed up on painkillers and pills, but that I would be checking into rehab shortly. He was seriously concerned. One of his mates had seen me out on the street and called Glen at home, saying his pal was falling over, effing and blinding in front of everyone. Glen knew that wasn't the real me.

Peter was equally horrified, as was his wife Karen, whom I'd actually introduced to Peter a few years before. All these people I'd known for so long were desperately worried about me but I was completely unaware of their distress. I've only realised it since, when they've told me how they felt.

I couldn't understand why I felt so tired all the time. So I bought wraps of speed – amphetamine sulphate – off people on the street and in pubs.

> **"Speed, that's what I need. That'll pick me up, of course it will." It's a wonder my heart didn't explode with all the speed, Valium and painkillers I was swallowing.**

At night I would hide in the bedroom at my mother-in-law's, only poking my head into the living room once or twice. Sometimes I'd wander to the off licence at the end of the road, where I'd buy bottles of booze and sit out in the back alley, guzzling Valium washed down with Hooch.

I'd hit rock bottom, as bad as it was ever going to get.

On Christmas Day I struggled down into the living room. I was completely out of it, wondering why everyone was staring at me. The kids were opening their presents, and I opened mine from

Chris. But I hadn't bought her anything for Christmas. It had never even crossed my mind. It was horrendous. Horrendous for them, not me – I was oblivious to all the hurt I was causing.

The plan had been for us to drive down to my dad's on Boxing Day. But Chris, not unreasonably, was refusing to spend any time with me at all, or to let me take the kids. So two days earlier I had phoned my dad and tried to break the news that I had a drug problem. I've no idea how it came across. It was a world he knew nothing about and this was the first he'd heard that I was in it up to my neck. But I had to come clean to explain why he wouldn't be seeing his daughter-in-law and his grandchildren. On Christmas Eve I broke my father's heart. It's very hard for me now even to think about it.

I vaguely remember the looks on people's faces as I staggered around the town. I vaguely remember being sat at my mother-in-law's. Some of the family were mad at me. Some were just bewildered by it all. I had turned all these poor people's lives upside down. That's the thing with being an addict. It's not just yourself you're damaging. You're affecting everyone you come into contact with. You make everyone else sick because you're dragging them into your problems. And if you deny that you're fooling yourself.

It took me six hours to drive the 120 miles from Blackpool. I could have killed 100 people on the roads, the state I was in. All I know about the journey was that when I got to my dad's house I had a bag full of cassette tapes with me that I hadn't had when I set out. I must have bought them at a service station on the way, though I had no recollection at all of having done so.

My dad opened his front door to see this terrible wreck on his doorstep. I dread to think what it must have done to him. People I'd grown up with – my godparents son Adrian, my cousin Graham – tried to talk to me while I was there about the mess I was in and what I was doing to myself, but I wasn't having any of it. I'd knocked everyone for six and they were all worried sick about me. My godfather Trevor and his girlfriend drove me back to Blackpool in my car, while my dad came up with my step-sister and brother-in-law to see Chris and the kids.

I vaguely remember the looks on people's faces as I staggered around the town. I vaguely remember being sat at my mother-in-law's. Some of the family were mad at me. Some were just bewildered by it all. I had turned all these poor people's lives upside down. That's the thing with being an addict. It's not just yourself you're damaging. You're affecting everyone you come into contact with. You make everyone else sick because you're dragging them into your problems. And if you deny that you're fooling yourself.

We flew back on 2 January. That was the flight I spent in a haze of gin, since I'd used up all my Valium.

When we got home I went straight up to my bedroom and locked myself in again.

13

Getting Better

On January 4, 1999, I checked myself in at the TRC. Fourteen weeks there was not an appealing prospect. I was back in the familiar system, though in a different apartment with different people. For the first few weeks I wasn't aware of anything. My head was still messed up and my system was still full of drugs. I wanted to run away every single second. For every waking moment I was thinking about how I could get away from there. I was going through the groups but can't remember anything about what we did in them. I rang

Bruce Prichard and Gerry Brisco all the time, pleading with them to get me out.

After three weeks, the doctors pulled me into an office for a conference call with Bruce and Gerry. The doctors had told them I wasn't getting it, they said. I was full of denial. "Yeah, I'm getting it. It's just that everyone is against me." Obviously not true, but a few things were starting to get through my thick skull. My head was clearing up and the drugs were leaving my system. Through the groupwork I started to realize little bits of what I had been doing and how it had ruined my life.

This was how it worked. We started off at 8.45 a.m. with a spiritual group in which everyone talked about their beliefs. Not my thing at all. Then at nine everybody on campus went into one big hall to listen to someone tell their story – what they call the First Step. You have to give five answers to various questions on your addiction – five ways it affected your finances, five ways it affected your social life, your work and so on. Five different preoccupations you had – what you were doing to get your drugs when you should have been doing something else. Five different ways you tried to stop using drugs or cut back, if you ever did.

This was how it worked. We started off at 8.45 a.m. with a spiritual group in which everyone talked about their beliefs. Not my thing at all. Then at nine everybody on campus went into one big hall to listen to someone tell their story – what they call the First Step. You have to give five answers to various questions on your addiction – five ways it affected your finances, five ways it affected your social life, your work and so on. Five different preoccupations you had – what you were doing to get your drugs when you should have been doing something else. Five different ways you tried to stop using drugs or cut back, if you ever did.

These added up to an hour's worth of your life story – or your drugs story, at any rate. Some had been doing it their whole lives. By this time I had been doing it for five years. Someone had to read out their story every day and when they finished everyone else got to rip it to pieces. Or rather, to call them on the bullshit. Others might say how they identified with something in the story. At the end one of the counsellors got to say their piece and gave it a pass or a fail.

After four weeks I'd written my own story down. It passed with flying colours, which meant I was allowed home on a weekend pass. After the Saturday morning group I would be let out, and was due back on Sunday night. Two weeks after that I would get a day pass which meant a whole Sunday at home, followed by another weekend pass two weeks later.

The most important part of the therapy for me was writing down everything I'd done. Gradually I understood how I'd affected myself and everyone else around me. I finally started to think that maybe everyone else had been right all along. So I got on with the programme and worked hard.

This was brilliant news. I could go home. I'd only been away for a month but it had felt like forever.

When I saw Chris, I expected everything to be okay again. I wanted her to say: "You're doing this, everything's fine again." Of course it wasn't.

She was sceptical. She'd heard me say too many times how I would never touch drugs again, only to go back on my word. She was reserved, waiting to see if the programme would work.

Soon I was back again and the following week Chris agreed to come to what they call Family Week. She came to all these classes and lectures with me and started taking some interest in my programme. I had buckled down to my work and my mind was made up. No more drugs and no more drink.

The most important part of the therapy for me was writing down everything I'd done. Gradually I understood how I'd affected myself and everyone else around me. I finally started to think that maybe everyone else had been right all along. So I got on with the programme and worked hard.

After six weeks I started doing something called MI – Mirror Image. Every morning, instead of going to a group, we were sent out to other treatment centres. In my case, I went with two others to a place in Atlanta which worked with kids off the streets. Many of them had a drug problem, many had been abused and a lot were living rough. If they got into trouble they were brought to this centre.

> I hated the idea that you were supposed to inform on your fellow patients if they broke the rules. It was totally alien to the way I had grown up and I would not do it. You do not grass on your mates.

I liked working there. I wouldn't want to do it for a living but it did me good to sit with these kids and hear how bad they had things. Their stories were tough. There were twelve- and thirteen-year-old girls who'd got into prostitution to pay for drug habits. There were kids out of street gangs. Being with them helped me a great deal.

There was one particular young lad called Xavier with whom I connected. He knew who I was. That was a big thing for me. He'd seen me on TV in WCW and wanted to know what I was doing there. So I had to tell him the truth. "I'm here because I'm a drug addict. This is part of my rehab programme." He was about fourteen and seemed like a real smart kid who'd just got caught up in a bad scene, as plenty of young people do. I think about him and I really hope he's doing well.

Five days a week I was there with the kids, then back to the centre for my regular groups. Soon ten weeks had gone by and I'd kept my head down and got on with my work.

Having to go everywhere in threes was one of the centre's rules. The idea was that if there are three of you and one is trying to persuade the others to fall off the wagon, there's more chance that someone else will be the voice of reason. I'm not sure if that's true but that is the way they did it.

I hated the idea that you were supposed to inform on your fellow patients if they broke the rules. It was totally alien to the way I had grown up and I would not do it. You do not grass on your mates. I felt as though it meant everyone in the centre was watching me, just waiting for me to slip up. And for all my hard work, I still disliked having to do everything together. We lived four to an apartment. They'd give us a voucher for so much money and we had to go out and shop together. We had to cook our meals together. I found all that very difficult. I understand why they wanted us to do it and I did it, but it was very strange to me.

Sometimes we would be walking around the local supermarket and someone would recognize me. But it was straight back to earth when I remembered what I was doing and why I was there.

In the ten weeks I'd been there I had been through a lot of stuff. The four weeks left were basically tidying-up time. I'd got on with all the work and thought I was doing really well. I thought a light bulb had switched on over my head and I was getting the message. Not so fast, though – I soon learned this was not the case.

One day the other two fellows who went with me to the treatment centre couldn't go. They weren't there when I went to pick them up, so I was allowed out on my own. I drove to the centre alone in my car, did my work there and left at lunchtime to drive back. As soon as I got in the car my head started playing with me again. "You know, you'll be going back to work soon. You still haven't been sleeping well, all the time you have been here. In ten weeks, the most sleep you've had straight is an hour-and-a-half. How are you going to manage when you go back on the road? You know how tired you get.

"Do you know what works? That Renutrient. You can buy it in a health store. Must be good for you. No one could have a problem with that. It works for you, puts you to sleep. Does all these wonderful things for you."

It didn't take me long to convince myself. So, as incredible as it may seem, I drove over to a health food store and bought myself a bottle. I had been telling myself I needed a good night's sleep, but I actually had that afternoon off. So I thought a little drink would bring a good sleep in the afternoon. Of course by the time I had bought it, the idea had snowballed to me guzzling it in the car on my way back to the centre. And the intention had changed from a nice afternoon nap to a lovely little afternoon buzz.

When I got back I had to report to one of the doctors. I went into

The next thing I knew, I was sitting naked on the couch in the front room of the apartment surrounded by people and ambulance men. I hadn't a clue what had happened. The next memory is of waking up in hospital with tubes in me. "What the hell's going on here?" I thought. I lay in a haze for a while, fell asleep and woke up again. I pieced together what I'd done. And then the strangest thing happened.

his office and he didn't spot that I'd taken anything. I went back to my apartment, drank some more and got into bed. Nothing seemed to happen – at any rate, I didn't go to sleep.

The next thing I knew, I was sitting naked on the couch in the front room of the apartment surrounded by people and ambulance men. I hadn't a clue what had happened. The next memory is of waking up in hospital with tubes in me. "What the hell's going on here?" I thought. I lay in a haze for a while, fell asleep and woke up again. I pieced together what I'd done. And then the strangest thing happened.

I'm not a religious man in any way. If that's your thing, good luck to you, but it's not for me. Yet what happened next was extraordinary. A feeling swept through me like a warm wave. It washed

right over me. And I absolutely knew that was it. I lay there and I knew the truth. I was not going to touch any more drink or drugs ever again.

I finally realized the simple lesson. Every time I did it, my life turned to shit. I knew now I wasn't going to do it any more. And I've felt exactly the same every single moment from that day to this.

People have often said how tough it must be going back on the road, how hard I must find it. Yet from that moment onwards it hasn't been hard at all. There have been times since then when I've been around drugs or seen people doing them and it doesn't interest me one little bit. It has never been hard. I don't have cravings, I haven't struggled, I don't even think about it.

> I have no idea what caused my moment of revelation. I'd just had enough. I had got to the point where I didn't want any more misery. I lay there on that bed and thought to myself: "It doesn't matter what happens from now on."

The only problem I had for a while was what they call using dreams, when I woke up convinced I'd been taking drugs again. I'd wake up feeling guilty, drenched in sweat and full of panic for a second or two before I realized it had only been a dream. Then that warm, grateful feeling would come over me again. I still have the dreams, though thankfully they're a lot rarer these days.

That's the way it's been for me ever since. I'm one of the lucky ones. A lot of people don't get to that stage, and struggle with their addictions for their entire lives. Other people I've met got to the same stage as me and simply said: "That's it."

I have no idea what caused my moment of revelation. I'd just had enough. I had got to the point where I didn't want any more misery. I lay there on that bed and thought to myself: "It doesn't matter what happens from now on."

I knew the company would fire me as soon as they found out about my latest relapse. But everything was going to be okay. I knew that whatever happened to me from then on, I'd be sober and so could handle it. You can always blot problems out for a while using drink and drugs. But once you've sobered up the problem will still be there – and most likely has got a lot worse. The best thing about being off drugs? Not waking up every morning wondering to whom I owe an apology. Not worrying about what havoc I've caused, in what messes I've landed myself and others.

> **And my family has got me back. There is only one thing I want out of life now and I don't care about anything else. It's that when I die, all I want them to be able to say is that I died sober. That's the only legacy I want to leave.**

Whatever happens in life now, I know I can handle it. I can take a deep breath, stop and sort things out. Before, my life was total and utter chaos. It was complete shit. I caused it all and whenever anything else happened on top of my antics it made everything a thousand times worse. There's no problem so big you can't get round it. I've had a few since that day and I've been able to deal with all of them. It never feels as bad.

And my family has got me back. There is only one thing I want out of life now and I don't care about anything else. It's that when I die, all I want them to be able to say is that I died sober. That's the only legacy I want to leave. My kids knew how bad I was. Daniel and Dane experienced the worst of it. Bailey, my youngest, will be told as he gets older and will be able to read this book. I really don't know how it affected the older two. We've had the odd little problem with them since then, but what happened is an open subject in our house now and I have never hidden away from it. I hope it will serve as an example to them of the dangers of drugs for when they grow up. But I want them all to be able to think that for the majority of their lives, I was a sober man. That's all that matters to me now. That I die sober.

Back then though, all these fine feelings were in the future.
I knew I'd never do drugs again. But no one else knew that this time I meant it. I still had to face all the trouble I was in. I was picked up from the hospital and put back in the Anchor, the nuthouse. This time I was in there for seven days, but it was okay – I knew I was being punished for what I had done.

It was a horrible place to be, but I just got on with things. Only this time, I realized what I must have been like the first time I was in there, because everyone else was exactly the same. They were all telling stories and lying about how they didn't need to be in there. But by now I was able to call them on their lies, because I could see things in a different way. I'd tell them: "Look. Stop making excuses and get on with it."

Easy to say for me of course – I'd come out the other side. I know it's hard when you're going through it. But I have little tolerance these days for people who make excuses for their drug failings. I won't listen to anyone's bullshit any more. I know because I've spouted it just like the rest of them.

> One of the counsellors told me: "We knew you had one left in you. We'd rather you do it while you're in here rather than on the outside." I often wonder whether it wasn't deliberate that those two other fellows couldn't come with me that day and I was allowed out on my own.

"I have to tolerate pain in my job. I've got a bad back. I'm homesick. I can't sleep. Life on the road is tough." All complete bullshit. I can understand people when they say stuff like that and I can empathize with it but I'm not going to stand for it.

"I know what you've been through, I've done it myself," I say. "This is what you are. A drunk and a junkie. You've got to do whatever it takes to sort yourself out because otherwise your life is going to remain shit." After my week in the Anchor I was allowed back in the centre, and expected I'd have to start the whole fourteen-week course again but I didn't. They could see I was doing good work and that something had clicked inside me. One of the counsellors told me: "We knew you had one left in you. We'd rather you do it while you're in here rather than on the outside." I often wonder whether it wasn't deliberate that those two other fellows couldn't come with me that day and I was allowed out on my own.

In my first week back on campus I was called to the main office where a couple of counsellors said there was a conference call waiting for me. It was Gerry Brisco and Bruce Prichard and they got straight to the point. "Sorry, but we've got to let you go."

It was totally the right thing to do. They stressed: "It doesn't mean the door is closed. Go and sort out your life and you are welcome back." It was hardly a great surprise. I thanked them for all they'd done for me. We left on friendly terms. And I was okay with it.

Chris, however, was not. I'd called her the day after I went back to the Anchor to tell her about my latest relapse. She didn't want anything to do with me and was refusing to speak to me. That was the hardest thing I had to deal with. I knew it would be all right in the long run because whatever happened, I was not going to do any more drugs or drink. In the short term, though, it was hard. She'd heard me say these things so many times before. Now, for the first time, it was rock solid in my head.

I came out of rehab on Saturday, April 14, 1999. And wondered what to do next.

14

Back in the Ring

I didn't know what I was going to do for employment. Luckily we had some money stashed away while I tried to think of the next step. I wanted to try Paul Heyman's Extreme Championship Wrestling in Philadelphia. I thought it would be the perfect environment to reinvent myself, get away from the Lord character and do something new.

I called them and never heard back. I also called Diamond Dallas Page at WCW and asked him if there was any chance he could sort me out with a job. He said he'd do what he could. Things were bad. I didn't know where my next pay cheque was coming from and had no idea how I was going to support my family. Chris had had enough and wanted to go back to England. She thought we wouldn't be able to support ourselves. I kept saying something would come up and we'd be okay. We've always been like that anyway – I say the glass is half full, she says it's half empty.

> Things were bad. I didn't know where my next pay cheque was coming from and had no idea how I was going to support my family. Chris had had enough and wanted to go back to England.

Six weeks after getting out of rehab, things were looking serious. ECW wasn't returning my calls. Then I got a call from Dave Penzer, a WCW ring announcer. He'd been driving in a car with Eric Bischoff who had asked him about me, since Dave lived nearby. Dave told him what I'd been through. Eric told him: "I've always liked Steve. Tell him to give me a call."

So I did, and was told to go to his office. All kinds of things had been going on in WCW since I'd been away. Eric had gone and come back and now business was on a big downslide. "You've done what you needed to do," said Eric. "Yes, you can have a job." Whatever anyone else says, I can only say good things about Eric. He always looked after me when I did the right thing. When I was a waste of time he did the right thing by getting rid of me.

Now he'd given me a job, I started going down the Power Plant again to train. A lot of the other lads I was training with have gone on to better things, and some of them are in WWE today. I enjoyed the training but physically I was still in a state. In the previous five or six years I had put my body through hell. The year before, I had been seriously unwell and still hadn't fully recovered from that.

The training was good, though. The younger wrestlers picked my brains and I've always enjoyed that. When I was learning the game plenty of people took time to teach me – Marty Jones, Robbie Brookside, Tony St Clair, Fit Finlay, Johnny South and Terry Rudge. If it wasn't for them I wouldn't be where I am. Because of that I've always tried to help people who've wanted to be helped. If they have a genuine interest in this business then I'll help anybody.

I still hadn't signed a contract, however, and for a month I trained at the Power Plant without getting paid. I was just happy to be going there so I could get in some sort of shape again. I was still heavy and my body felt like mush. Every last bit of muscle had gone. I was training the youngsters and training myself at the same time. When younger guys asked me questions, I had to delve into my memory banks and remember all the things I'd stopped doing myself, so it was really helpful.

I signed a WCW deal in the second week of June and eventually started again on TV. On my first night back I was put with Dave Taylor and Fit Finlay. They were having a match when I did a run-in and we were a group again. We were doing tags and things and it was good to be back. But the state of WCW's business was a massive shock. The difference between when I left and when I came back was enormous. Most of the crowds had disappeared, and the organisation was worse than it had ever been before.

I was just grateful to have a job again and regular pay cheques coming in. I was still struggling physically. Sometimes I'd feel all right, sometimes I'd be bad for quite a while. I was slowly getting better though – and I started training properly again. From the time I came out of rehab it took a long time for me to feel some benefit from training, but it was definitely worth it.

Working away that summer was fun. It was great to be back with Dave and Fit again. But not long after the three of us started, Fit got the injury which would end his career in the ring. He went through a table in a Hardcore match. The table broke and went through his leg. It cut all the major nerves and has left him with one leg that's not much use any more since it's dead from the knee down. You'd never know it to see him, which just shows the sort of fellow he is. He's never given into it and kept going – he's a good WWE agent today. WCW did that to him by providing poor equipment – formica tables. Going through any table is bad enough but formica breaks just like glass. The wound on his leg looks like a shark bite.

Then in September more bad news came. Vince Russo was taking over WCW. My one and only show for him was his first night in, a *Thunder* show in San Diego. A bunch of us were called into the office by Arn Anderson – an agent there then who now does the same for WWE.

> **He said: "Lads, I'm very, very sorry to have to put this to you. But this is exactly what I've been told to say by Vince Russo. You are all in an on-the-bubble battle royal. It means you're all on the bubble to getting fired. Whoever wins it will keep his job and the rest of you will lose your jobs. And we want Chavo Jr. to go over."**

> **We all looked at each other. "Is it for real?"**

> **Arn said: "I don't know."**

> **All I know is that Chavo Jr. won, Chavo stayed and everybody else got fired over a period of time.**

I don't know how you can do that to people. From that night onwards I was never on a single show that Vince Russo had anything to do with. The only TV work I did was the Saturday night TV tapings which were run by Jimmy Hart. Russo had nothing to do with them and so, once every two weeks I turned up to do those. Russo wouldn't return any of my calls, wouldn't have anything to do with me and wouldn't even get me into his office to say he wasn't going to use me. He didn't even have the backbone to face me and say I was out. He was the same with everyone else.

> **Russo wouldn't return any of my calls, wouldn't have anything to do with me and wouldn't even get me into his office to say he wasn't going to use me. He didn't even have the backbone to face me and say I was out. He was the same with everyone else.**

Just before Christmas 1999 Dave Taylor – who'd also been in that battle royal – came to tell me he'd been let go with no explanation. I spent the whole Christmas not knowing what was going on. I was getting guaranteed money every week and working every two weeks for Jimmy, but that was all. Despite all that, we had a wonderful family Christmas – a real contrast to the year before. Chris's mum and dad came over, as did her sister Kerensa and my niece Kelsey, and we had a real good time. Dave came over with his wife and we saw in the millennium in our house.

In January we still had no idea what was going on. I was obviously concerned but I thought something would turn up – it always had before. There was special cause for optimism too – I'd stayed drug-free since my relapse on March 12 the year before. I'd been clean and sober ever since.

In February came the inevitable call – from JJ Dillon again. "Steve, I'm sorry but we're going to have to let you go."

"Why's that, JJ?" I asked, knowing the answer I'd hear.

"You're not working enough days for the money we're paying you."

"That's not my fault, JJ. I'm ready to work but Vince Russo won't have me on the shows. He won't even talk to me so how can you say that?"

"That's just the way it is, Steve – I'm very sorry."

It wasn't JJ's fault and I didn't bear him any ill will – he'd always been good to me.

I put the phone down and wondered what to do. I was embarrassed to call World Wrestling Federation, considering all I had put them through before. But there was nothing else for it.

I called Paul – Triple H – to say: "Look, I'm totally clean and sober. I've got a lot more left in me. Whatever's needed, I'll do it. Just give me a chance, I know I can do it." He said he'd call back and within ten minutes he did, saying he'd spoken to Vince and yes, I could have a job. Someone would be in touch over the next couple of days.

I was surprised. One thing I had done when I came out of rehab was to sit down and write Vince McMahon a letter. It thanked him for what he had done for me. I know that Vince and his family saved my life. There's no question about it. If I had carried on the way I was going, I would be dead by now. It was just a short thank you note – not sucking up to him, just honest gratitude. He sent me a letter in reply. It read: "The door of opportunity is always open for you at the World Wrestling Federation." When I'd made that call I half-hoped he meant what he said. I wasn't sure he did. It was still less than a year since I'd been fired so spectacularly.

But Vince was as good as his word. Bruce Prichard and Jim Ross called me to lay down the law. Theirs was a very simple message. No more messing about. I understood, I told them. Whatever they wanted me to do, I'd do it. I just wanted the opportunity to prove I was good to go. Once again though, I had the problem of WCW's four-month no-compete clause. I knew it wouldn't stand up in Georgia but I didn't want to have to go to court – the company had put themselves out to sort it once before, after all. But JJ Dillon was good enough to say he knew I hadn't done anything wrong and sent me a letter clearing me to work for whomever I wished.

I finished getting paid by WCW on the last day of February 2000 and I started getting paid by the company the following day. Bruce Prichard and Jim Ross told me about a development territory in Memphis where they wanted me to go. I would be there for six months, I was told, and then I'd be brought up. That's exactly what happened. I started in Memphis on March 7. I drove to Tunica in Mississippi, which is where Memphis Championship Wrestling ran its TV shows from a casino. It was nice to see Bruce there. By now I was 255 pounds, training well and in the best shape I'd been in years.

I knew a couple of the other wrestlers in Memphis. Blue Meanie was one, Reckless Youth another. I wrestled Blue Meanie on my first night in. The guy who ran it was Terry Golden, who became a good friend. Terry, his wife Michelle and son were all very good to me. Ring announcer David Jett became another good friend. I look back on those six months very fondly. I worked the shows – three of them a week – and helped out with the training.

The person in charge of the training at the time hadn't been doing too good a job, so I was told to organize it. At first we didn't even have a place to train and used an old ring out in the back garden of Buddy Wayne, an old wrestler. When I train anybody I never ask anyone to do anything without doing it myself. We trained hard – me and the guys I was teaching.

Some might think I'd have found it hard to start again at the bottom in Memphis. Nothing could be further from the truth. I absolutely loved it there. It was a fresh start and I had a good time. I got on well with Terry and David, and I was getting in better shape all the time, too. I wrestled Reckless Youth a lot, who liked my style. Between us we kept coming up with things I hadn't done in a long time. Training others also meant having to come up with new things all the time, so that made me think and work hard.

New faces arrived as well. The Mean Street Posse came – Joey Abs, Pete Gas and Rodney. Rodney and I hit it off and we palled up together. Then four young lads turned up who'd trained at Shawn Michaels' wrestling academy – Spanky, Lance Cade, American Dragon and Shooter Schultz. I took an immediate liking to the lot of them, but especially to American Dragon and Spanky. I could see something special in the pair of them. Both were great lads, full of respect, and it was an absolute pleasure to train with them. When you watched them in the ring they made you proud to be in the business. Good luck to them.

My schedule meant ten days working followed by three days off. While working I'd stay with Terry and his family then I'd come home for three days. Things at home were better and improving all the time. After what I'd put my family through, saying sorry simply doesn't cut it. I'd already said it a million times so now it meant nothing. You can only put things right by doing the right things. Actions count, not your words.

That year I also had to pay tribute to a good friend who had passed away – Brian Pillman. Brian had been wild and out there but we hit it off in WCW. We spoke regularly – at least once a week – until near the end when I was heavily into my drugs and sadly Brian had gone down the same path. He was not as lucky as I was. All the wrestlers who knew Brian were devastated, and determined to do something for his family. That something became the annual Brian Pillman Memorial show, which would see wrestlers flying in from all the different wrestling companies to give their services for free.

Some of my favourite wrestling memories are of being with Brian. Once you got used to his sense of humour he was very funny. In 1995 the two of us were asked to go to Universal Studios in Hollywood to present a video game award on this live TV bash. The hosts were Leslie Nielsen and Jonathan Taylor Thomas, who played the kid in *Home Improvement.*

The show was going out live on TBS after the channel's highest-rated show, *WCW Saturday Night,* which went out from six till eight. We flew in on Friday afternoon for the dress rehearsal and found ourselves surrounded by all these luvvie and darling types – the sort of phoney people I can't stand.

We were due to do a skit which would have Leslie Nielsen at the podium at the front of the stage talking about violence in video games while behind him would be me and Brian, dressed in our ring gear and playing a wrestling game on a big screen that would descend into the two of us brawling. Leslie was going to carry on deadpan – just like he did on *Naked Gun* and *Police Squad* – while we created all sorts of havoc behind him. The skit would end when Leslie drew a gun and fired it.

That was the plan, anyway. When we got there it soon became clear we were a tiny part of a big show. A producer flounced up and said: "This is what we're going to do, darlings. You and Brian will go on from there and do your fighting bit all over this set."

The set was like the side of a mountain, all rock work with steps going up it. "Okay," we said. "We'll go here, here and here," showing them what we were going to do. Brian was going to do a crossbody dive onto me, and the producer thought it was all wonderful.

"Great," he said. "That's about the time we'll bring on the juggling midgets."

My ears pricked up. I had unpleasant midget memories. "Midgets? You've got midgets?"

"Yes, one of them juggles and rides a unicycle while the other one just juggles. They are going to come on, run between your legs and kick you up the backside."

I moaned internally. It got worse, too. At the side of the stage were two dickhead bodybuilders, all long hair and full of

Brian Pillman was one of a kind.
Here he is with Steve Austin as
The Hollywood Blondes.

themselves. I thought they were part of some other segment. But no, it emerged they were to come over, pull Brian and me apart and throw us off the stage. Didn't like the sound of that. Brian, as ever, saw the opportunity to wind me up.

"Hang on a minute," he told the producer. "This show is only on because it follows our show, which gets the best ratings on this channel, so you can get some of its viewers to watch you. We are two of its stars and you want these two nobodies to throw us off the stage?" Brian had got the hook right into me. I wasn't as pleasant then as I am now. I piped up: "If those two wankers come anywhere near me I'll fucking kill them."

They looked terrified and shrank away. The producer looked concerned. "They'll have to go to talk to their agent about this," he said. By now Pillman had got me steaming mad and he was roaring with laughter. The upshot was we got rid of the bodybuilders but the juggling midgets would have to stay. Brian thought it would be funnier with them in, so I went along with it, albeit reluctantly.

After a dress rehearsal like that, Brian and I were ready for a good Friday night out. We opted for the Viper Room on Sunset Boulevard. On a night out with Brian, even the taxi ride there was memorable. Brian asked the driver to take us to a diner near the Viper Room. He seemed like a nice old fellow and we started talking – only for Pillman to begin mercilessly winding him up.

"You don't sound like you're from here," Brian began.

"No," said the cabbie. "Back east, New York."

"How long have you been here, then?"

"Oh, thirty years."

Brian paused thoughtfully, then said: "It must really bother you."

"What?" asked the driver, genuinely puzzled.

"Thirty years ago it must have been wonderful here with all the movie stars and the sunshine. Now look at it – winos and bums on every corner."

The guy thought for a second. "Yeah, you're right!" he agreed. Within five minutes Brian had this fellow pulling up at traffic lights, screaming at the top of his voice at the winos in the street, "Get a job, you bastards!" Pillman had turned our perfectly mild-mannered cabbie into a screaming lunatic. He absolutely went. "These bastards, they've ruined this town!" When he dropped us off, I told Pillman: "That poor guy is going to go out and start shouting at someone tonight and get himself shot."

The Viper Room wasn't really my thing. The interior was completely black and everyone inside was dressed in black, too. We were stood at the bar when a pale apparition glided past us with a big tall blonde on his arm. The apparition had white hair, a white suit and was soon dancing around the floor with a bottle of champagne in his hand, while the blonde had one, too. It was Tony Curtis.

> **"That's Tony Curtis!" I told Brian.**
>
> **"No, it's not," he said. He looked again and changed his mind. "Come on," he said. "Let's introduce ourselves."**
>
> **We went over and Brian slapped the dancing Tony Curtis squarely on the back.**
>
> **"Hi Tony! I'm Flyin' Brian and this is Lord Steven!"**

"Hi guys!" beamed Tony. He didn't seem to mind our intrusion; on the contrary he seemed glad that someone had recognised him. Brian and I went back to our side of the bar, where we stayed until 2 a.m. As we were leaving, a Corvette with its top down pulled up alongside us on the road. It was Tony, arm around the blonde, with another bottle of champagne in his hand. He said: "Hey Brian! Hey Steve!" and zoomed off up Sunset Boulevard. Those sorts of things just seemed to happen whenever Brian was around.

We had to do the show the next day at 5 p.m. West Coast time. As we went out and were introduced to all these dinner suits from the video game industry, you could tell the whole crowd had but a single thought. "Who the hell are these two?"

We started pushing and shoving and fighting each other. The

more we did, the more people laughed – and that wasn't the reaction we wanted. Pillman and I upped the stakes, knocking seven bells out of each other. I was chopping him red raw and he was chopping me back so hard there was blood coming out of my chest. We were kicking lumps out of each other in frustration, and all the audience could do was giggle. Did they not see how hard we were working? We were hitting each other as hard as we could. Afterwards we realized they were right to giggle – it was supposed to be a comedy spot. But Brian and I had got it into our heads that they should have been *oohing* and *aahing*.

> As we were leaving, a Corvette with its top down pulled up alongside us on the road. It was Tony, arm around the blonde, with another bottle of champagne in his hand. He said: "Hey Brian! Hey Steve!" and zoomed off up Sunset Boulevard. Those sorts of things just seemed to happen whenever Brian was around.

Then it was time for the juggling midgets. They ran between our legs. One went down on hands and knees behind me and Pillman shoved me over him. Then he picked up another midget and slammed him on top of me. I grabbed the midget and hoisted him, throwing him up into the wall at the back. It was horrible. All I wanted to do was crawl up my own backside and die. I kept pleading inside: "Please let this be over with."

We had to go over and fight in front of Leslie Nielsen, who'd pull out his gun and fire it, and then this fiasco would be over. We went to our places, he pulled his gun out, pulled the trigger and ... nothing. Not a sound. He put the gun back in his holster and said: "Bang, bang."

Brian and I looked at each other, shrugged our shoulders and walked off the stage. God, it was embarrassing. I jumped in the shower and was just cooling down when a very camp dancer minced in. He took one look at me and lisped: "Ooh. Isn't your chest red?" Pillman thought it was the funniest thing ever. That was Brian, the king of the wind-up merchants. Just like my mate Peter in Blackpool. Those two would really have hit it off.

So when I was told I would be wrestling Chris Benoit at Brian's memorial show in Cincinatti, Ohio I was honoured – and a little excited. By then I'd got myself into good shape and was ready to go. There were WCW guys there, WWE, ECW and independent guys from all over the country. It was a great atmosphere and a great show. A lot of people there hadn't seen me in years. When I had gone back to WCW business had fallen away so much that not many people had seen me wrestle there. All that most of them knew was that I'd had a drug problem and disappeared.

I was apprehensive, wondering how the fans would react to me. I knew Chris and I would go out and have a good match because we always did. But I couldn't believe the reaction I got when I went out to the ring. I knew we'd get them once we started wrestling, but I never expected a reception like that. I thought people would be groaning: "Oh, it's not Regal is it?" But it was the exact opposite. People were already cheering for me when I came out. Some people were surprised by how good that match was. I was heartened by that reaction, but the truth is it's the sort of match Chris and I always have when we get the chance. It's just that those chances are very rare.

> A lot of people there hadn't seen me in years. When I had gone back to WCW business had fallen away so much that not many people had seen me wrestle there. All that most of them knew was that I'd had a drug problem and disappeared.

The heat we got, the crowd response, was absolutely incredible. It just built and built and built. Everyone there was a knowledgeable wrestling fan, there to enjoy all the different styles of what we do. We gave them our hard-hitting style of match and they reacted. Chris beat me at the end and both of us were given a standing ovation. They were all chanting my name, even before the finish. It gave me a much-need confidence boost.

I'd been wrestling in front of small crowds in Memphis – an average of 100 and once just seven people. The only time we got decent crowds was at state fairs in Tennessee and Arkansas. It wasn't glamorous but I loved it all the same. It had got me back on the map and that night was one of those times that make you proud to be in the wrestling business.

Another battle against Chris Benoit.

Plenty of people thought that match was what got me back into the company. I don't mind if they do, but it's not the case. I'd been told I would be in Memphis for six months and, to the day, that's when I was brought up. They were in Nashville and it was my first night back. I was nervous as hell.

15

The Goodwill Ambassador

Backstage in Nashville, I knew I would have to face a lot of people who had seen me at my worst. I had no idea how anyone was going to react. But everyone was as nice as they possibly could be. They all said they were pleased to see me and it was good to have me back. Most of them knew the real me – they realized I wasn't a bad person but just someone who had had a serious problem for a while.

Mideon was there, whom I'd known as Tex Slazenger from my first days in WCW. Triple H, too. Eventually I saw Vince and went up to shake his hand. It was a nerve-wracking evening but it turned out better than I could have hoped.

I went the next day when they were in Memphis and they told me from then on they'd be bringing me to all the TV shows. But nobody really knew what I was going to do. I had a few ideas and so did the writers, but no one had quite figured the whole thing out. All I was told was to get myself a suit. I did that and had some pictures taken in it, but I still didn't know the reason why.

Then Jim Ross started me off wrestling at house shows on the weekends. I still hadn't been on TV and usually wrestled Mideon, so I could rid myself of the ring rust and get used to their big rings again. I was still going backwards and forwards from Memphis but was soon told I had finished there. That was a sad day – I had enjoyed Memphis. So I was back living at home, going to house shows and TV but still without an idea of what I was going to do.

Then one day in Phoenix, Vince called me into his office and laid out the plan. "You're going to be the goodwill ambassador. You're going to go out and wave and smile at people. You're going to tell them how to live their lives. You're going to tell the American people how to become more civilized. And they are going to hate you for it."

It was a brilliant idea. No one likes being lectured – and particularly not the Americans when it comes from a stuck-up Brit. They gave me the script for my first time on TV. I sat at a table inside the ring, showing the good people of Phoenix how to use a knife and fork. We did it there for *SmackDown!* but the show ran long so my bit wasn't broadcast. So the following Monday I did it live for *Raw*. I came out as Steven William Regal and made my debut as the goodwill ambassador. By now we'd added Chris Jericho to the skit. He came along during my little etiquette class and with one swipe cleared all the cutlery off the table which led to us two going at each other. As soon as we did that I knew the ambassador idea was going to work.

I found myself listed as William Regal. That was my new name, Shane McMahon explained – the company already had too many Steves. It was the same reason Max Crabtree had used for calling me Roy, so I was glad to get William. There were a couple of reasons. A name change suited me because I was starting afresh – one career

An altogether superior
class of person . . . The
Goodwill Ambassador.

was over and a new one was beginning. And William was the name of my grandfather, who'd got me into wrestling in the first place, and is also my son Daniel's middle name. It was a happy coincidence that they picked a name with so much family history for me.

After just two months, I came in to tape the Thanksgiving Day *SmackDown!* two days before the big day. My name was down in a match against The Rock. And the opening segment read, "Promo segment: Regal – Rock."

Up until then I'd done my goodwill ambassador bit and a few little things but now I was being thrown in the deep end to see if I could swim. I was given a ten-minute promo to learn an hour before we went out and did it. I hit it word for word. I'd never done anything with The Rock before but we interacted well. Then we had a match, which was fine.

From then onwards everyone has had more trust in me to do stuff. Every day I've been here in the WWE has been a good one for me. After what I've been through I'm lucky to be alive and every day is a bonus. Sometimes I'd like to be in a better position on the card; that's only human nature, and I would be lying to deny it, but I'm happy with what I do and where I am. At time of writing I have the most years on the job of just about any one of the current wrestlers. I've done every aspect of the job and enjoyed every one of them. After all I have been through I know I'm lucky to be where I am today.

It's not always been plain sailing, however. Even though I've done pretty much everything in our business there are still times when I doubt my own ability. I'm better about it now but that's why I don't read reviews of the shows or care too much what others say about them these days. Don't get me wrong, I care deeply about my performance. But I don't worry what someone else thinks if they're not one of the people whose good opinion matters to me.

Here's how I rationalize criticism to myself. I purposely go out there and make millions of people around the world hate me. So why should I be bothered when someone genuinely dislikes me? Or doesn't like how I wrestle, or what I do on TV?

But when I first got to WWE I had a lot of trouble with anxiety. No matter how fit I was, before going out for a big match my mind would be playing tricks with me. And the doubts would always be the same. "You're not going to be able to do this. You're going to blow up, you're not going to be able to get through it. Your wind's going to go, your legs are going to go. There's no way you'll be able to get through." Yet every time I have had those feelings, they disappear as soon as I walk through the curtain.

The nerves were just the same in my first encounter with The Rock. Thinking about what I had to do made me jittery as hell. But as soon as I got out there I was word perfect. Then when I came back to put my boots on for our match, the doubts started up again. "You're not going to be able to do this. He is The Rock, you know. No way." Yet I vividly remember being stood in the ring when The Rock's music hit and he walked out through the *SmackDown!* set. I was so calm I could have laid down in the ring and gone to sleep. My mindset had changed to: "Let's get on with this and get this done."

It was the same story when I had a main event strap match against Steve Austin. My mind was playing all sorts of tricks on me and we went out and tore the house down. All my experiences have taught me that the mind is a powerful thing. Nowadays I can take a step back and put my worries in perspective. I tell myself: "Don't be such a silly bugger. You're going to be fine. You always have before and you will be now." Once I tell myself that, I'm okay.

I've always had a great deal of anxiety and fear. Those feelings certainly played a part in trying to hide from life through drugs. It's surprising how far I've managed to come when always – and even more so in my early days – I've doubted my ability to succeed. Anybody who hasn't will probably think it's foolish. Now I don't worry so much. I don't worry at all on house shows – the only time I get nervous then is if I know my family or friends are there.

I was certainly nervous when I appeared in front of two of the biggest wrestling gates in history, *WrestleManias X-Seven* and *X8*. The first was at the Houston Astrodome before it was knocked

WrestleMania X-Seven.
Chris Jericho and I both
want that Intercontinental
Championship.

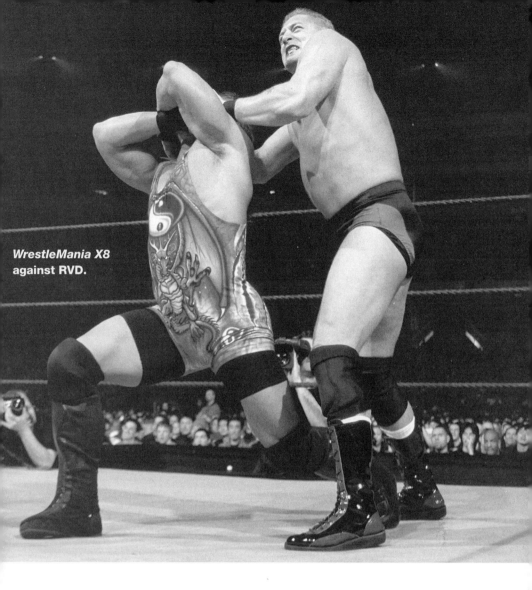

*WrestleMania X8
against RVD.*

down, when I wrestled Chris Jericho for the Intercontinental Championship in front of 67,925 people. Then the next year I took on Rob Van Dam, again for the Intercontinental title, at the Toronto Skydome with 68,237 watching.

I opened the show both times. Chris and I had done numerous angles, including him peeing in my tea. And both times I was more than a little overwhelmed. Usually, as soon as I walk out through the curtains, I am calm. But I can't say I enjoyed either of those matches until they were over. Particularly when you are opening

The Goodwill Ambassador 237

the show because you have the responsibility for setting the tone, I found it hard to relax. I didn't get the adrenalin rush until after, when the matches had gone well and I could sit back and enjoy the rest of the show.

I remember *'Mania X-Seven* well because Mötorhead were there, one of my favourite bands. It might sound strange coming from a Northern soul boy like me, but I've loved them since I was young, so it was great to hear them pumping out Triple H's ring music.

The other good thing about *WrestleMania* is the fan *Axxcess* we do beforehand. I've always enjoyed getting to meet the fans who've taken the time and trouble to come and see you. I don't understand people who want to rush through the signing sessions; I always take time to find out people's names, personalize their autographs and have a chat with them. People remember that – I certainly did when I was a kid getting autographs from my favourite wrestlers.

The *Axxcess* at *WrestleMania X8* felt like my first ever stand-up show. They had a ring set up and I was put in it with a microphone to take questions from the fans, who were all sat in bleacher seats. Some were serious, some you could have a laugh with and the whole thing was a blast. Illness meant I couldn't be at *WrestleMania XIX*. I watched it at home and thought it was a great show, one of the best I've seen from top to bottom. I was sad not to be there but I didn't sit around feeling sorry for myself. It just made me all the more determined to get fit and healthy enough to be on the show next year.

These days I feel like I can take on anything they throw at me. When I became the WWE commissioner I started doing skits with Tajiri, a brilliant wrestler they'd just brought in, who was playing my assistant. The sketches were so entertaining that they turned me into a good guy, a babyface. I wrestled house shows as a babyface and a few times on TV – but it's just not my thing. And I've never been a brilliant TV wrestler anyway. Getting a crowd riled up is more my style. Everybody seemed to like the Commissioner character and not one person said it was getting old – which is exactly why I thought the time was right to drop it. We can always go back to it later if needs be. Also, doing the character had limited my opportunities to wrestle.

Tajiri and I had great fun with our skits.

World Wrestling Entertainment draws more than its fair share of criticism. From some of the angles I've been in I know about this first hand. We'd had a big Pay-Per-View showdown between the two main factions at the time, World Wrestling Federation on one hand and a combined force of WCW and ECW on the other, who were invading the company. Of course I was on the evil side, and when they finally lost, the stipulation was that we'd all be off television.

So Vince had to think of a way to keep me on the show, and his solution upset a hell of a lot of people. Vince came to me in the afternoon before a show and told me his idea.

"What we're going to do is the Kiss My Ass club. You're going to have to get on your knees in the middle of the ring and kiss my ass to save your job."

The nerves were just the same in my first encounter with The Rock. Thinking about what I had to do made me jittery as hell. But as soon as I got out there I was word perfect. Then when I came back to put my boots on for our match, the doubts started up again. "You're not going to be able to do this. He is The Rock, you know. No way." Yet I vividly remember being stood in the ring when The Rock's music hit and he walked out through the *SmackDown!* set. I was so calm I could have laid down in the ring and gone to sleep. My mindset had changed to: "Let's get on with this and get this done." It was the same story when I had a main event strap match against Steve Austin. My mind was playing all sorts of tricks on me and we went out and tore the house down.

It sounded like fun, but Vince wasn't sure how real we should make it.

"What do you think? Should we actually do it? Or should we only tease that we are going to do it, and then I stop you and we hug each other?"

"No," I said. "Let's do the whole thing."

There were plenty of reasons why. Firstly, it made a lot of sense because I was about to have a hard-hitting programme with Edge. I wanted a reason to be as mad and as aggressive as I knew I was going to have to be, and there's nothing like being humiliated to make someone mad. I thought this was the perfect excuse. And I was totally at ease with actually doing it. I can look anyone in the eye and tell them I have never kissed anyone's backside to get a job. I've stayed in work by being good at what I do, being polite and professional. It's one reason I stayed in work so long when I was heavily into my drugs – because people knew what I had been like before.

In the ring I'm a villain, a heel, and here was something I knew everyone would hate me for doing. It certainly got people talking and will be replayed time and again – it means we can always show it again for any particular storyline. And kissing Vince's bum in the middle of the ring was no big deal. Some people have said to me: "That was a bit strong." Do they not get what I do?

It's interesting that a lot of wrestling's critics slag it off because it is scripted. But when we do something like that, it suddenly becomes all too real for those same critics. No one seemed to think I was acting a part anymore. The ones who reacted most strongly against it are the people who could recognize themselves in it; who suck up to their bosses in real life.

And they also fail to understand that I myself didn't kiss anyone's backside. William Regal, the character I play on TV, did but Darren Matthews didn't. William Regal is a double-snide, no-good bastard who would do everything that I would never do in my real life. He will snivel, grovel, suck up to the boss, hit women, anything. I play a character on a television show no different from any other villain on TV. My role just happens to include wrestling as well. When I'm

My showgirl outfit certainly turned some heads.

not at work, I'm not William Regal. I'm a husband and a father. I don't care about making a false impression on people just to be liked – as you can probably tell from this book. If you don't like me, fine. All that matters to me is whether the people I care about like me.

On another occasion we were doing *Raw* in Las Vegas and William Regal had to dress up as a Vegas showgirl for a match with Goldust. The storyline was that Regal hated it, and was horrified to be so humiliated. In reality, nothing could have been further from the truth. I had a real blast doing it. I threw in bits from all my old comedy favourites – Hilda Baker, Les Dawson, Larry Grayson – and thought it was hilarious. But one of the wrestlers asked me afterwards: "Didn't you mind doing that?"

He didn't appear to understand that when we get into that ring, we're playing a part. The guys like myself, Kurt Angle and Eddie Guerrero who will do things like this are comfortable with ourselves; we don't feel the need to prove we are tough guys.

Some people say our TV shows are too violent and too sexy for children to watch. Every parent has to make up their own minds about what their children should and shouldn't see on TV. If you don't think it's right for them then don't let them watch – it's that simple. If my children want to watch it then I let them, because they know the difference between right and wrong. They've had to learn the hard way that drugs, for example, are harmful, because they've seen me living with the consequences. But as with any television, it's up to parents to be responsible about it. Watch it with them and tell them the difference between right and wrong. Tell them it's wrong for a man to hit a woman. Or if you see us swearing, tell them that's wrong too.

As far as other critics go, the remedy is simple. If people don't like what we do then they should reach for the off button. Life is too short to spend your leisure time watching something you hate and moaning about it. Do something else instead.

Life as a professional wrestler is a privilege. But it's not easy. We're on the road four days a week, which can be hard. Take one week from 2002 as an example.

We flew on the Friday from Atlanta, near my home, to Washington D.C. for a house show that night at the MCI Center. From there I drove to New York in a rented minivan and the next night we wrestled another house show at Madison Square Garden. The following night we were at the Mohegan Sun casino in Connecticut. Then Monday night was a live *Raw* in Manchester, New Hampshire. On Tuesday morning I flew home, had Wednesday and Thursday off and was back away again on Friday.

If we're further afield, I usually get a red-eye flight back to Atlanta to arrive on Tuesday morning. When I do have time at home, I have to fit training in with spending time with my family. I have lots of training gear in my basement so I can do my workout without leaving home, meaning more time with the kids.

I also have to feed my lizards, which have been a lifelong love of mine. I've had a fascination with reptiles for as long as I've wanted to be a wrestler.

I got my first snake when I was about nine. I answered an advert in *Exchange and Mart* and it came through the post in a box. I opened it up and inside was a plastic bag full of moss with a snake curled up at the bottom of it – an Italian dice snake. That was the

I love all my reptiles. Nick Dinsmore (Eugene) and referee Chris Kaye don't look quite so sure.

start, and over the years I've had all kinds of reptiles. Nowadays I keep large lizards – a water monitor, a giant tegu, iguanas and some boas and pythons. I've a room in the basement for all my pets. Like wrestling, it's a passion I've stuck with all through my life.

In other weeks the travelling is even more arduous. The week before that stint I was in California which can throw you off a bit with the time difference. The 3,000 miles to California means having to deal with time zones. I've done shows in Washington state, which takes longer to fly to from my base in Atlanta than if I was flying to England. When we're on the west coast of Canada it takes a whole day to get home.

There's a great deal of flying and that means endless security checks to go through – more so after September 11. That can be a hassle when you hold one of the WWE titles. There are a lot of wrestling fans in Atlanta, so when my Intercontinental, European or Tag title belts have shown up in my baggage on the X-Ray machine, the staff often want to get them out, have a good look and hold them aloft for their friends. It's nice that they're interested but it soon becomes a pain when it happens every time and there's still a long trip ahead. I was almost glad when Spike Dudley won the European title off me.

So travel is the hardest thing, along with putting up with other people's incompetence. Little things matter more when you run into them so often. Like the hotel room not being ready, or the rental car not being there when I go to pick it up. All these minor hassles cut into my time, which is a very limited resource on the road. There's only so much time in a day and I have to get to where we're going, get food, get to the gym and quite often get to personal appearances we have to make. It usually happens that I get one day when everything goes wrong. These days, I'm able to take a step back and tell myself to stop moaning and get on with it. I have become more mellow and calmer as I've got older.

One reason we find the travel a grind is because there is no off-season for wrestlers, a fact many people don't realize. They don't know we work hard over 200 dates a year. In 2002, for example, I did 146 matches, and was at many more shows than that.

If it hadn't been for one or two little injuries it would have been even more. A week off is a very rare luxury. And we certainly don't want to miss Monday night's TV so a week off is never a full week anyway. In 2002 Chris and I went away from a Tuesday to a Sunday and it was only the second real break we'd had together without the kids – just the two of us on our own. The other had been a weekend in New York – and that had been because I was working there at the time.

There's a great deal of flying and that means endless security checks to go through – more so after September 11. That can be a hassle when you hold one of the WWE titles. There are a lot of wrestling fans in Atlanta, so when my Intercontinental, European or Tag titles have shown up in my baggage on the X-Ray machine, the staff often want to get them out, have a good look and hold them aloft for their friends. It's nice that they're interested but it soon becomes a pain when it happens every time and there's still a long trip ahead. I was almost glad when Spike Dudley won the European title off me.

But the way I came into this job we were taught to accept the hours, the travelling and all the little annoyances and get on with it. Anyone who doesn't like it should get another job. At the moment the coin's not bad either, though there have been plenty of times when it has been dreadful.

I feel privileged to do what I do. People come and pay their money to watch me and the rest of the crew perform. They might like it; they might not. But I still have to go out and give them all I can every single time. It doesn't matter if I've had a bad travel day, or if I'm hurt, or I just don't feel like it. Some nights are difficult. Sometimes when I put my feet in my boots and start to lace them up it feels like I'm at the foot of Mount Everest facing a long, impossible climb. That's when I have to take a step back and think about my life. I'm doing something that most people out there will never get the chance to – a job I love. And for millions of them, they can escape their daily grind when they come to watch me do my schtick. So I owe it to them to go out and entertain them.

Travel isn't always a chore, though. Seeing the world can be one of the best parts of what I do. We've gone to India; to the Far East twice; and I've been to Australia representing the company. That was a brief visit, but Chris came with me because she has a lot of family in Australia. She went to see them in Melbourne while I did a ton of press in Sydney. Being able to do something like that makes it such a great job. I fell in love with Australia. It had everything I love about America – the great outdoors and the warm weather –

Chris and I went away from a Tuesday to a Sunday and it was only the second real break we'd had together without the kids – just the two of us on our own. The other had been a weekend in New York – and that had been because I was working there at the time.

plus one of the things I miss most about home, a very British sense of humour. I was doing interviews from morning until night but I had a ball.

I've always enjoyed dealing with newspaper and TV guys – being a real-life ambassador for the WWE.

> **In Australia one guy was trying to knock us, asking, "When you and The Rock are rolling around on the floor, do you think it has gay overtones?"**
>
> **"I don't know," I replied, "but I do know he always closes his eyes when I kiss him."**

The guy loved my response and he wrote a good piece. I usually find I have a line for most situations.

On our Far East tour of Singapore and Japan in 2002 we wrestled in the Yokohama Arena. Japanese fans are incredibly knowledgeable and they were really up for it that night – which is why my match with Edge that night is my favourite so far in my career. They love all styles of wrestling in Japan. The *lucha libre* guys get so much respect there, as do people who do my hardhitting style.

In Singapore I had the pleasure of meeting the crown prince of Brunei. He's a huge fan and was walking around at the show, handing his business card out to all us wrestlers. His title on the card just reads, "Crown Prince". He told us that if ever any of us were in his part of the world and needed anything at all we should give him a call. You never know when something like that could come in handy.

Seeing so many places and having so many experiences is absolutely the best thing about my job. I was fortunate enough to see a lot of places even before I came over to America. I hope that by now, reading this book, you should be able to see wrestling has given me an incredible life, and I'm very grateful – even if I've screwed a lot of it up.

> In Singapore I had the pleasure of meeting the crown prince of Brunei. He's a huge fan and was walking around at the show, handing his business card out to all us wrestlers. His title on the card just reads, "Crown Prince". He told us that if ever any of us were in his part of the world and needed anything at all we should give him a call. You never know when something like that could come in handy.

Being in WWE allows me to do a lot of things I never dreamed I'd be able to. I wanted to be a wrestler and that was all. All the extra stuff that comes with being a WWE Superstar is an experience – and most of the time it's a great one. For example, WWE was asked to do a special celebrity version of the quiz show *The Weakest Link*. I went on it with Booker T, Big Show, Lita, Trish Stratus, Kurt Angle, Stephanie McMahon and Triple H.

It's entertaining to look back on – but it wasn't as much fun to do. I hadn't seen the show that many times and I didn't know much about it. As we flew to Hollywood I wasn't sure what I was expecting – but it was certainly different from what I got. By the time I was voted off, there was only me, Steph and Triple H left. The two of them got together to vote me off – obviously a conspiracy, which we won't go into.

But by that stage I was glad to leave the show. To film this single one-hour episode took three hours – very different to wrestling, when we do two two-hour shows a week pretty quickly. What viewers don't see when they watch the show is the break in between each round when Anne Robinson disappears to do whatever it is she does. Has a rest, puts her feet up and drinks a cup of tea, I expect. Meanwhile we contestants were left sweltering under the hot studio lights in front of the audience. It was worse for me than for most of the others because I was wearing my three-piece suit, so I was sweating buckets.

When it's time to fill in the little box with the name of the person you want to vote off, you write it while Anne is there; but then she leaves and you have to pretend to keep scribbling while the cameramen film you doing it. Then once she had left at the end of a round, the cameramen would film us from different angles.

> By the time I was voted off, there was only me, Steph and Triple H left. The three of them got together to vote me off – obviously a conspiracy, which we won't go into. But by that stage I was glad to leave the show. To film this single one-hour episode took three hours – very different to wrestling, when we do two two-hour shows a week pretty quickly.

But it wasn't only the lights that I found uncomfortable. We'd had a warm-up round when they'd asked us all questions and I couldn't get a single one right. They were all to do with America. So I piped up: "I'm English, I don't know any of these!"

That started everyone laughing. Whether my protest had something to do with it I don't know, but once the cameras were rolling I knew or guessed the right answer to just about everything they asked me. The only ones I got wrong were some American questions – there was one about JC Penney, an American department store, which I didn't know. So I came out of the whole thing smelling of roses. It made me look far smarter than I actually am.

Going in, I'd had the idea that if I was asked a series of questions I couldn't answer, I could walk off in a huff and it wouldn't matter – playing a villain, I could get away with it. Then I started getting all the answers right and I was thinking, "They're going to rumble me in a minute," but it never happened. And when Stephanie and Triple H voted me off, it looked as though the only reason I lost the show was because they had ganged up on me. It was win-win.

Coming back to England for WWE has been a thrill, too.
Before I lived in America, going to London had always meant jobs in places like Lewisham or Croydon. I'd drive straight in, do the match and drive straight out again. But coming to promote a Pay-Per-View, staying at a smart hotel and being driven around to different publicity engagements was the first chance I'd had to appreciate what a great city London is.

I was out for a curry with my friend Dominic, who works for WWE in London, when he told me they had a signing session lined up for me at the HMV record store in Oxford Street. I didn't think anyone would turn up. I could see people queuing up to see The Rock or another American superstar, but not Darren Matthews. I've never felt like a WWE Superstar – never lived like one, and I hope I don't act like a prima donna.

Yet when we got there the store was packed with 750 people at a ticket-only event. It brought it home to me how far I'd come – from working on a fairground in Blackpool to signing autographs for a massive queue of people in Oxford Street in London.

I was booked for an hour-and-a-half and was told not to personalize autographs. I wasn't having that. "Listen," I said. "These people have paid and they've all queued to see me. If you don't want me taking up that much time you shouldn't have brought so many people. These people pay my wages and put food on my table. You can't treat them like sheep."

I sat and signed for every single person there, talked to them all and had a great time for four-and-a-half hours. At the end the cleaners were there, frowning at us because we hadn't finished and were holding them up. I know what it's like trying to get an autograph off one of your wrestling heroes. But it was a shock to be treated like such a big celebrity.

It's the same in Japan. When we landed there people were waiting for us and screaming – it felt like being one of the Beatles. I wanted to put my head down, thinking, "They're not screaming for me." But in a way they were – they were screaming for all of us.

Another trip back home to England turned into one of the most enjoyable experiences I've had in WWE. Just before a Manchester Pay-Per-View, I went to Blackpool for a few days to do some filming for a *Before They Were Superstars* video and DVD. I got to revisit all my old haunts with a film crew in tow. It was the last Friday of the season, the beginning of November, and unusually for that late in the year, the sun was shining.

Michael Cole was there and Bubba Dean, one of the cameramen I get on well with. The production crew are all great guys and incredibly hard-working. They make our shows to such a high standard and the professionalism they demonstrate is outstanding – it's a pleasure to work with them all.

I was booked for an hour-and-a-half and was told not to personalize autographs. I wasn't having that. "Listen," I said. "These people have paid and they've all queued to see me. If you don't want me taking up that much time you shouldn't have brought so many people. These people pay my wages and put food on my table. You can't treat them like sheep."

I got my old friend Peter Thompson on board and we had a fantastic day. We started off at the Pleasure Beach and I talked about the good times I had there right at the beginning of my career. We rode in a horse-drawn landau and pointed out the different sights as we drove along the street on our way to the Tower. At the Tower Circus we were allowed to film inside. I talked about what a privilege it had been to wrestle there as a youngster of eighteen and nineteen. It still gave me such a rush to stand in my favourite venue. We even got some fish and chips from Harry Ramsden's. And then that night I met up with my old pals Glen, Alan and Joe; and Stuart who runs a pub there now. We were laughing and joking; it was so different from the time when things were at their worst and no one had wanted me around.

One of the biggest thrills about that trip was getting to stay in the Imperial Hotel. It was always the best hotel in town – the one the Prime Minister and the MPs use whenever they hold their party conferences in Blackpool. And now it was my turn – all in all it was one of the most memorable times in my life.

These are simple pleasures which people in the States might not appreciate. It's a strange existence – not just being a professional wrestler, but being a Brit living in America. Daniel and Dane were born in Blackpool's Victoria Hospital and it is a constant struggle to keep them British. All three of my kids have American accents, of course, but they watch a lot of the comedy shows I watch so they do share my British sense of humour. But I don't deny there are plenty of times when I hear them say something Americanised and I wince.

I expect I'll spend the rest of my days in America. I can't see my kids ever wanting to leave and I can't imagine ever wanting to be too far away from them, either. In an ideal world I'd live over here for most of the year and spend the summer months – June to mid-September – in England.

I'll never give up my British citizenship, though. You never know what the future holds. I could end up selling newspapers outside the back of Blackpool Tower – and as long as I was healthy and happy, that would be fine with me.

16

Lance and Me

September 11. Two weeks before, I was
doing some work for *Sunday Night Heat*,
which was shown on MTV at the time. I
had to go to *The World* to do it – the WWE
restaurant they had in Times Square in
New York. Seeing as we so rarely get
away together, I decided to take Chris
with me and make a weekend of it. Our
hotel was in a plum spot – the Marriott
right in Times Square. We did all the
sightseeing visitors do and went to see
Phantom of the Opera on Broadway,

which absolutely blew me away – I've seen lots of shows but the power of that was amazing.

On our sightseeing trip we'd gone to the top of the Empire State Building where Chris captured all the scenery on video. So we've got pictures of the World Trade Center's Twin Towers just two weeks before they were destroyed. It's very strange. Just a few days later they were gone. Not being very familiar with New York, I'd had no idea what and where the World Trade Center was until then. Two weeks later, everyone on the planet knew.

On September 11 we were in Houston, Texas to film a *SmackDown!* on that Tuesday night. We were staying at the Hilton at the airport and I was riding with Sean Waltman – X-Pac. I was in bed in my room that morning when Sean started banging on the door – loudly. "Steve, Steve, put the news on!"

"Sod off, leave me alone, I'm sleeping," I told him. I heard him muttering about planes crashing and the Twin Towers but I just thought: "Leave me alone, I'm going back to sleep."

I woke up a couple of hours later, put the news on and sat there in shock. Like everyone else around the world, I couldn't believe that what I was seeing was real. It was as though the news had become a *Die Hard* movie. We didn't tape our show that night. Instead we did it on the Thursday. At the start of the show the whole crew went out and stood on the ramp and looked around at the fans, tears streaming down their faces.

> Being from England, you get used to hearing about terrorist attacks and you become slightly inured to things like that because they are always on the news. It's terrible that you get hardened but you do, especially when you and the people you know have never been directly affected by it. Yet standing on that ramp, I felt absolutely gutted. It was the first time I'd seen the deep, personal effect that terrorism can have on people's lives.

Being from England, you get used to hearing about terrorist attacks and you become slightly inured to things like that because they are always on the news. It's terrible that you get hardened but you do, especially when you and the people you know have never been directly affected by it. Yet standing on that ramp, I felt absolutely gutted. It was the first time I'd seen the deep, personal effect that terrorism can have on people's lives.

Our first show back in New York after the attack came one month later, at Madison Square Garden on a Sunday afternoon. In the morning, before the show, we were split into groups and asked to visit various fire houses and police stations to meet some of the children of the victims of the terrorist attack. My biggest fear was that it would turn into some sort of ploy or stunt to publicise the company. But thankfully it wasn't, in any way, shape or form. There were no cameras or press in tow. It was just a wonderful gesture on the part of WWE to try to give back to the people in whatever way we could, and to show that we cared.

I was in a group of five or six – I can't remember exactly who was with me because it was such an emotional day. We went round to different fire houses in Manhattan and met so many children who had lost their fathers. One fire house had twenty-six people missing. But the kids were gloriously happy to see us.

I don't really understand the celebrity part of what I do; the way people treat us as heroes or as role models. I only want to be a role model to my kids. Yet this was one of those times when I realized what a marvellous job we have, to be able to put a smile on the face of a child who has lost his or her father, even if only for a short time. It showed me the power of television and the power of the company which employs us. And it showed what a privilege it is to be able to be a part of that. Everyone from all the police stations and the fire houses and all the children were invited to the afternoon show. We tried to entertain them and bring a bit of happiness to them, to take them out of themselves even if it was for a few short hours. I think we achieved that.

I don't really understand the celebrity part of what I do; the way people treat us as heroes or as role models. I only want to be a role model to my kids. Yet this was one of those times when I realized what a marvellous job we have, to be able to put a smile on the face of a child who has lost his or her father, even if only for a short time.

That was the day I got to wrestle Kurt Angle in a singles
match; our first since I'd made the switch from being the good guy
commissioner by turning on Angle and becoming the commissioner
of the Alliance, the WCW and ECW faction. I went to do a move I
do regularly, throwing Kurt from the floor up against the ropes of
the ring so the middle rope hits his neck, when I heard a 'ping!'
sound and looked down to see a hole in the top of my arm. I'd torn
my bicep – but at the top, which isn't as serious as if you tear it at
the bottom. It didn't hurt so I put Kurt in a chinlock before we
carried on and finished the match. I haven't had it fixed to this day.
It's the sort of injury you just have to put up with in my job. The
company gave me two weeks off to recover – I was still in the show
but I didn't actually wrestle.

Angle and I had some great chemistry and a programme between
us could have been one of the best things I had ever done. It wasn't
to be, but I really would have liked to have had that run with him.
On that day in New York I felt like we had something; something
you only get every now and then. It was a feeling I wouldn't get
again until I started tagging with Lance Storm.

After September 11, those in charge at WWE wanted to
turn Kurt Angle into a babyface. They thought it would be a good
time to have an all-American hero the crowd could rally behind.
The idea was for me to turn on Kurt and we would have that run
together with me as the heel and him as the babyface. It was
intended to be Kurt against the evil foreigner. It might have upset a
few people, but that wasn't why they dropped the plan – it was just
that Kurt is a great heel. That left me not being the commissioner,
being a heel again but with no one to do anything against. So that's
why we came up with the programme between Edge and me.

Everybody has high hopes for Edge and rightly so because he is so
good at what he does. It hadn't been long since his split from Christian,
his storyline brother and tag team partner and our programme was his
first big singles run. A lot of people didn't like the matches we had but
I loved them. We went out with the express purpose of making these
matches slightly different. Edge had done a lot of goofy comedy before
but we wanted to show he had a tough side.

We did normal stuff on house shows with me doing my house

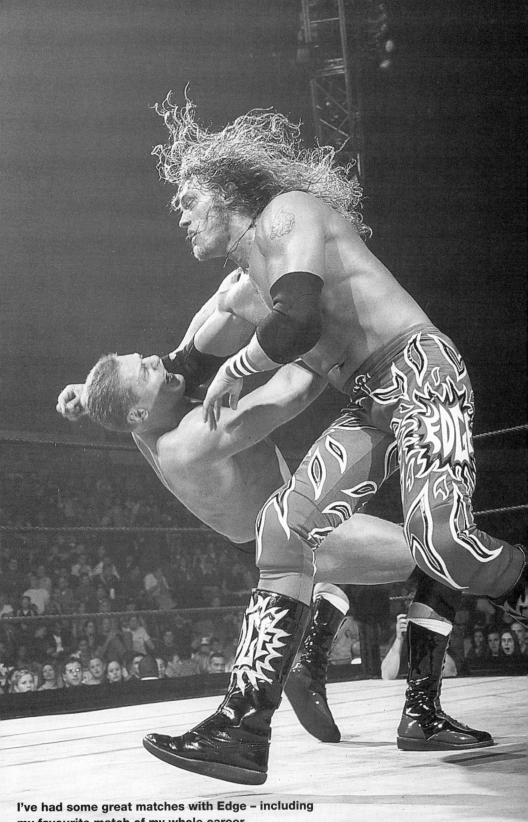

I've had some great matches with **Edge** – including
my favourite match of my whole career.

show heel routine and tearing the house down; but we wanted it to be more serious on TV. I was given new, more dramatic entrance music. For some reason it didn't work on TV – it was too serious, if anything. But I'm still proud of what we did. They were believable-looking pro wrestling matches. I challenge anyone to go back and look at them again. There's no reason why anybody who likes Japanese wrestling won't like our matches. The fans didn't take to them because they weren't used to that style. But it still served its purpose, to an extent – Edge has gone on from there and is bigger than ever today.

I'd always thought the Pillman Show crowd was the best I'd ever perform in front of, but the one that night in Japan was even better. Their energy and responses were unbelievable. There was just the most intense noise. Japanese fans stamp their feet up and down when they like what they see, so once they got going they were not only screaming and clapping but they were doing that as well. The atmosphere in the building was incredible.

My favourite match of my entire career was the match with Edge at the Yokohama Arena in Tokyo when we toured Japan. We opened the show with a fifteen minute effort and it was the best one we had. I'd always thought the Pillman Show crowd was the best I'd ever perform in front of, but the one that night in Japan was even better. Their energy and responses were unbelievable. There was just the most intense noise. Japanese fans stamp their feet up and down when they like what they see, so once they got going they were not only screaming and clapping but they were doing that as well. The atmosphere in the building was incredible. It's ideally shaped for wrestling, completely round like the Albert Hall in London, so the acoustics are perfect and it made for an amazing match. When the Japanese watch their own wrestlers they tend to be polite and only pop at certain moments, but when we've been there with WWE they react to us like American crowds because they copy what they've seen on TV.

In the autumn of 2002 I was asked to join a group called the Un-Americans which consisted of three Canadians; Lance Storm, Test and Christian. I jumped at the chance. They wanted someone who was a bit of a character; who wasn't frightened of having people hate them; and to be a spokesman for the group – even though they are all good at talking for themselves. My knack of getting people to hate me would be an extra ingredient to really build them up. It was perfect for me: bashing America is what I've been all about ever since I got to the States twelve years ago.

It worked, and they decided the natural progression would be for Lance and me to break out as a tag team. I was happy about that, since Lance is a terrific wrestler. He's a very talented athlete and can make everything he does look good. The fans know him as an unsmiling character whose catchphrase is: "If I can be serious for a moment . . ." And he can seem like that in real life. He's always got his head in a book and even encourages fans to read with a book club on his website. But when you get to know him you realise Lance can be a funny guy with a very dry sense of humour. Once we started tagging together, I'd always delight in trying to get him to laugh in the ring, just to drop his ultra-serious persona for a second.

Our partnership clicked straight away. It took a while to build on TV but we knew we had something going from our first house show together. We had a chemistry which worked right from the beginning, like the first time I wrestled Fit Finlay or Chris Benoit, or that one time I got in the ring with Kurt Angle. When you've been around and done as much as I have done, you just get a feeling that what you're doing is so right.

Tagging with Lance on house shows – often against Spike Dudley and the Hurricane or the Dudley Boyz – it was clear there was some magic there. We were giving everyone their money's worth and more. There were only so many tag teams in WWE at the time which made it difficult for us to come up with new material to do on television. But we were clearly going places.

It wasn't long before we ended up with the tag titles, and had two runs with them. We were what I call a solid backbone team. Any wrestling company needs people who have gone through their career as good backbone wrestlers. Arn Anderson comes to mind as the best example I can think of. It means being a polished performer who can be put in any position and, while not necessarily always having the best match of the night, can have a match with anyone, can talk well and is basically a reliable all-rounder.

I was tagging with Lance when we went on a tour of India in November 2002. The first day went well with a fine show in New Delhi. On the second day I was in a singles match with Kane. I'd eaten the same as everyone else and, as I had travelled to India before, I knew to drink only bottled water. I'd been as careful as anyone could but as I was signing autographs on my way from the hotel to the bus taking us to the arena, I was suddenly hit by a burning sensation in my stomach.

At the arena my discomfort got worse by the minute. I pushed it to the back of my mind because Kane and I were on last and I had

Lance and I made a great team. We had the right chemistry . . .

to think about the match. But by the time the bell went, my stomach was on fire. We got through the match and drove from the show to the airport to fly to Bangalore. As we waited for the plane I began to feel severely nauseous. I ran to the bathroom where I was violently sick – nicely complimented by a bad case of the runs.

I managed the flight and got to the next hotel, where I spent the next twenty hours straight alternately vomiting and suffering from diarrhoea. I had no idea what had brought it on – it must have been a bug that I'd picked up. They sent for a doctor who gave me some electrolyte to drink and some antibiotics and, by the end of those ghastly twenty hours, most of it had come out of my system.

I'd been hit so badly that on the final night of the tour I didn't wrestle, which is something I hate to do. I wouldn't have been able to if I had tried – there wasn't a second when I wasn't throwing up, or dry-heaving, or going to the bathroom. It still went against that old rule that had been drummed into me over the years – no matter what, you do the show.

I wasn't the only one suffering, though. Lance got sick and quite a few others did too – and all with different symptoms. When we got back to the States, Booker T ended up in hospital.

I went back to work in America and was really pleased with the stuff I was doing with Lance. We had a really good run from around October 2002 until February the next year and won the tag titles twice. We worked well together because he's a very talented wrestler and between us we were able to rile up the crowds at the house shows.

I got into a good training groove, working hard. But something was still not right. When I wasn't wrestling or training I didn't feel good at all. My sleeping problems were back worse than ever and now I was getting virtually no sleep every night. It was wearing me down, but because I was happy with my training and my matches, I kept going. January came around and another overseas tour, to South Korea and Japan; a trip I really enjoyed. I still wasn't sleeping well but the shows were such big events that I carried on.

Lack of sleep wasn't the only worry. I also noticed that my heart rate had sped up a lot. But I just blew it off and kept going. It all came to a head at the *No Way Out* Pay-Per-View in February 2003, when Lance and I wrestled Kane and RVD.

On the afternoon of the show, I started swelling up – my abdomen, my legs and my ankles. When the match started, the first time I got into the ring was with Kane. He picked me up and slammed me.

I can remember going up for the slam and the next thing I remember I was lying on the canvas, oblivious to everything going on around me. I felt

so calm and peaceful. The thought even passed through my mind: "I wish I could rest like this at night."

Suddenly Kane and referee Nick Patrick were leaning over me, asking if I was all right. It was only then I realised I'd been knocked out by Kane's slam. I felt like I'd been lying there peacefully for hours. "How long have I been out?" I wanted to know. We carried on and got through the match okay, but afterwards I noticed I was swelling up worse than ever.

The concussion meant I wasn't allowed to wrestle the next day, so I went to the ring with Lance while he had a match. But I was still swelling up. My stomach and legs were enormous. I got home on Tuesday and two days later I weighed 265 pounds, twenty pounds more than normal.

> I got into a good training groove, working hard. But something was still not right. When I wasn't wrestling or training I didn't feel good at all. My sleeping problems were back worse than ever and now I was getting virtually no sleep every night. It was wearing me down, but because I was happy with my training and my matches, I kept going.

I went to our nearest hospital and waited for five hours before they ran some blood tests on me. It was another two hours before I got their verdict: "There's something wrong but we don't know what it is. You'll have to see a gastroenterologist."

I went to see one a week later. In between I couldn't wrestle. By now I was twenty-five pounds overweight, my heart was pounding and I felt really bad. I was asked to come back for more tests the following week. Everyone was assuming it must have been connected with the bug I'd picked up in India. At no point did anyone put a heart monitor on me. That might have shown them what was really wrong.

What the doctors didn't know – and neither did I – was that I was about to face the biggest challenge of my wrestling career.

17

Don't Die a Little
Each Day

Eventually, after several more tests including an ultrasound on my stomach, the doctor seemed convinced it was all in my mind. When I told her I'd put on so much weight, she asked me if I was sure that I hadn't been eating too much. But, like any patient confronted by a doctor, I assumed that this one knew what she was doing. Then came yet another test when they pushed a tube down my throat to have a look inside me. None of this seemed to be getting anywhere – and in fact I never heard from that particular clinic again.

Meanwhile I got in touch with another doctor in north Atlanta who specialises in infectious diseases. I told him what had happened to me in India, asking whether perhaps I might have brought some sort of parasite home with me. He gave me some further blood tests and eventually he asked me to pack a bag and go to hospital – they were going to keep me in.

It was only there that I learned what the problem was – and it was a lot more alarming than parasites. A serious heart problem. Congestive heart failure. My heart got larger and was beating really fast, more than 100 beats a minute. The right side of my heart was fluttering and wasn't pumping the blood around my body properly. That's why my lower body had been swelling up – it was full of blood.

The people at St Joseph's Hospital in Atlanta were tremendous. I was there for eight days while they gave me test after test after test, and put me right. All those referrals to the gastroenterologist had been a waste of time. A simple heart monitor – a standard procedure, I would have thought – would have found out what was wrong right at the beginning and saved three weeks of tests and worrying.

> My heart got larger and was beating really fast, more than 100 beats a minute. The right side of my heart was fluttering and wasn't pumping the blood around my body properly. That's why my lower body had been swelling up – it was full of blood.

My heart had gone into abnormal arrhythmia, which was causing all the problems. They had to stick a camera inside me via my hip to check everything out. I woke up in hospital after that little procedure with eight wires sticking out of my neck where they were monitoring me. At first the doctor said he was going to send me home with some medication and if things didn't go right, then after a few months they would have to stop my heart electrically and start it again.

"Why don't you do it now?" I said. "Let's get it out of the way." No, he said, we should wait and see. But before the end of that day a nurse walked in, looking grave, and shut the door behind her. She was about to tell me that I might need a new heart.

She said: "Whatever you were planning on doing for the rest of your life, just forget it. Everything will have to stop. What you've got, people have heart transplants for. That's probably what you're going to have to have too."

I wasn't having any of it – I wasn't buying into anything this nurse was telling me. If you give in to something you're in trouble. My dad has always been my greatest example. When he had a stroke fifteen years ago it would have been so easy for him to have given up – and that would have finished him. But he kept going and is still going strong now. If I ever felt sorry for myself – and there were plenty of times over the next fifteen months when it did get to me – I would just think of my dad and how much he had to put up with. He works with one hand now and recently celebrated his seventieth birthday. He kept fighting and never gave up and that's what I had to do too.

They didn't know how determined a wrestler could be. I knew that if I looked after myself the way the doctors and nurses wanted me to then yes, I would have been done in – no question about it. I knew better. I had to eat right and look after myself right.

That was my mindset. But there were more immediate problems to worry about. Suddenly, even though I didn't feel any different, all these alarms started going off all around me. Doctors and nurses came running in from everywhere. I was lying in the middle of all this activity, wondering what it was all about. They told me my heart rate was 180 beats a minute – it had really flipped out and was all over the place. And then they decided they would have to stop my heart and re-start it the next day. I was proper wound up because that was exactly what I had asked them to do in the first place.

The following morning they got me ready for this procedure by putting pads on my chest and, just before they gave me the anesthetic to put me out, they told me that as soon as my heart re-started I would wake up.

The next thing I can remember was sitting up in bed screaming. I fell back and fell asleep again. When I woke up later – I'm not sure how long I'd been sleeping – the doctor said: "You can go home now." He said my heart was back in normal rhythm and running fine again. He told me I'd have to stay on the medication they gave me and that I should take things easy – go for nice walks in the park, that sort of thing.

All the doctors said my wrestling career was over. Pretty much everyone else around me thought so, too.

What the doctors didn't know was that it was far from the first time I'd heard those words. If I'd believed every doctor who said I could never wrestle again I would have retired at the age of twenty, when I was told I needed an operation for an arm injury. I went to see a physio instead, who sorted me out without too much trouble, and I was back in the ring in next to no time.

After experiences like that, I've always been sceptical of doctors – and I've certainly seen enough of them over the years. They aren't used to someone like me. When they tell most of their patients to cut down on fatty foods, drink less, give up smoking or exercise more, they know that people will agree with them but not do what they're told. Whereas I'll do all the right things. I'll eat right, train right and do whatever it takes so I can wrestle again. If none of my other trials have defeated me, I didn't see why this latest one should. The whole episode reinforced my belief that you get out what you put in – and that goes for all walks of life.

> All the doctors said my wrestling career was over. Pretty much everyone else around me thought so, too.

In truth, as soon as I was told what was wrong with me, there was no fear, panic or depression. Only relief. Relief that they'd worked out what was wrong. That there had been a reason why I'd been feeling so bad for months. It was a load off my mind to know why I was feeling poorly.

It is a strange feeling to be told something has gone wrong with your heart. And you do want answers. The doctor said that he could not truthfully give me any. When people of my age get congestive heart failure, some say it comes from a viral infection. When I told the doctor about the drug abuse in my past, he said it could have been an underlying problem caused by that. I think he's right. It had taken a few bouts of sickness, combined with my trouble sleeping, to bring it to the fore.

I know I have abused my body in my life. I really shouldn't be here. I should have died several times. So I felt lucky to be in the health that I was in. I was determined not to let it get to me. And I simply would not stand for the idea that I'd never wrestle again.

I started feeling better right from the moment of that electric shock. My resting heart rate was back down between 58 and the low 60s and I felt good.

But I was on seven different types of drugs for my heart, which prevented my wrestling. For one thing, I was taking a blood-thinning drug which meant that if I got cut in a match I'd bleed all over the ring. And by the time I left hospital I had ballooned up to 278 pounds.

If none of my other trials have defeated me, I didn't see why this latest one should. The whole episode reinforced my belief that you get out what you put in – and that goes for all walks of life In truth, as soon as I was told what was wrong with me, there was no fear, panic or depression. Only relief. Relief that they'd worked out what was wrong. That there had been a reason why I'd been feeling so bad for months. It was a load off my mind to know why I was feeling poorly.

I was so determined that on the same day that I was released from hospital I got back on the treadmill. And the next day I had a long think about what to do. I cast my mind back, trying to think when I had felt at my absolute best condition. It was when I was doing very old-style conditioning training – push-ups, Hindu squats and all those kinds of exercises. That was when I felt my best, when I'd been doing that.

When I came to America I still did little bits of my old routine, but everyone else was lifting weights and getting on Stairmasters, so that's what I started doing. I never thought about it at the time. But all that old-fashioned training that wrestlers and rugby players have done for decades works. That's why people have been doing it for thousands of years. You use your own body weight in multiple joint exercises. That was going to be my way back.

I got on my computer and typed "Hindu squats" into an Internet search engine and the same name kept coming up over and over again – Matt Furey. I logged on to his website and found out that he was an all-round martial arts man. He was a champion amateur wrestler, he won championships all over the world, and had spent his last few years being trained by Karl Gotch. Not only was Karl a famous wrestler but in terms of training techniques he was famous for being a conditioning freak. He did 9001 squats in four and a half hours once without stopping.

Matt Furey had taken the time to go and learn all this old stuff and was now trying to tell other people about it. I got interested in his ideas and the right techniques – I found out I had been doing a lot of them wrong. I did all that and I got my diet right, too. In hospital most of the doctors had absolutely no idea about nutrition whatsoever. It's not their fault; they are not specialist nutritionists or dieticians. Instead of finding out what's really wrong with you, it's a lot easier for them to give you a lot of drugs to take. You're more likely to find out what's wrong by looking at someone's diet. I also got a lot of information from England, a lot of research that had been done with fish oils and the like. It was all stuff that I had read about over the years but never taken much notice of until now.

I was still going back for tests and one by one the doctor took me off the various medications, although he said I would never get off all of them. I told him: "Look, you've got to admit it. I'm getting healthier." He called me up that same night and refused to see me anymore. He said: "You shouldn't be getting as healthy as you are getting."

Doctors are bound by insurance and were petrified of saying that I could get back in the ring again, in case anything went wrong. Like I say, they're not used to people like me. My attitude is if you've got something wrong with you, you find out what it is and you sort it out. If your nose is bleeding, you figure out why it's bleeding and don't just keep stopping it when it happens.

Most people at the WWE thought my in-ring career was finished. I got a call from the WWE's John Laurinaitis asking me if I wanted to become an agent; so I did that for about six weeks. But I came back far too soon. I thought I could do everything, and I was wrong. The doctor was right in that respect at least. I was fine training at home but once you throw in all the travel and the long hours I was taking backward steps.

But while I was an agent I had to come back to England to do some publicity for the company which was good fun – and provided me with some much-needed light relief. While I was there I discovered that there was a wrestlers' reunion at Ellesmere Port in Cheshire. It was run by a guy called Bob Bell for whom I'd wrestled once when I was sixteen. I was able to get to the reunion and it was grand, seeing so many people I'd worked with years before. Johnny Saint was there; Jack Cassidy, Ian Wilson and many others. It was a brilliant day.

> I had never considered myself as having a great ego but, once I was away from the ring, I realised that wasn't true. I'm an entertainer and I found that I missed being out there in front of the crowds

That same week while I was in London I also had a night out with Mal Saunders, Steve Grey, Lee Bronson, Ian Muir and one of my all-time heroes – Cyanide Sid Cooper. We went for a curry and ended up drinking tea outside a mobile café for hours telling jokes and wrestling stories. Top entertainment.

But being an agent was incredibly frustrating – and it taught me something about myself.

I had never considered myself as having a great ego but, once I was away from the ring, I realised that wasn't true. I'm an entertainer and I found that I missed being out there in front of the crowds and doing my act – so I do have more of an ego than I thought. The meaning of life, for me, is to go out and entertain people. Whether I've got three or four in a gym or thousands, that's what gets me going. Being backstage and watching everyone else do it without being able to do it myself was very hard. And all through the time I was off, I would have a good month, health-wise, and then it would be bad again; especially with the swelling in my legs, which didn't help.

When I was booked to be an agent on a show in Australia, I had a long look in the mirror and took a reality check. I was already struggling with two- and three-hour flights. I wouldn't be doing myself any favours by going on such a long trip. I told the doctor what I thought and he said that if I went he would have to increase my medication. The amount I was taking already was making me feel more than a bit worse – like any drugs, it had side-effects. So I decided to call it a day. If I was going to get better, it wouldn't be by going on thirty-hour plane rides. I called WWE and explained and

It was fantastic to see so many of my old heroes. Left to right: Mal Saunders, Steve Gray, Lee Brunson, me, Ian "Bully Boy" Muir and one of my all-time heroes, "Cyanide" Sid Cooper.

they were fine about it – do whatever you have to do so you can get better, they said.

Training on my own at home, I had real ups and downs.
November was one month-long down. It was a constant struggle to get up every day and do something; it was as if I was suffering from depression. I kept fighting it off but it was constantly there. I was still positive that I could get back to the ring, but everyone else around me said I couldn't. That gets to you. When you feel like you've no one on your side, that's when you start questioning yourself.

By this time, I had found myself a new doctor, Dan Sorescu at Crawford Long Hospital, who was as good as gold with me. He took me straight off the main medication I wanted rid of, assuring me that I didn't need to be on it. I wanted to stop taking the blood-thinning drug, for example, because if you fall and cut yourself you can bleed to death. Hardly ideal when you have a house full of lizards and you're getting whipped and scratched all the time. He gave me some new stuff and said I could go back to work and train in the ring, but I still couldn't do any actual wrestling.

> The blessing in disguise was that I got to spend a lot of time with my family. That was good. It made a real change to be there when my children came home from school every day.

The blessing in disguise was that I got to spend a lot of time with my family. That was good. It made a real change to be there when my children came home from school every day. Chris and I also had to readjust to me being around the whole week and I found out she watches some bleeding awful TV.

There were times I would go and watch some of my own favourites. Going through such a tough time, I was cheered up by some of the British comedians I'd always taken for granted – people like Ronnie Barker and Tony Hancock. I spent many hours going through their old shows and I learned to appreciate what geniuses they were.

At Christmas I came back to England with my family. It was the first time Chris and the kids had been back in five years. We had a lovely couple of weeks. It was all a family Christmas should be. You couldn't imagine a greater contrast to the last time we'd all been over together in 1998.

On our return to America I was back to my new routine – going to see the doctor regularly. I kept on at him: "I feel fine. I can do 500 squats, 200 push-ups, with no problems."

Eventually he said to me, "Let me tell you the absolute truth. If it was up to me, you could go and do anything you wanted to. But for insurance reasons, there is no way this hospital will let me release you to wrestle in case something happens to you."

He was being as truthful as he could with me. There was nothing more he could do. At that point, I was about to flip. I knew I was okay but it looked like I just could not get cleared to wrestle. Then Bob Clarke, from the company, called me.

I explained to him that there was nothing wrong with me but no one would allow me to wrestle. It was the first release of tension I'd had and I exploded, ranting down the phone to him.

He rang me back five minutes later with some good news: "We've got a different doctor for you to see."

In Birmingham, Alabama there's a cardiologist called Dr Morris. They'd sent me to see him because he works with Dr Andrews, the guy who does the operations for any of the wrestlers. Everyone wants him to do them because he's an incredible surgeon and is good at dealing with athletes.

That meant Dr Morris knew athletes, too, in a way that other doctors and hospitals didn't. The first time I saw him, he told me straightaway he would take me off all this medication and, if I was okay after being monitored for a month, I could go back to work. And that is how it went. When the month was up he said I could go back on the show and run around if I had to, but I still had to take it slowly: he didn't want me to become a full-time wrestler again at that time.

WWE came to Atlanta and I went to the show so everyone could see me. Most people thought I was still at death's door because they had only heard the doctors' versions of what had happened. I turned up, met Vince and he told me that as soon as something came up they would put me back in the show.

In the middle of June I went back to the hospital in Alabama and after some tests the doctors told me I could go back wrestling again – exactly what I wanted to hear.

I had spent fifteen long months thinking about my wrestling. With the time off I'd had, I used it to look back at all my matches. I started with the old WCW stuff and watched to see how I had gone over with the fans. I saw how my original style had worked. And when I came to watch the stuff I'd been doing in WWE it was the total opposite. I was trying to fit my stuff into everyone else's. This is no knock on anybody else, but I could see that I was working down to several people's levels when I should have been making them work up to mine. And I couldn't do that because I wasn't working at the level I should have been, so it was my own fault. Instead of doing my aggressive, hard-hitting style, I had fallen into the trap of doing the same kind of routines the other middle and lower-card guys were doing. I had dropped my standards without realizing it.

Looking back, I could see there were times when I was trying to fit into a formula for TV matches. I can really do this business and I don't fit into any kind of formula. Now that I've come back, when certain agents ask me what I am going to be doing in the ring, I tell them that I don't know. I'd been worrying too much about doing everything right in the right amount of time, instead of doing what came naturally. I was always thinking ahead to how I would be doing the next move and that took the edge away from what I was good at.

Shortly before I got sick, when I was tagging with Lance, I had been working more like my old self again. I got into a command position, being what is termed in our business a ring general – making sure everyone was in the right spot and properly organised. I was good at that, which was why I was enjoying it.

Within a couple of weeks I got a call from the office telling me they wanted to put me in a manager's role with a new character. I turned up at a TV and straight away I was with this guy Eugene.

On my first night back it felt like I had never been away. All the time I'd been off had dragged by and I had been through a lot of emotional difficulty, not knowing what was happening to me and not knowing if I would be able to get over it. Wondering what I was going to do. In the back of my mind had always been the thought that I might not be able to do it any more. I really did feel like a little bird locked in a cage when I wasn't out entertaining. I knew I would always be able to do something, even if it wasn't wrestling. If I had to resign myself to being an agent, then that would be what I would do. I would rather do an on-camera role, but so be it.

Eugene and I just clicked from the start.

But with me and Eugene, it worked well from night one. I've known Nick Dinsmore, who plays Eugene, for a long time. He was in the developmental territory of Ohio Valley Wrestling for some years. We'd always got on well and we hit it off straightaway. It was like the chemistry I had with Tajiri. Nick is a brilliant wrestler and the whole idea of Eugene was his. The creative team tweaked it a little, but he came up with it in the first place.

The storyline was that Eugene was a little simple but a brilliant wrestler, who wanted to fulfil his life's dream of getting into the WWE. On TV, his uncle Eric Bischoff was in charge of *Raw* and he was getting me to make Eugene's life hell. But as the weeks went by, I became fond of the fellow and started looking out for him. I had chemistry with Eric Bischoff too, and I'd never done anything on camera with him before.

Everything worked. I couldn't believe how quickly people took to Eugene because he was a different type of a character. He was a disadvantaged person. It caused a bit of trouble at first because some critics said we were making fun of the mentally handicapped; but Eugene was a very positive character because

> In the back of my mind had always been the thought that I might not be able to do it any more. I really did feel like a little bird locked in a cage when I wasn't out entertaining. I knew I would always be able to do something, even if it wasn't wrestling. If I had to resign myself to being an agent, then that would be what I would do. I would rather do an on-camera role, but so be it.

he kept coming out on top. The whole idea behind it was that whatever goal you set yourself, if you stick at it you can come out on top.

As soon as I was back I was doing a full schedule of house shows alongside my new pal. It meant I could get back in to the swing of travelling and everything without actually wrestling. Everything was fine because I had a nice easy progression into wrestling again. I would wrestle in the day time without having to do it in the shows.

The first match I did was in Canada with Steven Richards. I

wrestled every night that week – Dave Batista was one of my opponents – and when I got to TV on the Monday they told me I was having a match with Triple H; and that was my first one back on television. Going back and wrestling in front of people was great and my confidence began flowing back on TV.

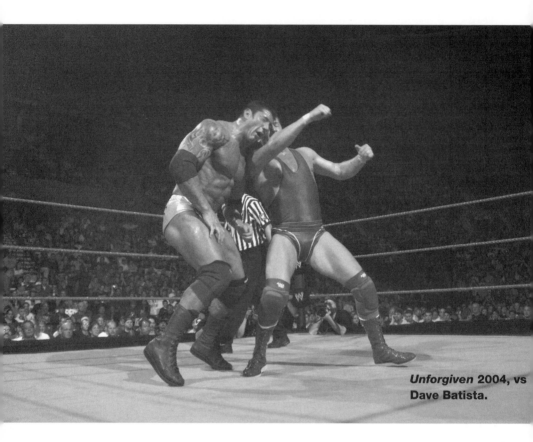

Unforgiven 2004, vs Dave Batista.

I felt it especially after one Monday night in particular. I'd come back into the middle of a cracking storyline. The group Evolution was trying to destroy the young lad Eugene and because Triple H was picking on him, I took against Triple H. I kept in my old character the whole time. I was still diabolical and snide but I believed that Triple H had taken a liberty with Eugene. Even though I hadn't changed in any way, people started cheering me, for almost the first time in my career, because I was sticking up for Eugene.

The week beforehand, Triple H and Chris Benoit had wrestled for an hour in Pittsburgh in one of those moments that makes me proud to be in this business. Watching that match from backstage, it was an unbelievable effort by both guys. Both of them are friends of mine but even if they weren't I would still say it was incredible.

The thought of trying to do that for an hour is mind-boggling, even for me. I've wrestled for an hour straight myself but not like that – they did some really physical stuff. And at the end of it Eugene came in and messed it up for Triple H.

So a week later, Triple H was screaming on TV that he wanted Eugene, and I got the opportunity to do a promo, which I enjoyed so much because I hadn't had the chance to do something like that for such a long time. I went out with a list of bullet points to get over and the freedom to spew out what was on my mind. It came out really well.

"*Dear, dear, dear, dear,*" *I said to Triple H as I came onto the entrance ramp. "Someone has lost their temper haven't they? I hate to be the one to inform you lad, but Eugene isn't here this week. You honestly don't think that I would lead that lamb to slaughter? No, no, no. What kind of a man do you think would let Eugene into the building last week? Rather a perplexing question, isn't it? What kind of a diabolical villain do you think would tell Eugene to get involved in your match? It was me, sunshine! You see, me and you know each other very well indeed, don't we?*

"*Let me give you people a little history lesson. Eleven years ago me and you were a tag team in WCW – in fact, I was your mentor wasn't I? Yes, indeed I was. Well, what can you say? Let's face facts. Some people, people like us, we are just born naughty. We are – that's why we gravitated towards each other. And if you would have used and abused anyone else except for that poor dear boy Eugene I would have applauded your cunning. But for a*

clever man like yourself it was very foolish to take advantage
of a disadvantaged boy because now you have made an
enemy out of me. And if you want a fight, look no bloody
further! Because I will quite happily go and change into my
ring attire and I will join you back in that ring and I will
battle you with every ounce of vile and venom that runs
through my veins!"

That set up a very violent match, which was needed to get over the angle we were doing. I finally found out what it's like to get punched in the face with a genuine set of knuckledusters. He hit me right in the eye and it certainly makes a real clunk in your skull.

He also hit me three times with his favourite toy, a sledgehammer. Then I was strapped into a neck brace and onto an ambulance stretcher. Triple H grabbed the stretcher and tipped me onto the floor, with my arms strapped to my sides so I had no chance to break the fall. It was violent and bloody but it was done for the right reasons and at the right time, to help with the story. To do material like that for no reason at all makes no sense. Here there was a reason, we went for it, and my head had to be stitched up

I let him know what I think of the way he was treating poor Eugene.

Triple H and I are building up to our showdown.

backstage afterwards – gory footage which the company later put out on the Internet.

It's great to be back on TV, having matches and playing the sort of despicable character William Regal has always been. It's good to know I was able to get back when so many had written me off.

In general, I'm fitter these days than I've ever been. A while back I discovered I was allergic to wheat and it has made an enormous difference to my life. I used to blow up with water all the time. I would feel sick and have a lot of bad stomachs. Sorting out my diet has made a world of difference to me. If I eat wheat now it throws me right off tilt. I train smarter these days, too – which is very different from just training harder.

In October 2004 when WWE was doing live TV from England for the very first time, I came out on to the ramp for *Raw* at the MEN arena in Manchester waving the union flag and the crowd nearly raised the roof. I heard afterwards it was pretty much the biggest pop of the night. It felt like I'd come home. It was brilliant; it made it all worthwhile.

I get a sledgehammering for my trouble.

Any minute now I'm about to be tipped off the stretcher.

I don't have any big plans for my life once I retire from wrestling. Some people who've seen me on the show say I could get acting work. We'll see. Right now I'm happy doing what I do – being a WWE entertainer. I'd like to be a part of the show for as long as I can. I seem to have a knack for helping and training people, and that's something I really enjoy. I've had a hand in training a lot of people who are top guys today. Many people ask me for advice and if they genuinely want it, I'll give it to them – just as others did for me when I was starting out.

Other ambitions? If someone ever made a film about the life of Tommy Cooper, I'd love to play him. I don't know if I could do him justice but I'd have a bloody good go. I would like to play a villain in a pantomime at the Grand Theatre in Blackpool one day. Trying to explain pantomime to an American is as hard as explaining professional wrestling to someone who has never seen it. Imagine the conversation.

> In October 2004 when WWE was doing live TV from England for the very first time, I came out on to the ramp for *Raw* at the MEN arena in Manchester waving the union flag and the crowd nearly raised the roof. I heard afterwards it was pretty much the biggest pop of the night. It felt like I'd come home. It was brilliant; it made it all worthwhile.

"You're in a ring and are pretending to fight. But you have to make it look like you really are fighting. You're in there with guys who are good and others who aren't so good. You have to learn how to do basic things. Some are better than others, some are good at psychology."

"What's psychology got to do with it?"

"It's knowing what to do at the right time, how to make people react and drag emotions out of them."

It's no wonder that virtually all the people who excel at pro wrestling have grown up watching it. The exceptions are very rare – people like Kurt Angle, who is one in a million.

I'm happy in my work. But I'll never forget what I've been through. And I'll never forget how Chris stuck with me through thick and thin. I'm astonished she never walked out. I know I would have done had the situation been reversed. There were several times

It feels so good to be back.

when she was on the brink of going. She's told me how, during the worst of it, she was convinced I'd kill myself in a road accident while I was high on drink or drugs. I'm lucky I never did. But Chris used to wonder whether she could look sufficiently upset when the police came to give her the bad news.

One reason she didn't go was sheer bloody-mindedness. "Why should I have to leave our lovely home?" she'd think. I'm glad of that stubbornness today.

Anyone who could put up with me has to be amazing. And Chris really is amazing. Now, after all we've been through, we get on better than ever. It is true that whatever doesn't kill you makes you stronger. After all, we met when I was seventeen and she was eighteen and she's stuck with me ever since. So she's the best.

Now, I don't do the right things in life – helping out around the home, doing family things – because I have to or because I feel I should. I do them because I want to. Loving my wife and my children is not a chore.

I've got three great children. Daniel, the eldest, looks very much like me. He's quiet; he's into his music, skateboarding and drawing and he reminds me a lot of certain aspects of me when I was a youngster. My middle son, Dane, looks just like I did at his age. There were times when I'd be the clown and that's how Dane is – always trying to make people laugh. And little Bailey is a rum bugger, into everything. It's tough for Chris, having to cope with everything on her own for most of the week while I'm away working, but she does a great job and we love her for it.

I love to read and I always have a book on the go. I'm always reading biographies. It gives me something to do when I'm away from home and I'm always on the lookout for things I can

> Anyone who could put up with me has to be amazing. And Chris really is amazing. Now, after all we've been through, we get on better than ever. It is true that whatever doesn't kill you makes you stronger. After all, we met when I was seventeen and she was eighteen and she's stuck with me ever since. So she's the best.

Dane loves to play the comic – just like me.

Bailey is into everything – including my lizards.

Chris is a star for sticking with me. I owe her everything.

Daniel is into his music.

I'm so proud of my kids. Daniel (standing), Bailey, Dane and my nieces Kira and Kelsey.

incorporate into my act. I like reading about other people who have had interesting lives – comedians, actors, gangsters and fighters, they are a constant source of enjoyment. I lent Triple H a book by Dave Courtney and that's when he suggested I start using the knuckledusters Courtney was so fond of in our show.

I also have bareknuckle boxer Roy Shaw and his book to thank for something that made a big impression on me. He wrote: "Never live in the past because you'll die a little each day." A light bulb went on in my head when I read that. I can't live in the past. If I do I'll start feeling sorry for myself. I've seen it happen to a lot of people – and it usually ends with them falling off the wagon again. I know I've been fortunate. I've got to the point where I can tell myself: "You've done a lot of bad things. There's nothing you can do to change them."

All I can do is go forward and be the best I can.

That's what I've got to do. Get on with life the best I can.

To the victors belong
the spoils . . .

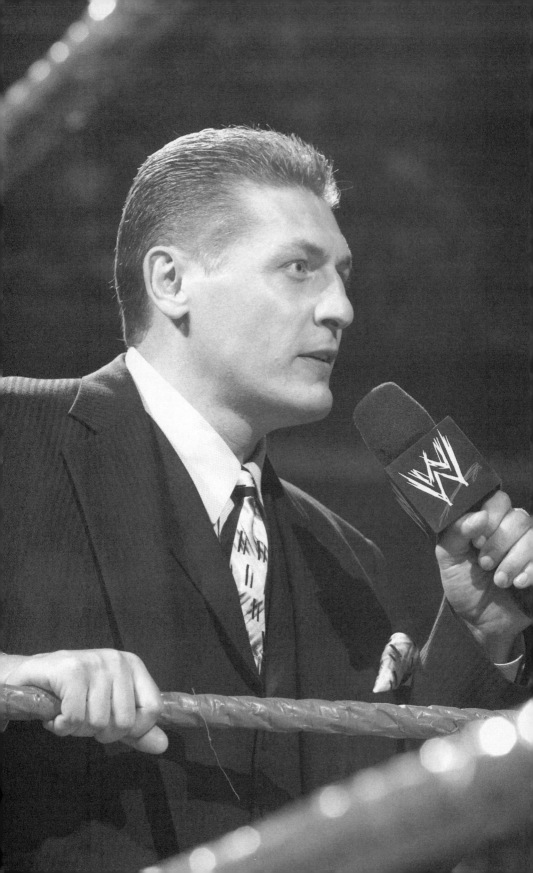

GLOSSARY

It has come to my attention that many of my American fans unfortunately have difficulty speaking the Queen's English. In order to continue my education of the American people, for which I know they are very grateful, here is a guide to some of the terms, phrases, people and places referred to in this book.

advert

a commercial (short for advertisement).

Alan Partridge

fictional fading TV personality and ex-chat show host created by comic and satirist Steve Coogan.

alcopops

bottled alcoholic drinks flavoured with fruit cordials and cynically designed and packaged to make alcohol attractive to younger drinkers.

Albert Hall, The

large circular venue in Kensington, south-west London, host to concerts, exhibitions and sometimes sporting events. Built in the nineteenth century during the reign of Queen Victoria and named after her husband Prince Albert.

barmy, barmier

crazy, nuts.

bait

to provoke someone by making remarks that you know will annoy them.

bent

crooked, open to bribery and corruption, not averse to cheating or to potentially criminal or illegal activity.

Bernard Manning

northern club circuit comedian renowned for the political incorrectness of his jokes.

Bertie Bassett

the company symbol of confectionery (candy) manufacturers Bassett's, Bertie Bassett was a jolly-looking cartoon figure with a cane, whose head, body and limbs were made up of the different shapes of Liqorice Allsorts, the company's best-known product.

Billy Connolly

Scottish comedian, musician and actor best known in the U.S. for his roles in Mrs Brown, The Last Samurai and Lemony Snicket's A Series of Unfortunate Events.

blinding

from "effing and blinding" (see **effing**). Swearing constantly and unpleasantly. Generally someone who is either extremely angry or out of control.

bloody-mindedness

stubbornness; grit and determination, especially when things are against you. Almost always appears as "sheer bloody-mindedness" or "absolute bloody-mindedness".

bollocking

to give someone a bollocking is to give them a severe telling-off. To get a bollocking off someone means to get a telling-off from them. A right bollocking is an even more serious telling-off than an ordinary bollocking.

bollocks

slang anatomical term for balls. Also colloquial expression of disagreement or indication that someone is talking nonsense.

bottle well gone

bottle is nerve, courage, guts. To lose one's bottle is to lose one's nerve. So when your bottle has gone it indicates that you are scared. "Bottle well gone" means that you are effectively no longer capable of doing whatever it is that you need the bottle to do.

Bristol

Large city and historic port in the west of England, once a hub of transatlantic trade.

bristols

Cockney rhyming slang for breasts, from the football team Bristol City (Bristol Cities: titties).

bugbear

an annoyance, something that constantly bugs you.

bugger

1. An exclamation ("Oh bugger!") 2. An affectionate insult or term of abuse (see **rum bugger**, **silly bugger**.) An extremely common expression in the U.K. at which almost no-one takes offence.

bugger off

go away, get lost. See **sod off**. On the other hand, "we buggered off" simply means we left, or we made a quick exit.

Butlins

see **holiday camp**.

camp

(adjective) having an affected, effeminate manner, especially someone who deliberately exaggerates their gestures, appearance and behaviour.

Cheshire

part of north-west England renowned for its wealth.

Chester

the county town of Cheshire, founded by the Romans in the first century A.D.

climbdown

accepting less than you would normally hold out for: a lowering of position, status or prestige. Also to admit defeat in an argument.

cobblers

nonsense, garbage. Hence "a load of old cobblers" is someone talking garbage. Originally Cockney rhyming slang from Cobblers' Awls, hence balls.

Comedians, The

British television programme from the 1970s which showcased comic talent drawn mainly from the traditional stand-up club circuit in northern England.

cooker shop

store specializing in stoves and ovens.

cookers

stoves and ovens (electric or gas).

councillor

an elected local government official serving on a City Council, County Council or District Council, depending on whether urban or rural.

cracking

excellent, top class. Sometimes "cracking good".

creamed

defeated, wrecked, destroyed. So "double creamed" means completely and utterly wrecked.

cricket

the English national game, exported throughout the territories of the British Empire in the nineteenth century, hence now also the national game of India, Pakistan, Bangladesh,Sri Lanka, South Africa, Australia, New Zealand and the West Indies. Also played in numerous other countries which once had English or British connections. It is said that baseball originated in the games of cricket played by English colonists in Boston during the 1700s.

Croydon

a satellite commuter town on the far south east outskirts of London.

daft

stupid, ditzy.

darling

"luvvies and darlings" are affected, theatrical types, from their tendency to address one another as "darling" or "love".

Dave Courtney

London underworld figure and author of several true crime books based on his life.

dick

a dickhead, an idiot. Also the body part, although this use is less common in England where we have plenty of other traditional and modern slang terms to choose from.

done in

exhausted, finished, washed up.

double creamed

see creamed.

effing

"F"-ing: euphemism for fucking or, as verb, for swearing generally ("He was effing and blinding"). See **blinding**.

Exchange & Mart

weekly newspaper in which all kinds of goods are offered for sale.

F.A. Cup Final

the biggest sporting event in the British calendar. The F.A. (Football Association) Cup is the U.K. equivalent of the SuperBowl.

football

soccer.

for six

cricketing term: six runs is the maximum score in cricket and is scored by hitting the ball through the air over the boundary of the playing area without it touching the ground. So to hit something for six or to knock someone for six is to give them the maximum possible blow.

Frank Carson

Irish comic based in the north of England who achieved TV fame in the 1970s in The Comedians.

full shilling

"not the full shilling" is to be not quite all there, to have something missing. From the days when British currency was in Pounds, Shillings and Pence (now just Pounds and Pence).

gawping

staring open-mouthed.

get on

to get on with someone or is to be at ease in their company, to have things in common, to be (casual rather than close) friends with: to get along.

git

an irritating, unpleasant person.

gob

slang term for mouth. Someone who is "a bit gobby" is someone who shoots their mouth off or talks a lot. Can also be a verb meaning to spit.

gobsmacked

astonished, dazed, speechless. Literally, the sensation of being smacked in the mouth.

grafter

a hard worker. Graft is work.

grass, grass on

to tell on someone, to rat on them. A grass is U.K. criminal slang for an informer.

Guernsey

one of the Channel Islands off the coast of France which has its own legislative parliament but is politically part of the United Kingdom. See **Jersey.**

Grumbleweeds, The

pop band who turned to comedy and had a British radio and TV show in the 1980s, combining sketches with songs and impressions.

hard slog

see **slog.**

Harry Ramsden's

famous traditional restaurant chain based mainly in the north of England and specializing in fish and chips (fries).

heaving

crowded, packed with people: a room so full that people are pushing and jostling against one another.

holiday camp

a uniquely British institution where families could have an inexpensive holiday in simple chalet-style accommodation set in a self-contained complex where food, drink and organised entertainment were all part of the deal. The holiday camp phenomenon was affectionately satirised in the British TV sitcom Hi-de-Hi.

hump

> to get the hump or have the hump with someone is to take offence and go into a sulk. To "have the hump on" is to be in a bad mood and spoiling for a fight.

Jersey

> one of the Channel Islands off the coast of France which has its own legislative parliament but is politically part of the United Kingdom. See **Guernsey**.

kick off, kicked off

> to start, to begin. From the opening move in a soccer game. Sometimes used to indicate the beginning of trouble or a fight in a crowd.

knack

> a skill, a technique, a particular way of doing something. Not to be confused with knackers (see below); or with a knackers' yard, which is a slaughterhouse; or with knackered, which means exhausted.

knackers

> anatomical slang for balls.

knobbly knees contest

> traditional fun event at British working-class seaside resorts where men would line up and compete to see which of them had the boniest knees.

knocking seven bells

> originally a nautical expression, meaning to give someone a thrashing. In the navy, eight bells signifies the end of each watch, so to knock seven bells out of someone is to beat them almost to the limit.

knuckleduster

> brass knuckles.

landau

> an elegant four-wheeled open horse-drawn carriage.

Leeds

> largest city in West Yorkshire, north central England.

Len Faircloughs

Len Fairclough was a character in Coronation Street, *Britain's longest-running soap opera. In 1983 the actor who played him was charged with indecently assaulting two young girls while teaching them to swim, although he was subsequently found not guilty.*

Lenny Henry

British comic, impressionist and actor who also starred in his own TV sitcom, Chef!

Les Dawson

British TV and club comedian of the 1970s and 1980s famous for his dry sense of humour and for his ability to contort his face into some truly extraordinary expressions.

Lewisham

a borough or district of south-east London, at one time fairly deprived and run down.

Liberty-taker

to take a liberty with someone is to go too far, to push their boundaries or presume on a friendship or acquaintance. A liberty-taker is someone who does this a lot, who is always trying to see how far they can go.

lilo

a small inflatable airbed for floating in swimming pools.

Littlehampton

a small seaside harbour town on the south coast of England.

luvvie

derogatory term for British actors, theatre and movie folk, from their supposed habit of calling one another "love" and "darling", irrespective of gender.

Manchester

the commercial, cultural and industrial capital of north-west England.

mental

out of control, chaotic. Can be used of a person or of a place or situation, such as a noisy club or party. *"It was mental in there"* means that all hell was breaking loose.

Mick Miller

popular northern stand-up comic who is known for his adult routines and blue humour.

Midlands, The

the central part of England.

mindedness

see **bloody-mindedness**.

mobile café

a motorized sandwich bar or hamburger bar as used at outdoor sporting events.

moody

fake (so double moody means doubly fake, fake twice over).

Morecambe and Wise

comic double act who dominated British TV from the late 1960s to the early 80s. Famous for their musical finales and for relentlessly making fun of their (willing) celebrity guests. Eric Morecambe died in 1984 but the Morecambe and Wise Christmas Specials are still shown on British TV at Christmas time to this day.

mucking about

general horseplay, messing around, having fun.

mug

someone who is easily fooled; a sucker, a fall-guy, a patsy. Hence *"a mug's game"* is something only an idiot would fall for or stick at.

navvy

a manual worker originally on the canals (known as navigations in the eighteenth and nineteenth centuries); more recently on the railways and in general construction.

needle

to needle someone is to annoy them, and to have the needle with someone is to be annoyed or irritated by them. See also **right needle**.

nick

(verb) to steal. Often used colloquially between friends to mean "borrow" as in "I've nicked your pen, I'll give it back in a moment." Also a slang term for prison. "In the nick" is equivalent to "in the slammer".

nicked

stolen. Also to be arrested. British policemen are popularly supposed to say, "You're nicked, son."

Norwich

historic old medieval city and the largest city in East Anglia, the rounded part of eastern England that sticks out into the North Sea.

nutters

eccentrics, psychos, crazy people, madmen.

off licence

store licensed to sell alcoholic liquor.

old cobblers

see **cobblers**.

Only Fools and Horses

long-running British sitcom about the misadventures of a working-class family of schemers and dealers in a South London community. The title comes from the proverbial expression: "Only fools and horses work."

Peter Kay's Phoenix Nights

TV sitcom set in a shabby northern social club where despite the unfailing optimism of both owner and customers, the night's entertainment invariably ends in disaster.

physio

short for physiotherapist.

pillock

slang derogatory term for an idiot, someone who repeatedly makes a fool of themselves.

pitch

an outdoor playing area for cricket, soccer or rugby football.

plain sailing

straightforward, and therefore easy (as opposed to tacking against the wind in a boat, which is complicated and difficult).

Plymouth

naval port in the far south-west of England from which admiral Sir Francis Drake sailed out to defeat the Spanish Armada in 1588.

Pontin's

see **holiday camp.**

posh

a term which tends to be used by the middle classes of the upper classes and by the working classes of the middle classes. Posh people have more money than you do, a bigger house than you do, a better car than you do. Posh also implies an element of style and good taste, though. People who flash their money around are not posh, however much they might want to think they are.

poxy

general expression of distaste (originally meaning diseased, rotten, or unattractive, as in the scars left by smallpox).

prat

a fool, an idiot. A pratfall is a fall onto one's backside.

Prestatyn

a seaside resort on the north coast of Wales.

Preston

a town in Lancashire, the same county (region) as Blackpool.

properly stuffed
see **stuffed.**

punters

originally, people who bet or gamble. Now often a slang term for any paying customers or audience.

queue

a line (noun); to wait in line (verb).

rabbited on

rabbit is Cockney rhyming slang for talk (from "rabbit and pork" as in ingredients of a mixed pie or stew). A person who rabbits on is someone who talks endlessly and will not shut up.

right

(adjective) an all-purpose expression of emphasis.

right needle

as in **needle** above except "the right needle" adds emphasis, meaning to be extremely and obviously annoyed by someone or something, to the extent that other people notice.

right pillock

a complete idiot.

Rochdale

a town in Lancashire, the same county (region) as Blackpool.

Ronnie Barker

comedian and stalwart of British television for almost fifty years. Starred in the classic sitcoms Porridge (set in a prison) and Open All Hours (set in a grocery store) as well as in the sketch show The Two Ronnies with fellow-comic Ronnie Corbett.

Royle Family, The

unusual and hugely successful TV sitcom first screened in 1998 and featuring a northern working-class family. There was no studio audience, no laughter track and almost all the "action" takes place on the sofa in front of the television, where the family members air their views on life, the universe and everything.

Roy Shaw

bareknuckle fighter whose account of his life as an East London hard man has achieved cult status.

Rugby

Midlands town where the game of rugby football was invented in the nineteenth century on the playing fields of Rugby School.

rumble me

to rumble someone is to see through them; to realize that they are out of their depth or that they are pretending to be something or someone they are not.

rum bugger

a peculiar character. "Rum" is often used in this context to mean odd, mysterious, puzzling.

screw

a prison guard.

shop

a store. Also (verb) a slang term for snitching on someone.

Skegness

holiday resort on the windswept east coast of England best known for a 1933 railway advertising poster with the slogan: "Skegness is so bracing."

slog

(noun and verb) effort, struggle, something you have to work hard at.

scruffy

messy, untidy, dirty: generally unkempt.

Shetland Isles

group of islands north-east of Scotland and politically part of Scotland, but historically with mixed Scots and Scandinavian heritage.

silly bugger

a fool (usually meant affectionately rather than offensively).

skint

broke.

Slade

glam rock band who first made it big in the 1970s, famous for their thumping beat and the eccentric spelling of hits like "Coz I Luv You", "Mama Weer All Crazee Now", "Cum On Feel The Noize" and "Skweeze Me, Pleeze Me".

slag off, slagging off

to slag something or someone off is to make insulting, critical or derogatory comments about them to others.

slate-layer's nailbags

a slate-layer is a roofer: someone who lays tiles or slates to make a house roof. Such workmen tend to keep their nails and tools in cloth bags hanging from their belts in order to leave their hands free.

sod off

an impolite way of suggesting "go away". U.S. equivalent would be "get lost".

Southport

coastal town in north-west England famous for its long stretches of sand where racehorses are trained, among them Red Rum, the only three-time winner of the Grand National, the world's toughest race.

Spit the Dog

spiky-furred canine glove puppet handled by comedian Bob Carolgees who first appeared shortly after the heyday of punk rock wearing a tartan collar and making ostentatious spitting gestures. Credited with reviving the ailing fortunes of TV-AM, Britain's first commercial breakfast television station, when viewers tuned in specially to watch him.

Steptoe and Son

classic British sitcom from the 1960s about a father and son team of "rag-and-bone men" (also known as "totters"); men who toured the streets with a horse and cart collecting old clothes, furniture and household goods for resale. Inspired the American TV show Stamford and Son.

strides

Australian slang for trousers (U.S. pants).

stuffed

stuck, stymied, unable to finish the task in hand usually because of circumstances outside one's control. Hence "properly stuffed" is roughly equivalent to being up the creek without a paddle.

syrup

Cockney rhyming slang for a wig. From Syrup of Figs (an old medicinal preparation): hence wigs.

take the mick

to make fun of, to make jokes, to tease (usually with some sarcasm involved). Also "take the mickey".

Terry-Thomas

British cinema actor of the 1940s, 50s and 60s, legendary for perfecting an upper-class British drawl and for playing shady upper-class characters or con-men pretending to be upper-class.

the hump

see **hump**.

thick ear

to give someone a thick ear is to give them a swift blow or a cuff around the side of the head. At one time a fairly common "instant" punishment in schools or from parent to child.

Thora Hird

British comedy actress and television presenter, one of the elder stateswomen of British theatre and television, who died in 2003 aged 91.

toffs

aristocrats, gentlemen, the upper classes generally.

Tommy Cooper

anarchic British comedian from the 1960s and 70s, famous for his backfiring magic tricks, his unruly hair and wild eyes, the red fez he wore, and his celebrated catchphrase: "Jus' like that."

Tony Hancock

> *legendary TV comic from the 1960s, famous for his monologues, for his gloomy persona on screen and for classic sketches such as "The Blood Donor". Committed suicide in 1968 while on tour in Australia.*

trouser beast

> *a sexual predator; someone with a high sex drive; unable to keep it in his trousers (pants).*

up people's noses

> *to get up someone's nose is to persistently annoy or irritate them.*

Victor Meldrew

> *British TV character from the BBC sitcom* One Foot in the Grave. *A short-tempered senior citizen who criticizes everyone and everything.*

Wembley Arena

> *premier music and entertainment venue, adjacent to Wembley Stadium in north-west London.*

wind me up

> *to wind someone up is to tease them or taunt them. Can be either affectionate or malicious.*

windscreen

> *windshield.*

wind-up

> *the act of playing a joke on someone or teasing them. "This is a wind-up, right?" means, "you are joking, aren't you?"*

wind-up merchant

> *someone who delights in teasing people or winding them up.*

Wolverhampton

> *industrial city in the West Midlands known for the distinctive regional accent of its inhabitants.*